Windows Vista™ Plain & Simple

Jerry Joyce and Marianne Moon

PUBLISHED BY
Microsoft Press
A Division of Microsoft Corporation
One Microsoft Way
Redmond, Washington 98052-6399

Library of Congress Control Number: 2006937015

Printed and bound in the United States of America.

7 8 9   QWT   2 1 0 9 8

Distributed in Canada by H.B. Fenn and Company Ltd.

A CIP catalogue record for this book is available from the British Library.

Microsoft Press books are available through booksellers and distributors worldwide. For further information about international editions, contact your local Microsoft Corporation office or contact Microsoft Press International directly at fax (425) 936-7329. Visit our Web site at www.microsoft.com/mspress. Send comments to mspinput@microsoft.com.

Acquisitions Editor: Juliana Aldous Atkinson
Project Editor: Kathleen Atkins
Typographer: Kat Marriner, Pineleaf Productions
Proofreader/Copy Editor: Alice Copp Smith
Manuscript Editor: Marianne Moon
Indexer: Jan Wright, Wright Information
Technical Editor: Jerry Joyce Indexing Services

Body Part No. X12-48748

Contents

What do you think of this book? We want to hear from you!

Microsoft is interested in hearing your feedback so we can continually improve our books and learning resources for you. To participate in a brief online survey, please visit:

www.microsoft.com/learning/booksurvey/

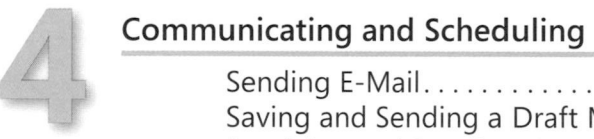

Exploring the Internet 79

Playing Games 97

Working with Pictures   109

Working with Multimedia   127

Using Voice and Sounds   169

Printing and Scanning   183

11   Managing Files and Folders   193

12   Networking   215

13 Setting Up 237

14 Customizing 253

15 Maintaining Security 277

16 Managing Windows Vista 301

What do you think of this book? We want to hear from you!

Microsoft is interested in hearing your feedback so we can continually improve our books and learning resources for you. To participate in a brief online survey, please visit:

www.microsoft.com/learning/booksurvey/

Acknowledgments

This book is the result of the combined efforts of a team of skilled professionals whose work we trust and admire and whose friendship we value highly. Kat Marriner, our wonderful typographer, did the work of two people and did it graciously. She not only refined and produced the graphics but also laid out the complex design, wrestling with problems ranging from limited space to logical arrangement of numbered steps. We appreciate her excellent work. Our dear friend Alice Copp Smith has helped us improve every one of the books we've written. Alice does so much more than proofread and copyedit: Her gentle and witty chiding on countless yellow sticky notes makes us groan (and laugh) but teaches us to write better and, always, to get rid of those danglers! And we are fortunate indeed to be able to work with indexer *par excellence* Jan Wright, whose index reveals in microcosm the soul of the book. We thank this dedicated and hardworking trio for their exceptional work and their unwavering good humor in the face of grueling deadlines.

At Microsoft Press we thank Lucinda Rowley and Juliana Aldous Atkinson for asking us to write this book, and we thank Kathleen Atkins for her valuable insight and helpful suggestions. Thanks also to Jim Kramer, Sandra Haynes, Victoria Thulman, Bill Teel, and Sally Stickney. We also thank Dan Polivy and Jen-Hung Ho at Microsoft for helping us with the Windows SideShow tools.

Thanks also to the Seattle Audubon Society for allowing us to use images from BirdWeb, their beautifully designed and comprehensive Web site about the birds of Washington State.

We thank, in spirit, Oscar Tschirky, longtime maître d'hôtel at The Waldorf (now The Waldorf-Astoria) in New York City, whose book *The Cook Book by "Oscar" of The Waldorf*, first published in 1896, is a family heirloom and the source of the sample text in many of our screen shots.

On the home front, we thank our wonderful grandchild, Zuzu, for love, laughter, and many hours of Monopoly, at which she routinely beats both of us and winds up with more money than the bank. We also thank puppies Baiser and Pierre for graciously allowing us to publish their private playlist.

Last but not least, we thank each other—for everything.

1 About This Book

If you want to get the most from your computer and your software with the least amount of time and effort—and who doesn't?—this book is for you. You'll find *Windows Vista Plain & Simple* to be a straightforward, easy-to-read reference tool. With the premise that your computer should work for you, not you for it, this book's purpose is to help you get your work done quickly and efficiently so that you can get away from the computer and live your life. Our book is based on the Home Premium Edition of Windows Vista. If you're running another edition of Windows Vista, you can still use the information you'll find here. Just be aware that the Home Basic Edition doesn't provide all the features that we talk about, and that our book doesn't deal with some of the additional features—joining a domain or sending and receiving faxes, for example—that you'd find in the Windows Vista Business, Enterprise, and Ultimate Editions.

No Computerspeak!

Let's face it—when there's a task you don't know how to do but you need to get it done in a hurry, or when you're stuck in the middle of a task and can't figure out what to do next, there's nothing more frustrating than having to read page after page of technical background material. You want the information you need—nothing more, nothing less—and you want it now! *And* it should be easy to find and understand.

That's what this book is all about. It's written in plain English—no technical jargon and no computerspeak. No single task in the book takes more than two pages. Just look up the task in the index or the table of contents, turn to the page, and there's the information you need, laid out in an illustrated step-by-step format. You don't get bogged down by the whys and wherefores: Just follow the steps and get your work done with a minimum of hassle. Occasionally you might have to turn to another page if the procedure you're working on is accompanied by a *See Also*. That's because there's a lot of overlap among tasks, and we didn't want to keep repeating ourselves. We've scattered some useful *Tips* here and there, pointed out some features that are new in Windows Vista, and thrown in a *Try This* or a *Caution* once in a while. By and large, however, we've tried to remain true to the heart and soul of the book, which is that the information you need should not only be available to you at a glance—it should also be *plain and simple!* So, whether you use Windows Vista on one home computer, on several computers that are part of a home network, or in a home office, we've tried to pack this book with procedures for everything we could think of that you might want to do, from the simplest tasks to some of the more esoteric ones. We've also tried to find and document the easiest way to accomplish these tasks. Windows Vista often provides a multitude of methods to achieve a single end result—which can be daunting or delightful, depending on the way you like to work. If you tend to stick with one favorite and familiar approach, we think the methods described in this book are the way to go. If you like trying out alternative techniques, go ahead! The intuitiveness of Windows Vista invites exploration, and you're likely to discover ways of doing things that you think are easier or that you like better than ours. That's exactly what the developers of Windows Vista had in mind when they provided so many alternatives.

A Quick Overview

Your computer probably came with Windows Vista pre-installed, but if you do have to install it yourself, the Setup Wizard makes installation so simple that you won't need our help anyway. Next, you don't have to read this book in any particular order. It's designed so that you can jump in, get the information you need, and then close the book and keep it near your computer. But that doesn't mean we scattered the information about with wild abandon. The tasks you want to accomplish are arranged in two levels. The overall type of task you're looking for is under a main heading such as "Finding Something on the Internet," "Using Shortcut Menus for Quick Results," and so on. Then, in each of those sections, the smaller tasks within the main task are arranged in a loose progression from the simplest to the more complex. OK, so what's where in this book?

Section 2 covers the basics: starting Windows Vista and shutting it down, changing users without having to log off, starting programs and working with program windows, using shortcut menus, taking a class at Mouse and Keyboard School, and getting help if you need it.

Section 3 focuses on running programs, including programs such as Sticky Notes and Journal that come with Windows Vista, and using the various little gadgets on the Windows Sidebar. You'll find information here about everyday tasks: composing, editing, saving, opening, and closing documents; copying material between documents; capturing screen images with the Snipping Tool; and using the Calculator and the On-Screen Keyboard. There's a short section here for MS-DOS fans, and another about running older programs.

Sections 4 and 5 are all about using Windows Vista as your window on the world at large—exploring, communicating, and using some of the tools that let you work and play out in cyberspace. We'll talk about communicating via Windows Mail—composing, sending, receiving, forwarding, and organizing e-mail messages; subscribing to newsgroups; managing and adding to your Contacts list; and using the Windows Calendar to keep track of your appointments and to schedule meetings and tasks. We'll surf with you as you explore the Internet—searching for people and places, finding and revisiting Web sites, designating your home page, viewing Web pages off line, saving and copying material from Web sites, and so on. You'll also learn how to block those annoying and occasionally dangerous pop-up windows.

Section 6 is devoted to playing games, including Chess Titans, Mahjong Titans, and six other familiar games to keep you challenged and entertained, as well as three new games—Comfy Cakes, Purble Shop, and Purble Pairs—that will delight the youngest members of the family.

Sections 7 and 8 cover working with different types of pictures in your Windows Photo Gallery; working with pictures from digital cameras and videocameras; assembling multimedia slide shows and creating transitions between video clips; playing and recording CD music; and creating and listening to your own music playlists. You'll be amazed by the professional results you can achieve with the combination of your own creativity and the Windows Vista tools—among them Media Player, Media Center, and Movie Maker.

Section 9 is about sounds—controlling the volume of the sounds your computer makes, creating sound files, associating sounds with events, and so on—but the majority of this section is devoted to Windows Vista's powerful speech-recognition system that makes it possible for you to direct your computer with voice commands. You'll step through a tutorial that teaches you the commands you have to use so that the program can understand your voice and the way you pronounce words. Alternatively, you can have a program called Narrator read aloud to you the contents of your computer screen—an especially valuable feature if your eyesight isn't what it once was!

Section 10 is the place to go with questions about printing your documents or problems setting up your printer. Windows Vista makes it a snap to print your photographs, and we'll also show you how to print readable Web pages. This section of the book also covers creating documents in the XPS format, which makes it possible for your documents to look exactly the same regardless of the computer you use to open or print them—a very useful feature when you need to preserve a document's design and formatting. We also discuss scanning and digitizing images in this section.

Section 11 covers managing and organizing your documents, files, and folders: moving or copying files, and creating a system of folders in which to keep them; sharing files with other users; recovering deleted items; using compressed folders to minimize large files; storing files on CDs, DVDs, or other types of removable memory devices; re-arranging the items on your Desktop; and navigating with toolbars.

Section 12 is the networking section—the types of networks you might encounter, how to find what you need on your network, and how to use the power of a network to your best advantage. We'll show you how to share files, folders, and printers, and how to connect to your network in several different ways. We'll talk about connecting to public wireless networks, hosting or participating in network meetings—even conducting wireless meetings—and making sure that your wireless communications are secure.

Section 13 is about setting up your computer. This is where you'll find information about transferring your files, folders, and settings from one computer to another without losing any of that precious information. You'll learn how to turn Windows components on or off and how to set up your Windows Mail, your Internet access, your local and network printers, and any other hardware.

Section 14 is all about customizing, and it'll make you realize that *you're* the boss of your computer and that you can customize just about everything in Windows Vista. You can change the overall look by changing themes and colors, or you can create your own themes. You can try out the new Windows Aero glass effect; you can customize your Desktop background, screen saver, folders, Desktop icons, account picture, taskbar, and Start menu; and you can change the way the mouse works and the way a CD starts. You can check out some alternative ways of working, and, if you sometimes work in another part of the world or use another language, you can customize your keyboard to that language and add clocks to the taskbar so that you can see what time it is in that other city or country.

Section 15 deals with what's possibly the most important topic in the whole book: Security, with a capital "S"! In this section, we cover all the ways you can protect yourself and your computer from the activities of others, whether they have direct access to your computer or are lurking in some faraway place from which they attempt to prey on you over the Internet. We'll show you how to set up secure passwords to deny access to your computer when you're not around; create *trusted contacts;* use parental controls to keep children safe; set up a firewall to prevent intrusions from the Internet; protect your personal information on the Internet; and increase your protection against dangerous e-mail viruses.

Last but not least, section 16 concentrates on doing some basic maintenance to tune up Windows once in a while. And if something does go wrong with your system, we'll help you diagnose the problem, get help, and get the system running correctly again.

What's New in Windows Vista?

One of Windows Vista's remarkable new features is its ability to conduct any type of search from almost anywhere on your computer. If you need to find a document, just search for it from the Start menu or from any window. If you're saying, "Well, what's so new about *that*?", try this: Press the Windows key, and then type part of the name of any program, folder, or file. The Windows key opens the Start menu, and, as you type, the results of your search appear on the Start menu. Type another letter or two, and the search results get narrowed down. Another great thing about the search feature is that not only can you search your computer, you can Search the entire Internet from the Start menu or any window.

You'll find other features that make working on your computer easier than ever, including links in each window—some set up by Windows and others you create yourself—that allow you to jump to your favorite locations; and the Address bar, which helps you to locate all the different places you want to explore. Windows Vista has also grouped many of the tools and features you need into task-oriented centers. For example, there's the Welcome Center, which helps you learn about your computer and shows you how to set up and customize it; the Mobility Center, which helps you set up your portable computer when you're on the road; the Network Center, which helps you configure, control, secure, and navigate your network; the Ease Of Access Center, which helps you modify computer settings to improve your access to the computer; and the Security Center, where you can make sure that you and your computer are protected from all the nasties lurking out there in cyberspace.

One of the first things you'll notice about security in Windows Vista is what you'll probably come to think of as an *extremely* annoying dialog box that's constantly popping up and asking you for the password for an Administrator's account (or, if you're logged on as an Administrator, asking your permission to continue). This feature, called the User Account Control, is central to the new and very powerful Windows Vista security features. Each time that dialog box appears, it's because you (or a program) are trying to do something that will change Windows, that will affect what other users can do, or that will introduce something onto the computer that could be dangerous to the system. By requiring permission, Windows is not only alerting you that these types of actions can't be conducted by someone who isn't authorized to make them, but is also preventing hackers, viruses, and other software from misusing or damaging your system. Aside from your frequent encounters with the User Account Control, you'll find that although many security features are running, they rarely interfere with your work. For example, Internet Explorer runs in Protected mode, which allows full access to features and tools on the Internet but isolates Internet Explorer from the rest of your computer to protect your system. Windows Defender watches your computer for spyware and other intrusive programs, and the Windows Firewall blocks unauthorized access to your computer and unauthorized transmission of information from your computer. A quick visit to the Windows Security Center shows you what Windows Vista is doing to protect your computer and also lets you know what you need to do to help keep your system secure. You can keep your children safe from harm when they're using the computer: With Windows Vista's Parental Controls feature, you can block Web sites, videos, games, TV shows, and any other media you consider inappropriate, and you can limit the amount of time during which your children (or anyone) can access the computer.

An impressive new feature of Windows Vista is the Aero glass appearance. If your computer's hardware supports this feature, parts of windows and other Windows components can be transparent, semitransparent, or colored as you want. You can see dazzling 3-D effects when you switch between windows, and everything on your screen looks really clear and sharp. You'll also notice improvements in other visual effects, including the increased clarity of pictures and videos.

You'll notice some significant differences between the components of Windows Vista and those of previous versions of Windows. For example, the Start menu doesn't have all those cascading submenus to navigate, and the folder windows aren't cluttered up with different toolbars; instead, the toolbar that remains changes its content depending on the types of folders or files contained in the window. You'll also notice that the menus seem to have disappeared. Fear not! They're still there (just press the Alt key) but are hidden and are mostly unnecessary. You'll see that folder windows can have different panes so that you can easily navigate among folders, see detailed information about an item, and even see a preview of a file without opening the file. There's also a special section of the Desktop, called the Sidebar, where you can store gadgets that show the time, get news headlines, run a slide show of your pictures, and do various other useful tasks.

Okay, we've talked about the way Windows Vista looks, the way it works, and the way it protects your computer system. Now we'll explore some of the many new features included in the Windows Vista Home Premium Edition. Available previously only in special editions of Windows, Media Center and Tablet PC tools are now included in Windows Vista. With Media Center, you can watch movies and even live TV. You can record shows, play music, and make your computer the center of your entertainment world. The Tablet PC tools are specialized tools that give you the power to do most of your work directly on the screen, especially if you use the Ink feature, which enables you to use your own handwriting in your programs.

You'll find an assortment of other new tools too. There's Windows Photo Gallery, a great photo organizer; and tools for making DVDs, whether they're data discs, photo slide shows, or movies. Windows Calendar makes it possible for you to track your schedule and publish it so that others can see it, and to download calendars from the Web. No more excuses for missing that dentist's appointment or being late for a meeting! Some of the other new Windows Vista features are really pretty remarkable. For example, for quite some time there have been several ways to conduct a secure electronic meeting over a network or over the Internet. Well, now—provided both computers are in the same room and that each has a wireless network adapter— you can hold a meeting between two computers that aren't connected to either a network or the Internet! And if you've always wanted to yell at your computer—or at least tell it what to do—you can use Windows Vista's powerful speech-recognition program.

You'll also find that Windows Vista comes with new and improved versions of programs from earlier versions of Windows. Windows Media Player now gives you the power to purchase and download music directly from the program; and Windows Mail replaces Outlook Express, providing greater security and power, and giving you the ability to automatically download Internet feeds (RSS feeds) so that you can see the latest news, conversations, or anything else you want.

So what's new in Windows Vista? Aside from all the new tools and features we've just described, perhaps what's new for *you* in Windows Vista is a feeling of renewed confidence that you can easily and safely do what you want on your computer without worrying that someone or something will cause you all sorts of trouble.

A Few Assumptions

We had to make a few educated guesses about you, our audience, when we started writing this book. Perhaps your computer is solely for personal use—e-mail, surfing the Internet, playing games, and so on. Perhaps your work allows you to telecommute. Or maybe you run a small home-based business. Taking all these possibilities into account, we assumed that either you'd be using a stand-alone home computer or you'd have two or more computers connected so that you could share files, a printer, and so on. We also assumed that you have an Internet connection.

Another assumption we made is that—initially, anyway—you'd use Windows Vista just the way it came, and that your computer is capable of using all of Windows Vista's features, meaning that your computer supports the Aero glass transparent appearance. Also, although we assumed you'd be using your mouse to execute commands and navigate around your computer, we know that many people prefer to accomplish just about every task by using the keyboard only.

If you decide to change Windows Vista's appearance—by reverting to the look of a previous version of Windows, for example—or to hide some screen elements and display others, you can quickly and easily customize almost every-thing. However, because Windows Vista's default setup makes accomplishing your work so easy—and because our philos-ophy is that work should be as stress-free and pleasant as possible—that's what we've shown in the procedures and graphics throughout this book.

A Final Word (or Two)

We had three goals in writing this book:

- Whatever you want to do, we want the book to help you get it done.

- We want the book to help you discover how to do things you *didn't* know you wanted to do.

- And, finally, if we've achieved the first two goals, we'll be well on the way to the third, which is for our book to help you *enjoy* using Windows Vista. We think that's the best gift we could give you to thank you for buying our book.

We hope you'll have as much fun using *Windows Vista Plain & Simple* as we've had writing it. The best way to learn is by doing, and that's how we hope you'll use this book.

2 Jump Right In

Windows Vista is designed to work for you, not you for it. You'll find that there are often several ways to accomplish one task. Why? Because people work differently. Because different tasks have different requirements. And because you want to find the way that works best for you, get your work done quickly, and then get away from the computer and live your life!

The procedures described in this book are simple and straightforward, and you can often use automated methods to get the more complex tasks done easily. This section of the book covers the basics: starting Windows Vista and shutting it down, starting programs, switching users without having to shut down all your running programs, accessing your documents, arranging your open windows, using the mouse, getting online help, and so on. There's also a handy visual glossary on the following two pages that will help you become familiar with the various components of the Windows Vista environment.

You'll want to feel comfortable with the basics before you do any customizing, so don't do anything yet. The best way to learn about running programs, managing windows, and getting help if you do get into trouble is to jump right in and try things out.

What's Where in Windows Vista?

Windows Vista is your working headquarters—the operating system that lets you run different programs simultaneously and share information among programs if you need to. Most of the programs you'll use have common characteristics that were designed to work together in the Windows Vista environment so that once you learn how to do something in one program, you'll know how to do it in other programs.

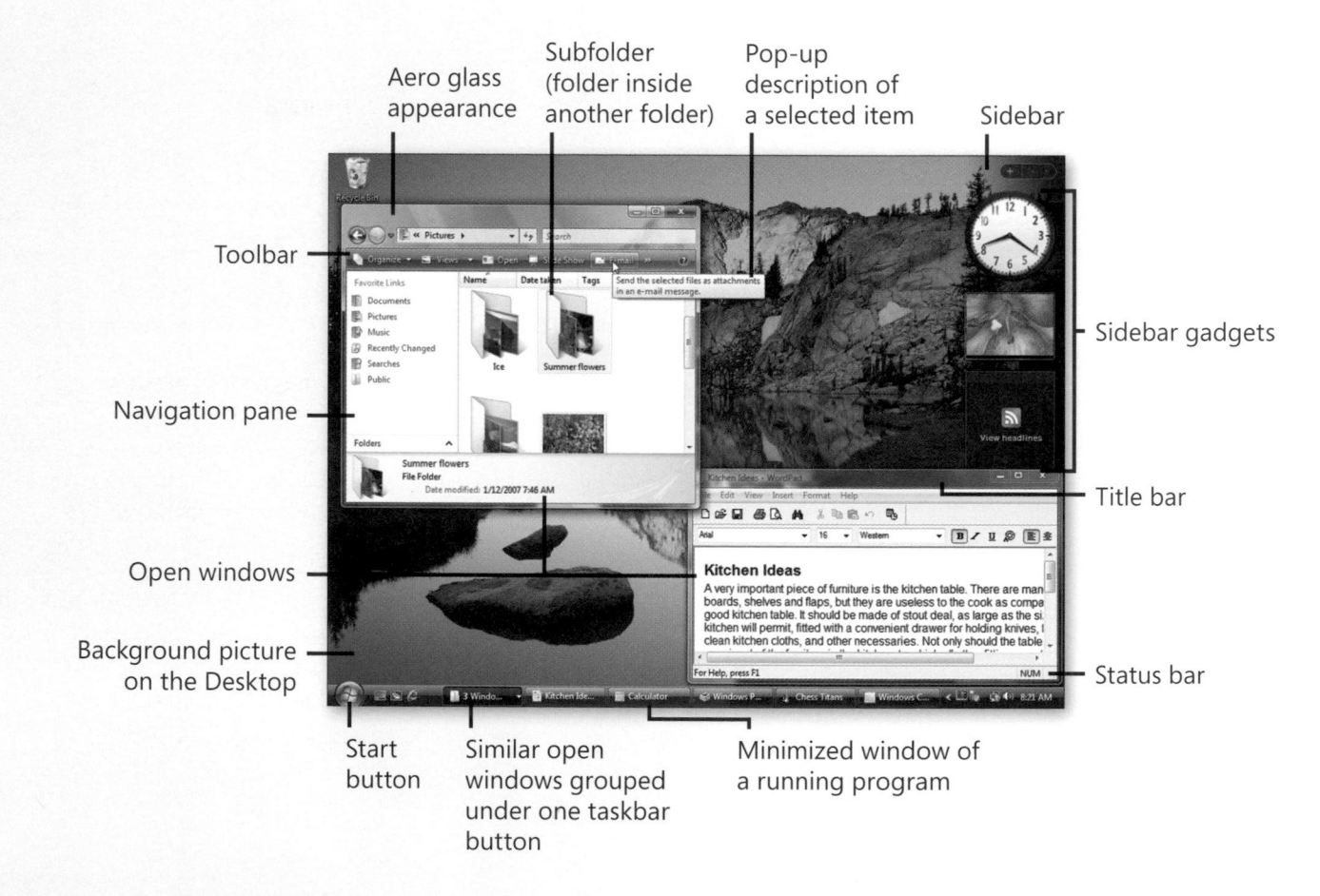

Aero glass appearance

Subfolder (folder inside another folder)

Pop-up description of a selected item

Sidebar

Toolbar

Sidebar gadgets

Navigation pane

Title bar

Open windows

Status bar

Background picture on the Desktop

Start button

Similar open windows grouped under one taskbar button

Minimized window of a running program

Take a look at the different parts of the Windows Vista environment displayed on these two pages—what they do and what they're called—and you'll be on the road to complete mastery. The way Windows Vista was set up on your computer, as well as the many ways in which you can customize Windows Vista, can make drastic changes to the look of your Desktop, but the basic concepts are the same. And, if you need to, you can always come back to this visual glossary for a quick refresher on Windows Vista terminology.

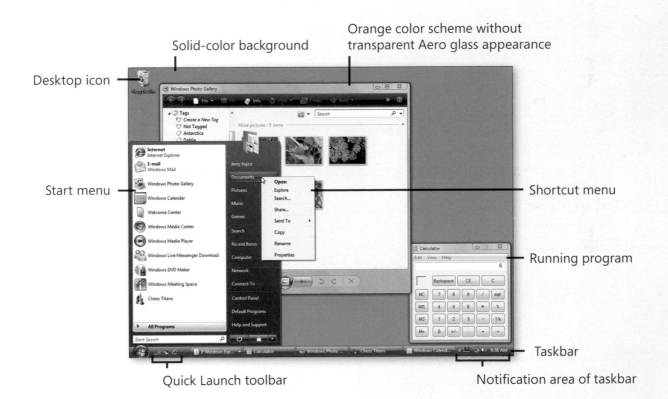

Solid-color background

Orange color scheme without transparent Aero glass appearance

Desktop icon

Start menu

Shortcut menu

Running program

Taskbar

Quick Launch toolbar

Notification area of taskbar

Starting Up

Windows Vista and your computer are designed to exist in more states than just being on or off. If you've been gone for a while, you've unplugged your computer, or you're using it for the first time, you'll need to bring it to life from its "off" state. Just like humans, Windows Vista and your computer both love to sleep. In the computer world, "sleep" is a state in which the computer stores your information on the hard disk and keeps it in memory, enters a very low-energy state, and then returns to full activity very quickly.

Start or Wake Up a Computer

(1) Move the mouse button or press a key on the keyboard to see whether the computer is really off or just sleeping, or if it's simply resting with the screen off.

(2) If nothing happens, turn on the computer, the monitor, and any peripheral devices—your printer, for example—and wait for Windows Vista to load.

(3) Click your name. If a box for a password appears, type your password, and then press Enter to log on to Windows Vista.

How to Get Your Computer Going

Its state	What you can do
Off	Press the Power button, and log on.
Sleep	Press the blinking Power button or lift the laptop cover, and log on if required.
Hibernate	Press the Power button, and log on if required.
On, with a blank screen	Move the mouse or press a key.
On, with a screen saver	Move the mouse or press a key, and log on if required.
On, locked	Enter your password, or click Switch User to log on using a different name.

Caution

Personal accounts are very powerful in scope. Each user of the computer has his or her own folders for storing documents, and each user has individual and specific settings. You should never use someone else's account! If you do, everything from files to e-mail messages could be misplaced or lost.

See Also

"Leaving Your Computer" on the facing page for information about putting the computer to sleep, turning it off, restarting it, or locking it.

Leaving Your Computer

If you walk away from your computer for more than a few minutes—or even for a few seconds if your computer is accessible by others—you'll want to either lock the computer or switch it to a low-power state that saves energy. That way, the computer can still function, but your files, settings, and programs aren't accessible and can't be viewed by others.

If you want to grant access to another user, you can let the other person log on and use his or her own settings. If you need to be away from the computer for extended periods, or you want to add components or move the computer to a new location, just turn it off.

Leave It

① Click the Start button.

② Do any of the following:

- Click the Sleep button, and wait for Windows to save your work and then go to sleep.

- Click the Lock button to deny access to anyone except those you've authorized to log on to this computer.

- Point to the arrow and choose Switch User to keep your programs running in the background (but inaccessible until you log on again), allowing another user to log on.

- Point to the arrow and choose Log Off to close all your programs but leave the computer running so that another user can log on.

- Point to the arrow and choose Restart to shut down the computer and then restart it.

- Point to the arrow and choose Shut Down to close all your programs and turn off the computer.

See Also

"Controlling the Power Options" on pages 308–309 for information about setting a power plan that automatically puts the computer to sleep, and for information about changing what happens when the power button is pressed or your laptop's lid is closed.

Starting a Program

The real work of an operating system is to run software programs. Windows Vista comes with a wide variety of programs, and you can install additional (and often more powerful) ones. Most programs are listed on the Start menu, but Windows gives you several ways to start your programs so that you can choose the way you like best. The programs listed below are only some of the programs that come with Windows Vista. You'll find descriptions of the others elsewhere in this book.

Start a Program

 Do any of the following:

- Click the Start button or press the Windows key, and choose a program from the Start menu.

- Click the Start button or press the Windows key, type the first few letters of the program you want to run, and, after the search results on the Start menu show the program, press Enter or click the program.

- Click the Start button, click All Programs, click any relevant folders to display or expand their content, and click the program you want.

- Point to and then double-click the program icon on the Desktop.

- Click Computer on the Start menu, navigate to the folder that contains the program you want, and double-click the program.

- Click Documents on the Start menu, locate the document that's associated with the program, and double-click the file.

- Insert the disc or removable drive that contains a program that's designed to run from the disc or drive, and choose to run the program.

② Use the program, and close it when you've finished.

Frequently Used Windows Vista Programs

Program	Purpose
Windows Contacts	Stores names, addresses, and other contact information.
Calculator	Does arithmetic calculations and complex mathematical calculations.
Character Map	Inserts special characters from installed fonts.
Calendar	Shows dates and records appointments and tasks.
Internet Explorer	Functions as a Web browser and an HTML document viewer.
Photo Gallery	Organizes pictures and picture tasks.
Notepad	Creates, edits, and displays text documents.
Windows Mail	Provides e-mail, newsgroup, and directory services.
Paint	Creates and edits bitmap pictures; imports and edits scanned images and digital pictures.
Media Player	Plays sounds, music, and videos.
Movie Maker	Converts, edits, organizes, and distributes video files.
WordPad	Creates, edits, and displays text, Rich Text Format, and Word documents.

Accessing Your Documents

The Documents folder is a personal storage area in which you should store all—or at least most—of your documents, unless you're using a network-sharing system such as SharePoint or a document-management program.

Open a Document

1 Click the Start button, and choose Documents from the Start menu to open the Documents window.

2 Click a file to select it.

3 Review the properties of this file.

4 Review the contents of this file.

5 Double-click the file to open it, or press Enter to open the selected file.

6 Click the Close button when you've finished.

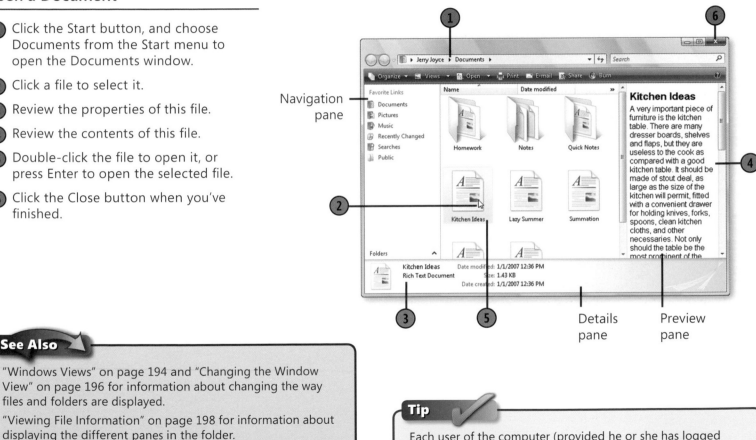

Navigation pane

Kitchen Ideas

A very important piece of furniture is the kitchen table. There are many dresser boards, shelves and flaps, but they are useless to the cook as compared with a good kitchen table. It should be made of stout deal, as large as the size of the kitchen will permit, fitted with a convenient drawer for holding knives, forks, spoons, clean kitchen cloths, and other necessaries. Not only should the table be the most prominent of the

Kitchen Ideas
Rich Text Document
Date modified: 1/1/2007 12:36 PM
Size: 1.43 KB
Date created: 1/1/2007 12:36 PM

Details pane

Preview pane

See Also

"Windows Views" on page 194 and "Changing the Window View" on page 196 for information about changing the way files and folders are displayed.

"Viewing File Information" on page 198 for information about displaying the different panes in the folder.

"Organizing Your Files" on pages 204–205 for information about arranging the files in the folder.

Tip

Each user of the computer (provided he or she has logged on) has a separate Documents folder, as well as other personalized settings.

Finding Any File

You know it's there somewhere, but where? Instead of wasting time digging through all the folders you think might hold that file you need, why not have Windows Vista do the searching for you? With the Search feature, not only can you search for a file name or even part of its name, you can also search for words that are contained in the file.

Search for the File

① Click the Start button, and start typing in the Search box the name, or part of the name, of the file you want.

② As you type, you'll see the search results. If there are too many results, type more of the name to narrow the search, or include the file extension if you know it.

③ When you locate the file, do either of the following:

- Click the file to run the default action for that type of file. For a document, this means to open it in its default program; for a program, it means to run the program; for a folder, it means to open the folder.

- Right-click the file, and choose the action you want from the shortcut menu.

Tip

When you search from the Start menu, Windows Vista searches only files that are indexed. If you search for a file that you know is on the computer but it doesn't appear in the search results, use the Advanced search and specify that you want to search for files that aren't indexed.

Try This!

Open a folder where you think the file you want is located (even if it's in a subfolder), so that you limit the search only to the contents of the folder and its subfolders, whether or not the folder has been indexed. In the Search box of the Start menu, start typing the file name or part of it. Type just enough of the name so that the file you want is easy to locate in the search results.

Run an Advanced Search

1. Click the Start button, and choose Search from the Start menu to display the Search Results window.

2. Type your search text.

3. Select the type of file you want to search for.

4. If you want to search a location other than the default location, click the down arrow, and select the location you want to search.

5. Select the file property you want, select the search function, and enter the search parameters.

6. Enter any additional identifying information you want to use in the search.

7. Select this check box if you want to search every file, including system files and files that haven't been indexed.

8. Click Search to find the file or files.

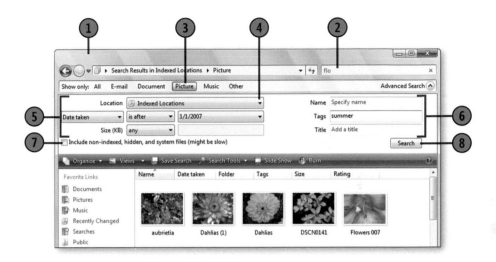

See Also

"Sorting Your Files and Folders" on page 197 for information about displaying only selected files by filtering the contents of a folder window without running a search.

Try This!

Create and run a search that you know you'll probably want to redo in the future. Click the Save Search button, and name the search. In the future, click Searches in the Navigation pane of any window, and double-click the saved search. Windows will run the search and will show the updated results.

Accessing Everything

The Computer folder is the gateway to your computer's contents, and it displays the icons that represent all your local storage areas: removable disk drives, hard disks, CD and DVD drives, and so on, as well as shared network files. From here you can venture as deep into the folder structure of your computer as you dare.

Open Any Folder

1. Click the Start button, and choose Computer from the Start menu to open the Computer window.

2. Double-click a drive icon to open a window for that drive.

3. Point to a folder and review the properties and content of the folder.

4. Click a new destination if you want to work in a different folder.

5. To open a folder, double-click it, or, if the folder is already selected, press Enter.

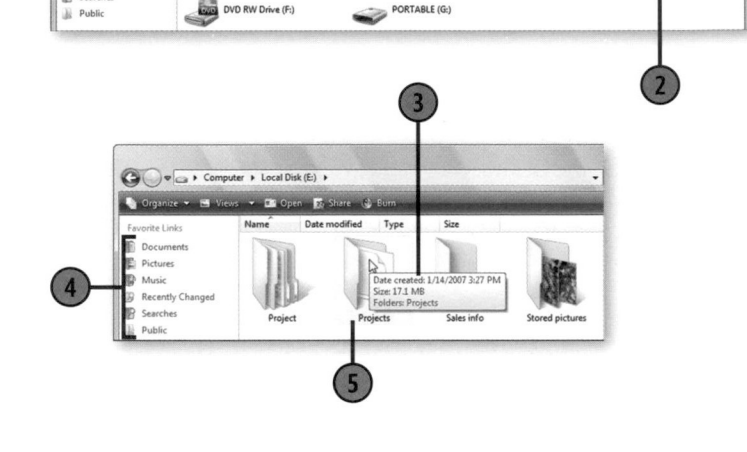

See Also

"Windows Views" on page 194 and "Changing the Window View" on page 196 for information about changing the way files and folders are displayed.

Tip

To open a file that you used recently, point to Recent Items on the Start menu and choose the file from the list that appears.

Explore

① Do either of the following:

- Click a location to return to it.

- Click a down arrow to see a list of locations you can go to, and click a location to go to it. If the scroll arrows appear, use them to find all available locations.

② Click the Back button to return to the previous window, or click the Forward button, if available, to move to a folder you visited previously and then left using the Back button.

③ Click a link in the Navigation pane to go to that location.

④ To open a folder in a new window, hold down the Ctrl key and double-click the folder.

⑤ If you want to explore everything, click Folders in the Navigation pane to show all your drives and folders. Click a folder to go to that folder.

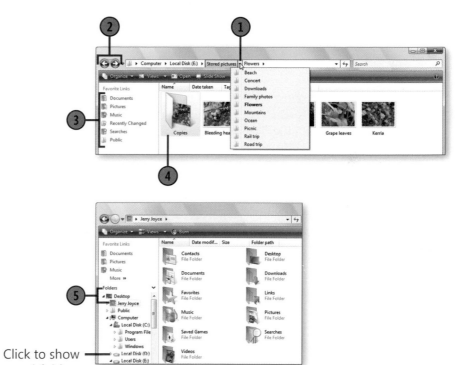

Click to show any subfolders

See Also

"Adding a Link to a Folder" on page 201 for information about adding your own destinations to the Favorite Links list.

Tip

When you use the Address bar to navigate, you're using the traditional "path" structure in which items are organized in a hierarchy—a drive contains certain folders, a folder contains subfolders, those subfolders contain more subfolders, and so on.

Switching Among Open Windows

Whatever your working style, it's likely that you'll end up with more than one window open on your computer—your Documents window and the Network window, perhaps, or a couple of program windows. Instead of closing one window to get to another, you can simply switch windows.

Select a Window

① On the taskbar, point to the window you think you want, and use the thumbnail image of the window to confirm that it's the one you want.

② Click the window on the taskbar to switch to that window.

③ If Windows has grouped similar types of windows under one button, click the button for the grouping, and then click the window you want.

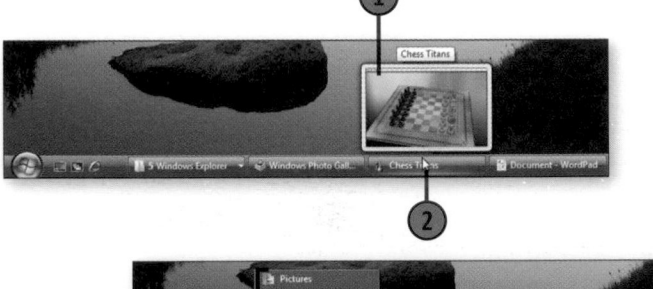

Tip

If there isn't enough room on the taskbar to display a button for each open window, Windows groups similar types of windows under one button. To rearrange all the windows in the group, right-click the button, and choose the arrangement you want from the shortcut menu that appears.

Try This!

Hold down the Windows key and press the Tab key. If your computer system supports the effect, each window will be shown in 3-D. Continue holding down the Windows key and pressing the Tab key until the window you want is on top.

Switch Windows

① Hold down the Alt key and press the Tab key to display the open windows. Continue pressing the Tab key while holding down the Alt key to cycle through the open windows.

② Release the Alt key when the window you want is selected.

Mouse and Keyboard Maneuvers

Windows lets you work the way you want. You can move around, choose items, and do much of your work using only the mouse, only the keyboard, or a combination of the two. With the mouse, you can jump directly to the point you want, grab and move things, and quickly choose commands. With the keyboard, you can do most things by using keyboard shortcuts or by moving around using the Tab key or the arrow keys. The way you work is up to you, and you might find that a combination of the two methods gets things done quickly, efficiently, and, most important, comfortably for you.

Mouse Moves

Point: Move the mouse until the mouse pointer (either a small arrow-shaped pointer or a tiny hand) is pointing to the item you want.

Hover: Point to an item and keep the mouse stationary.

Click: Point to the item you want, and then quickly press down and release the left mouse button.

Double-click: Point to the item you want, and then quickly press down and release the left mouse button twice, being careful not to move the mouse between clicks.

Right-click: Point to the item you want, and then quickly press down and release the right mouse button.

Select: Point to an item, and click to select it. To select an icon when the system is set to open an item with a single click, point to the icon but don't click. A selected item is usually a different color from other similar items or is surrounded by a frame.

Multiple-select: To select a list of adjacent or sequential items, click the first item, hold down the Shift key, and click the last item. To select or deselect nonadjacent items, hold down the Ctrl key and click each item you want. (Note that not all windows and dialog boxes permit multiple selection.)

Drag: Select the item you want. Keeping the mouse pointer on the selected item, hold down the left mouse button and move the mouse until you've "dragged" the item to the desired location; then release the left mouse button.

Keyboard Moves

Keyboard shortcuts: Press two or more keys in combination or consecutively. Keys you press in combination are linked with a plus sign, so Ctrl+C means hold down the Ctrl key and press the C key, and then release both keys. Keys you press consecutively are separated by a comma or commas, so Alt, F, X means press and release the Alt key, press and release the F key, and then press and release the X key.

Windows key: A special key that displays the Windows logo: Press it by itself to open the Start menu. Many programs have keyboard shortcuts that use the Windows key.

Arrow keys: Four keys, each with an arrow pointing in a different direction: Use them to move the highlight, the insertion point, or the selection in the direction of the arrow.

Tab key: This key has different functions. In a document, it inserts a tab character or moves you to the next column; in a window or dialog box, it moves you from section to section. To go in the opposite direction, press Shift+Tab.

So Many Ways to Do It

To work without the mouse or keyboard, see "Directing Your Computer with Voice Commands" on pages 172–173, "Dictating Text" on pages 174–175, and "Letting Your Computer Do the Talking" on page 178. To modify the way the mouse works, see "Customizing Your Mouse" on pages 260–261 and "Customizing Your Folders" on pages 268–269.

Managing Windows

"Managing" a window means bossing it around: You can move it, change its size, and open and close it. Most programs are contained in windows. Although these windows might have some different features, most program windows have more similarities than differences.

Use the Buttons to Switch Between Sizes

 Click the Maximize button, and the window enlarges and fills the screen. (If the window is already maximized, you won't see the Maximize button.)

Click the Restore Down button, and the window gets smaller. (If the window is already restored, you won't see the Restore Down button.)

Click the Minimize button, and the window disappears but you can see its name on a button on the taskbar.

Click the window's name on the taskbar button, and the window zooms back to the size it was before you minimized it.

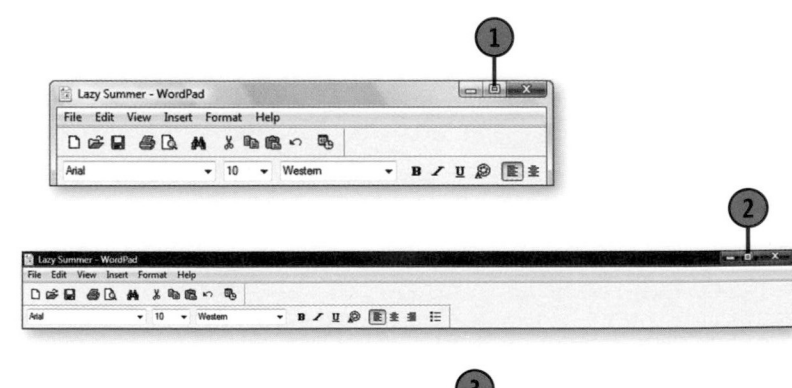

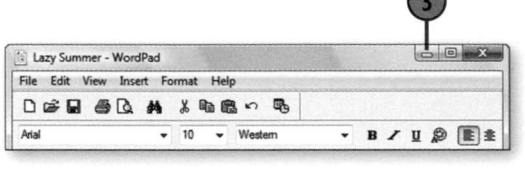

Tip

To automatically arrange all the windows on your Desktop, right-click a blank spot on the taskbar, and choose the arrangement you want from the shortcut menu.

Try This!

Double-click the title bar of a maximized window to restore the window to its original size. Double-click the title bar again to return the window to its maximized size. Now press Alt+Spacebar to open the window's Control menu, and choose the action you want from the menu.

Use the Mouse to Resize a Window

1 Move the mouse over one of the borders of the window until the mouse pointer changes into a two-headed arrow. Drag the window border until the window is the size you want. The directions of the arrowheads show you the directions in which you can move the window border.

See Also

"Mouse Moves" on page 19 for information about dragging items with the mouse.

Try This!

Move your mouse over a side border, and drag the border to change the window's width. Now move your mouse over the bottom border, and drag the border to change the window's height. Finally, move your mouse over one of the window's corners to change both its height and its width.

Tip

You can't manually resize a maximized window, so if the window you want to resize is currently maximized, click the Restore Down button.

Move a Window

1 Point to the window's title bar, and drag the window to a new location.

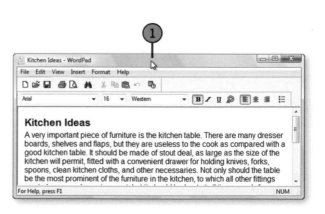

Using Shortcut Menus for Quick Results

Windows Vista and the programs that work with it were designed to be intuitive—that is, they anticipate what you're likely to want to do when you're working on a particular task, and they place the appropriate commands on a shortcut menu that you open by clicking the right mouse button. These shortcut menus are dynamic, which means they change depending on the task in progress.

Use a Shortcut Menu Command

(1) Right-click an item.

(2) Choose a command from the shortcut menu to accomplish the task at hand. If the item or action you want isn't listed on the shortcut menu:

- From the shortcut menu, choose an item whose name has an arrow next to it to see whether the item or action you want is on one of the shortcut menu's submenus.

- Check to be sure you right-clicked the proper item.

- Check the program's documentation or Help files to verify that what you want to do can be accomplished from the item you right-clicked.

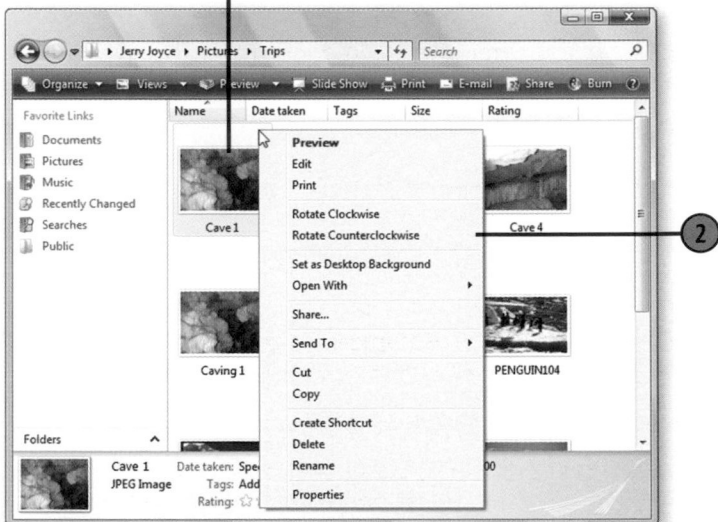

Tip

The tasks listed on the toolbar in a folder window are also dynamic, depending on the types of files in the folder, but they usually provide actions that are less specific than those listed on a shortcut menu.

Tip

When in doubt, right-click! If you're not sure how to accomplish what you want to do, right-click the item in question, and you'll usually see an appropriate command on the shortcut menu.

Try This!

See what's on the shortcut menus. Right-click the Start button, and note the commands on the shortcut menu that appears. Right-click a button on the taskbar, and then right-click a blank spot on the taskbar. Open the Start menu, and right-click an item. Continue experimenting by right-clicking the Recycle Bin icon on the Desktop, other items on the Desktop, and various files and folders in folder windows. Amazing, isn't it?

Getting Help

What are big and colorful; packed with information, procedures, shortcuts, and links to online information; and sadly underutilized? The Help programs! Of course, they couldn't possibly replace this book, but you can use them to find concise step-by-step procedures for diagnosing and overcoming problems, and to explore many aspects of managing Windows. You can access Help from the Start menu or from within a program.

Browse the Help And Support Center

1. Click the Start button, and choose Help And Support from the Start menu to open the Windows Help And Support Center.

2. Do either of the following:

    • Click a topic, and browse to display a list of topics you can choose to view.

    • Type a question or keywords, and press Enter to search Help.

3. Click a link to the main topic of interest. If the item has subtopics, click the subtopic you want.

4. Review the content of the Help topic.

5. If the content doesn't answer your question, use the Back button to return to the previously viewed topic, and choose a different item to read. Use the Forward button, if available, to look at a previously viewed item.

6. To print a displayed topic, click Print, and select your print preferences in the Print dialog box.

7. To look up another topic, use the Search box to search Help.

8. To continue browsing the Help topics, click either the Home button to select another topic or find additional help, or the Browse Help button to see the Help table of contents.

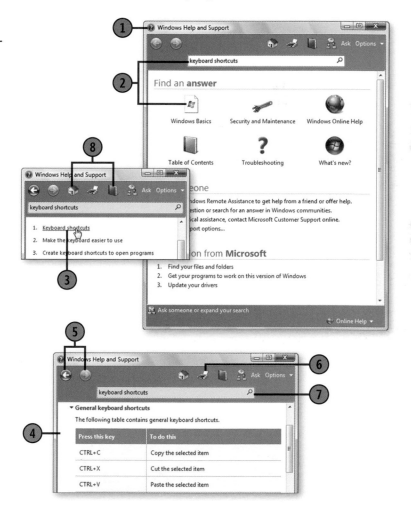

Windows Vista and You

Your version of Windows Vista might look quite different from, and work quite differently from, your friend's or your coworker's version. Different versions of Windows Vista have different features, but even the same version will look and run differently, depending on the capabilities of the computer on which it's installed. You'll find the greatest number of tools and features in the Ultimate version. The two Home versions—Home Basic and Home Premium—provide features that are a subset of the Ultimate version, and they're designed to work on a stand-alone computer or on a small network. Although the Home Basic version contains a subset of the Home Premium version's features, it doesn't include Windows Media Center, the Tablet PC tools, and the advanced graphics features such as the Windows Aero glass appearance. The two business versions—Business and Enterprise—provide features that are different subsets of the Ultimate version. They're designed to work on a business network using a domain, and they provide high levels of file management and security.

But wait—there's more! Once you're familiar with which features your version of Windows has, you need to understand what your computer can do with those features. Because Windows is scalable to the capabilities of your computer—meaning that Windows will do only what it can based on your computer's hardware—it can present varying features and appearances. The Aero glass appearance, thumbnail previews of your open windows, and 3-D effects require a lot from the graphics adapter in your computer, so many computers can't display these features. If you have a slightly underpowered graphics adapter, you'll see the Vista Basic color scheme—an attractive but less dramatic look, which doesn't support either the Aero glass appearance or the 3-D effects.

So, if your version of Windows Vista doesn't do something you expect it to, check out which version you're running and what your computer is capable of doing with that version. To find that information, see "Checking the Status of Windows" on page 306. And, if you realize that the version of Windows Vista you have isn't the right one for you, see "Upgrading Windows Vista" on page 324.

The Windows Vista Aero glass appearance

The Windows Vista Basic appearance

3

Running Programs and Gadgets

Getting to know the programs that come with Windows Vista is a bit like moving into new living quarters. Just as your new abode has the basics—stove, refrigerator, and (dare we say it?) windows—the Windows Vista operating system comes with many basic accessories and tools. Just as you'll add all the accoutrements that transform empty rooms into a cozy home, you'll add programs to Windows Vista to utilize its full potential.

But let's cover the basics first. We'll do some everyday tasks in WordPad: composing, saving, and printing a document; creating and editing text; copying items between documents that were created in different programs; and inserting characters such as © and é that don't exist on your keyboard. We'll look at the Calculator, which is handy for scientific calculations as well as basic arithmetic. We'll explore the Tablet PC tools, including the Input Panel for entering text, either with handwriting or the On-Screen Keyboard; onscreen Sticky Notes for jotting down quick notes; the Snipping Tool for copying just about anything on your computer; and the Journal, where you can write and annotate to your heart's content. We'll show you the little Gadget programs that you can run on the Sidebar or on your Desktop. And, for all you MS-DOS fans, we'll discuss working at the command prompt and running MS-DOS programs.

Composing a Document

WordPad is a powerful little word processor you can use to create documents either in Rich Text Format or as plain Text Documents. In most cases, you'll want to create a document with formatting for a well-designed, professional look. Save the document as you create it, and print it when you've finished.

Create a Document

1. Click the Start button, type **wordpad** in the Search box of the Start menu, and click WordPad to start the program. If WordPad is already running, click the New button on the toolbar, click Rich Text Document in the list, and click OK.

2. Type your text. Press Enter only when you want to start a new paragraph.

3. To edit the text, click in the document where you want to make the change. An insertion point indicates where your edit will be placed.

4. To insert additional text into a paragraph you've already typed, click where you want to insert the new text, and type it. If the text you want to insert is stored on the Clipboard, click the Paste button on the toolbar (or press Ctrl+V) instead of typing the text.

5. To delete text, select it, and press Delete. To save the text for later use instead of deleting it, place it on the Clipboard by clicking the Cut button on the toolbar (or pressing Ctrl+X).

6. To replace existing text with different text, select the text, and then type the new text.

The New button

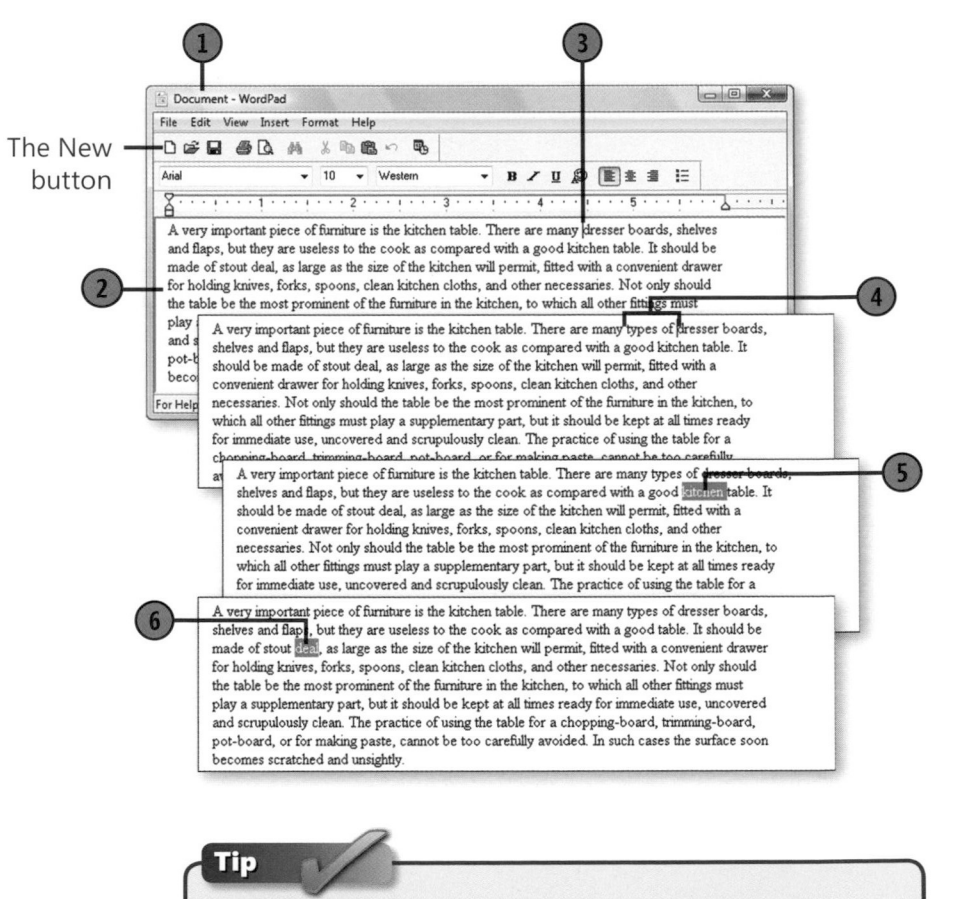

Tip

The Windows Clipboard is a temporary "holding area" for items you copy or cut; it holds only one item at a time.

Format the Document

1. Select the text to be formatted.

2. Specify the font, font size, and font script (the locale or type of font). Apply bold, italic, underlined, or color emphasis as desired.

3. Click in the paragraph you want to format, or select all the paragraphs to which you want to apply the same formatting.

4. Use the Alignment buttons to align your text, or use the Bullets button to create a bulleted list.

5. Drag the indent markers to set the left, right, and first-line indents. Click in the ruler to set a tab stop.

6. Save the document.

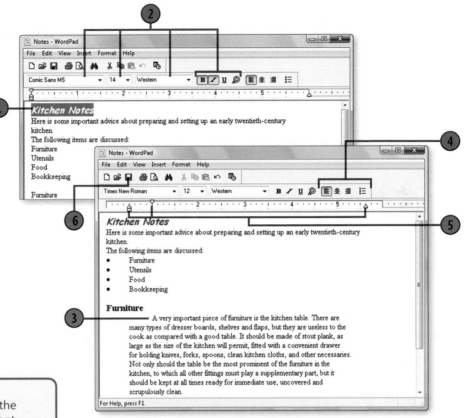

Try This!

Select some text in a document, and choose Font from the Format menu. In the Font dialog box, specify a font, a font size, and any emphasis you want, and then click OK. Now click in a paragraph, choose Paragraph from the Format menu, and use the Paragraph dialog box to set exact measurements for the paragraph indents you want. Click OK. Choose Tabs from the Format menu, and use the Tabs dialog box to set the exact position of any tabs you want in the paragraph. Click OK. Now move to the end of the paragraph, press Enter, and type some text. You'll see that all the paragraph formatting from the previous paragraph has been copied and applied to the new paragraph.

Caution

If you're planning to save your document as a plain Text Document, don't apply any formatting to it. If you do, all the formatting will be lost when you save the document.

Saving, Closing, and Opening a Document

After you've created a document, you'll probably want to save it for later use. When you've finished creating the document, close the program in which you created it so that the program isn't using space or taking power from your computer. When you're ready to work on your document again, you can easily restart the program and open the document directly from the running program.

Save a Document

1 Click the Save button on the toolbar, or, if the toolbar isn't visible, choose Save from the File menu.

2 If you don't want to save the document to the default folder, specify a different location. If the Favorite Links list isn't displayed, click the Browse Folders button.

3 Type a name for the document. The name can be up to 255 characters long (including any path and file extension); it can contain spaces but can't contain the * : < > | " \ or /characters. Note that long file names are often truncated by programs, so a descriptive short name is best.

4 If you want to save the document in a different format from that of the default file format, select the format.

5 Click Save. As you work with the document, click Save frequently. Windows will now save the file without displaying the Save As dialog box.

Try This!

Many programs can stay open for additional work after you close the document you're working on. Open the File menu and look at the commands. If there's a Close command, click it to close the document without closing the program. If there's a New command but no Close command, choose New to see whether it closes the open document.

See Also

"Accessing Everything" on pages 16–17 for information about navigating to different folders or drives.

Tip

In many programs, you can press Ctrl+S to quickly save a document.

Close a Document

① Click the Save button one last time to make sure that you've saved all the changes in the document.

② Click the Close button to end the program.

Tip

Most, but not all, programs use the Save As and Open dialog boxes, just like the ones in WordPad. If you have a program that uses its own style of dialog box, you'll probably need to consult the program's documentation for additional help.

Open a Document

① With the program you want to use running, choose Open from the File menu to display the Open dialog box.

② If necessary, specify the location of the document you want.

③ If necessary, double-click a folder to navigate to the document. Continue double-clicking folders until you locate the document.

④ Specify the file type of the document you want to open. Only documents of the specified file type will be displayed in the list of files.

⑤ If you can't locate the document, type its name, or part of the name, in the Search box.

⑥ Double-click the document to open it.

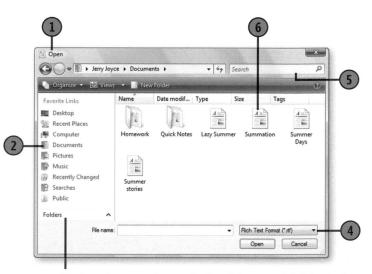

Click to browse through the drives and folders of the computer and the network to specify a location.

Copying Material Between Documents

It's easy to copy material from a document that was created in one program to a document that was created in another program. The way you insert the material depends on what it is. If it's similar to and compatible with the receiving document—some text that's being copied into a WordPad document, for example—you can usually insert it as is and can edit it in the receiving document's program. If the item is dissimilar—a sound clip, say, inserted into a WordPad document—either it's *encapsulated* (isolated) as an object and can be edited in the originating program only, or you simply are not able to paste that item into your document.

Copy and Insert Material

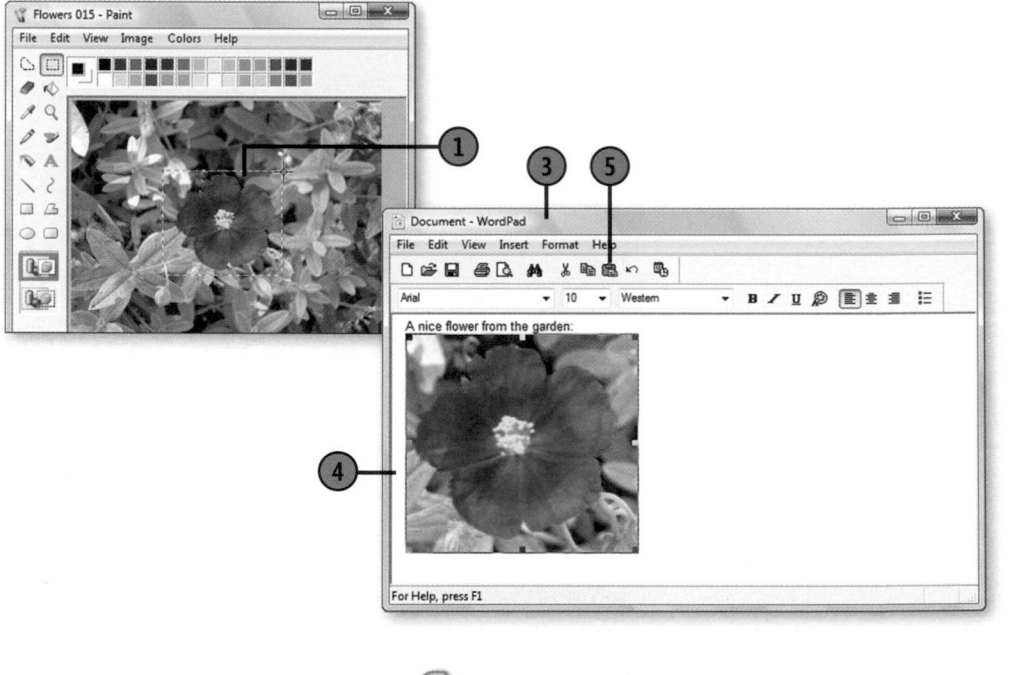

1 In the source document, select the material you want to copy.

2 Choose Copy from the Edit menu (or press Ctlr+C). Windows places copied items on the Windows Clipboard. (You can copy only one item at a time, so always paste the Clipboard contents into your document before you copy anything else, or you'll lose whatever was on the Clipboard.)

3 Switch to the destination document.

4 Click where you want to insert the material.

5 Click the Paste button, choose Paste from the Edit menu, or press Ctrl+V.

Tip

Some programs—those that are part of Microsoft Office, for example—have their own Clipboard, which allows you to store and retrieve multiple copied items from Office programs.

Tip

To insert the copied material in a different format, or as an icon for an online document, choose Paste Special from the Edit menu (provided the command is available on the menu) instead of choosing the Paste command.

Copying Your Screen Content

You use the Snipping Tool program to capture an image—or a snippet—of a Web page or just about anything else on your computer screen. You can then e-mail the image, save it, or paste it into a document in another program. When you save or e-mail a snipped image, it's saved as a single-page HTML document. When the image is that of a Web page, the URL (the Web address) is automatically inserted into the document.

Snip an Image

(1) If the Snipping Tool isn't already running, click the Start button, type **snip** in the Search box of the Start menu, and then click Snipping Tool to start the program.

(2) Click the down arrow next to the New button, and select the type of snip you want:

- Free Form Snip to capture in any shape

- Rectangular Snip to capture a rectangular snip

- Window Snip to capture a program or a folder window

- Full-Screen Snip to capture everything on your screen

(3) Capture your snip. For free form and rectangular snips, drag out the shape with the mouse (while holding down the left mouse button) or a stylus. For a window snip, click or tap anywhere in the window. The full-screen snip is captured automatically.

(4) In the Snipping Tool window, use any of the tools to save, copy, send, or modify the snip.

(5) Click New to capture another image, or click Close to exit the Snipping Tool.

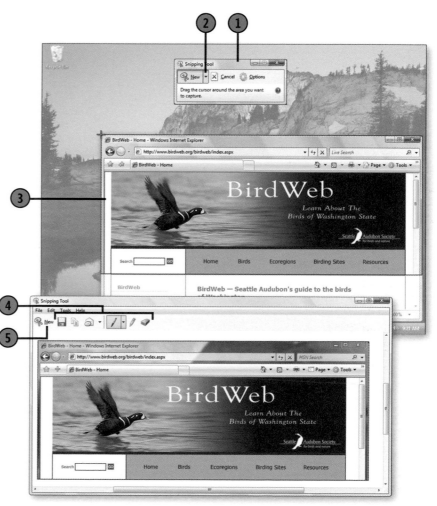

Dialog Box Decisions

You're going to be seeing a lot of dialog boxes as you use Windows Vista, and if you're not familiar with them now, you soon will be. Dialog boxes appear when Windows Vista or a program—WordPad, let's say—needs you to make one or more decisions about what you want to do. Sometimes all you have to do is click a Yes, a No, or an OK button; at other times, there'll be quite a few decisions to make in one dialog box. The Print dialog box, shown below, is typical of many dialog boxes and is one you'll probably be seeing frequently, so take a look at its components and the way they work.

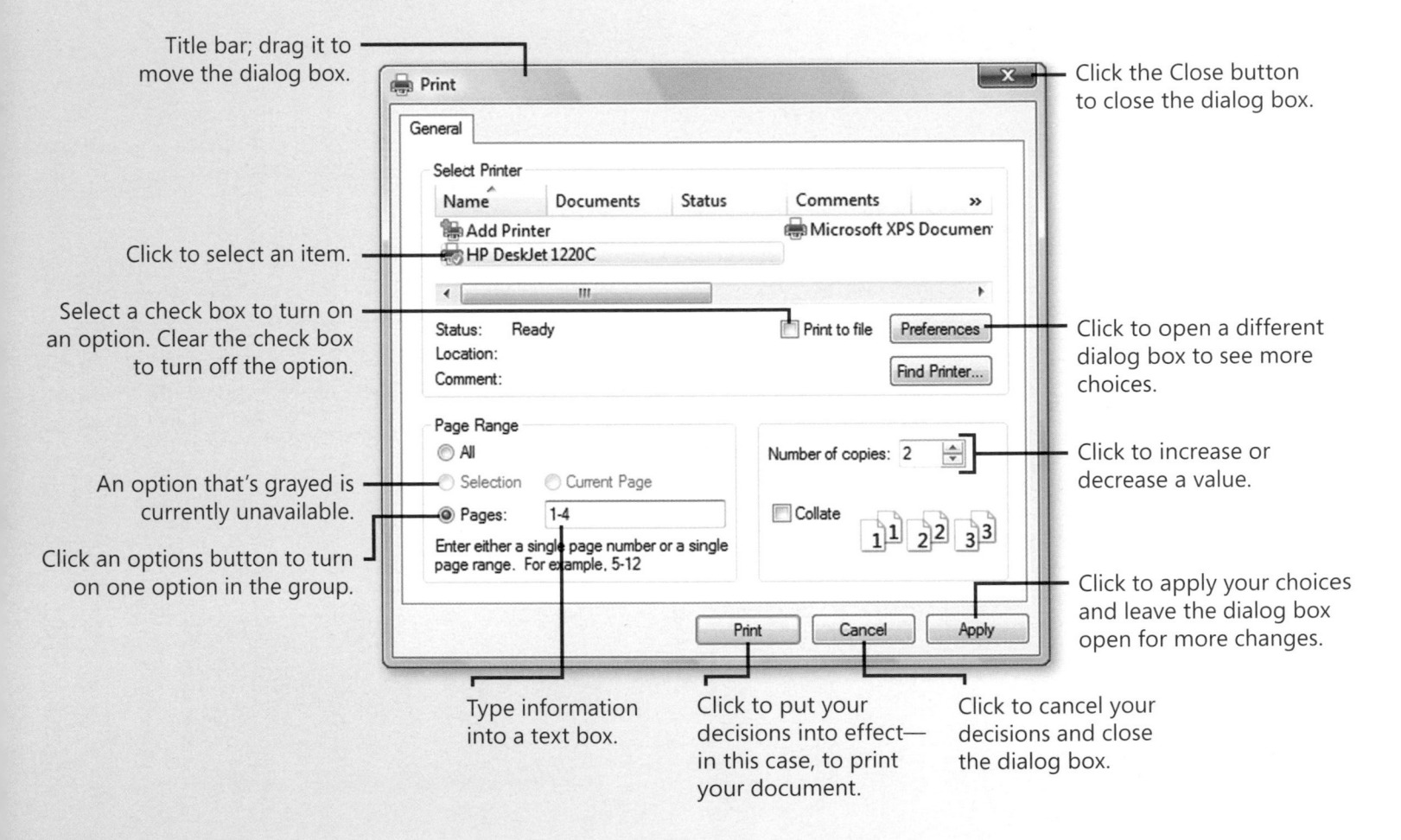

Title bar; drag it to move the dialog box.

Click the Close button to close the dialog box.

Click to select an item.

Select a check box to turn on an option. Clear the check box to turn off the option.

Click to open a different dialog box to see more choices.

An option that's grayed is currently unavailable.

Click an options button to turn on one option in the group.

Click to increase or decrease a value.

Click to apply your choices and leave the dialog box open for more changes.

Type information into a text box.

Click to put your decisions into effect— in this case, to print your document.

Click to cancel your decisions and close the dialog box.

Inserting Special Characters

Windows Vista provides a special accessory program called Character Map that lets you insert into your programs those characters and symbols that aren't available on your keyboard.

Character Map displays all the characters that are available for each of the fonts on your computer.

Find and Insert a Character

1. Start Character Map from the System Tools folder of the Start menu, or click the Start button, type **char** in the Search box of the Start menu, and click Character Map to start the program.

2. Specify a font.

3. Double-click the character you want to insert. Double-click any other characters that you want to insert at the same time.

4. Click Copy to place the character or characters on the Clipboard.

5. Switch to your program, click where you want to insert the character or characters, and choose Paste from the Edit menu (or press Ctrl+V) to paste the character or characters from the Clipboard into your document. Format and edit the inserted text as desired.

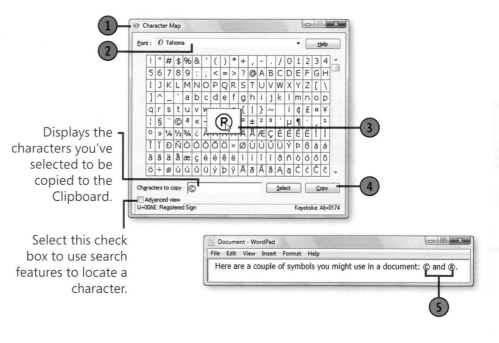

Displays the characters you've selected to be copied to the Clipboard.

Select this check box to use search features to locate a character.

See Also

"Turning Windows Components On or Off" on page 242 for information about installing Character Map if it isn't already installed.

Try This!

In Character Map, select a character you insert frequently, and note the keyboard shortcut for the character in the bottom-right corner of the Character Map dialog box. Switch to the program into which you want to insert the character, hold down the Alt key, and use the numeric keypad to enter the numbers. Format the inserted character with a different font or font size if desired.

Crunching Numbers

Need to do a quick calculation but don't have enough fingers? Want to convert a decimal number into a hexadecimal or binary number? You can do these procedures, and even a few complex geometric and statistical calculations, with the Calculator.

Use the Calculator

1. Start the Calculator from the Accessories folder of the Start menu, or click the Start button, type **calc** in the Search box of the Start menu, and click Calculator to start the program.

2. Either click the number buttons or type the numerals you want. Continue until you've entered the entire number.

3. Click a function.

4. Enter the next number.

5. When you've entered all the numbers, click the equal (=) button. Press Ctrl+C to copy the result if you want to paste it into your document.

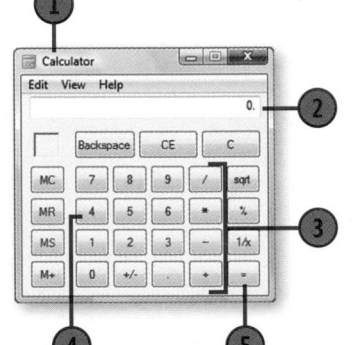

Make Complex Calculations

(1) Choose Scientific from the View menu.

(2) Choose a numbering system if you don't want to calculate using the standard decimal system.

(3) Enter a value.

(4) Use any of the function keys to calculate a new value.

(5) If you want to do statistical calculations, click Sta to display the Statistics Box dialog box.

(6) Enter the first number to be used in the statistics, and click Dat. The number you entered will be added to the Statistics Box dialog box. Continue entering the data you want to use, clicking Dat after each entry.

(7) Review the data in the Statistics Box dialog box. If you need to delete an entry, click the entry to select it, and then click CD to delete that entry.

(8) Click the button for the statistic you want:

• Ave for the average of all the data

• Sum for the sum of the data

• s for the standard deviation

(9) Close the Statistics Box dialog box when you've finished.

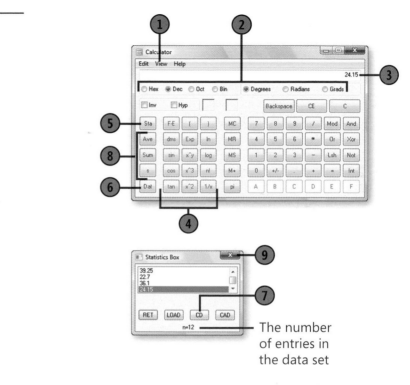

The number of entries in the data set

Try This!

With the decimal numbering system selected, enter a number. Click Hex to see the number in the hexadecimal system, click Oct to see the number in the octal system, and click Bin to see the number in the binary system.

Writing Your Text

The Tablet PC Input Panel isn't just for Tablet PCs any more! You can enter text in a program by writing on the Input Panel using a pen-sensitive computer (such as a Tablet PC), or you can use a digitizing pad, a stylus or similar interface tool, or even just your mouse. The Input Panel has two writing modes—the Writing Pad, where you can write anywhere on a line, and the Character Pad if you want to write one character at a time. However, these two modes are similar—you can even use the Character Pad to make corrections to your text when you use the Writing Pad. Whichever method you use to write your text, the program recognizes your writing and converts it into standard digital text. You can then insert the text into a document.

Write Your Text

① Make sure that the program into which you want to insert your text is running. Then click the Start button, type **inp** in the Search box of the Start menu, and click Input Panel to start the program. If the Input Panel is already running but minimized, click or tap on the Input Panel tab.

② Click the Writing Pad button if it isn't already selected.

③ Write your text.

④ If your text isn't recognized correctly, click the incorrect word.

⑤ Do any of the following:

- Click one of the alternative words.

- Rewrite the incorrect letter or letters.

- Point to an incorrect letter, click the down arrow, and click the alternative letter or action you want.

⑥ Click OK.

⑦ Click Insert to insert the text into your program.

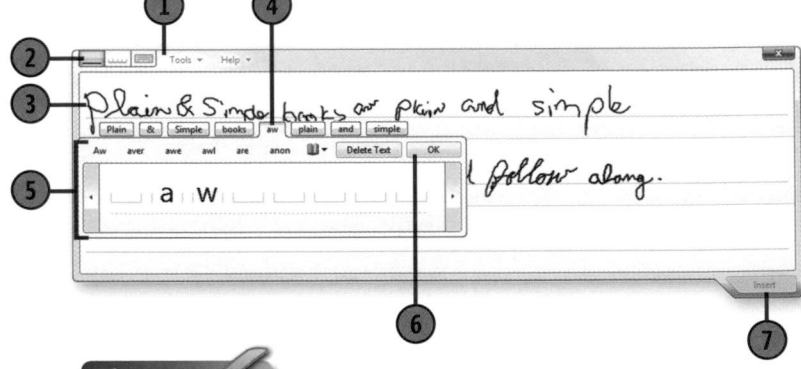

Tip

With so many different input methods and types of hardware, we can't describe in exact detail all the ways you can use your equipment. For example, if you're using your mouse, hold down the left mouse button to write. If you're using a stylus, just write and tap to execute a mouse-click. You'll need to experiment to find the best way to use your input system with these Tablet PC tools.

Tip

If you want to edit the text that you've imported into the program, select the text, and it will automatically be returned to the Correction pane of the Input Panel.

Add Other Elements

1 With no written text in the Input Panel, use the navigation buttons to move the insertion point to the location where you want it in the program.

2 Tap or click any of the following:

- The typographic element you want

- The editing keys to delete any content

- The Num button to display the Number pad, the Sym button to display the Symbols pad, or the Web button to display the Web Quick Keys pad, and then the item you want to insert into your document

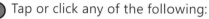

Bksp and Del are editing buttons.

Tab, Enter, and Space are typographic buttons.

← and → are navigation buttons.

Number pad

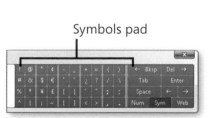

Symbols pad

Web Quick Keys pad

Tip

To modify the Input Panel's location; to improve the handwriting recognition; or to change the way the Input Panel opens, edits existing text, and displays handwritten text, open the Tools menu before you write any text.

Typing on Your Screen

The On-Screen Keyboard mode of the Tablet PC Input Panel lets you enter text directly onto your screen instead of using a physical keyboard. The content you enter appears in the document of your currently running program.

Type Your Content

① Make sure that the program into which you want to insert your text is running. Then click the Start button, type **inp** in the Search box of the Start menu, and click Input Panel to start the program. If the Input Panel is already running but minimized, click or tap the Input Panel tab.

② Click the On-Screen Keyboard button.

③ Tap or click each character to enter it.

④ To modify the keyboard, tap or click a modifier key—for example, the Shift, Caps, or Func key. Tap or click the key a second time to turn off the change.

⑤ To enter keyboard shortcuts, tap or click the Alt and/or Ctrl key and then the assigned key. The Alt and/or Ctrl keys will be turned off automatically when the keyboard shortcut is completed.

⑥ Tap or click the navigation and editing keys to use them just as you would on a standard keyboard.

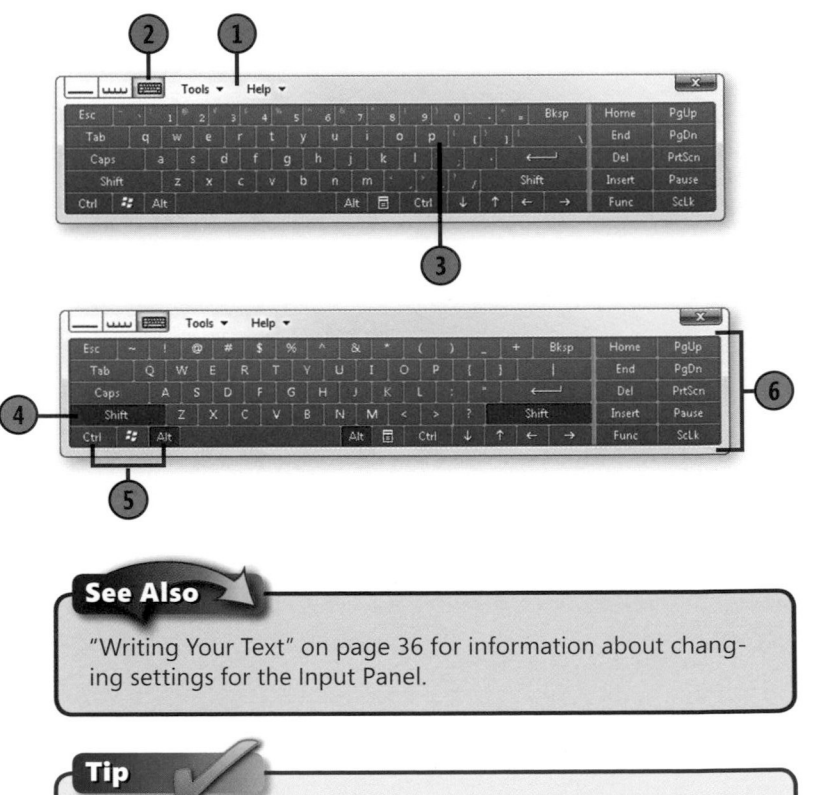

See Also

"Writing Your Text" on page 36 for information about changing settings for the Input Panel.

Tip

Windows Vista has another On-Screen Keyboard that isn't part of the Tablet PC Tools and that is available in all editions of Windows Vista as one of the Ease Of Access tools. To access this keyboard, click the Start button, type **key** in the Search box of the Start menu, and click On-Screen Keyboard.

Writing Quick Notes

Just like those little sticky notes that clutter up your desk or parade around the edges of your computer screen, the Tablet PC Sticky Notes tool is a great way to jot down a reminder, an idea, an address, or a phone number—and, because these particular Sticky Notes stack up in one container, bye-bye clutter! But there's another big difference—not only can you write a note, you can record up to a 30-seconds-long sound note, too.

Write and Read Your Notes

1 If Sticky Notes isn't already running, click the Start button, type **stic** in the Search box of the Start menu, and click Sticky Notes to start the program.

2 Use your writing input device or hold down the left mouse button, and write or draw your note. The note is saved automatically.

3 If you want to create another note, tap or click New Note, and write your content.

4 Tap or click the Record button to use a microphone to record a note. Click Stop when you've finished recording.

5 Tap or click the Next Note or Previous Note arrow to review your existing notes.

6 If you want to insert your current note as a picture into a document, click the Copy button, and then paste the picture into the document. However, note that not all types of documents accept pictures.

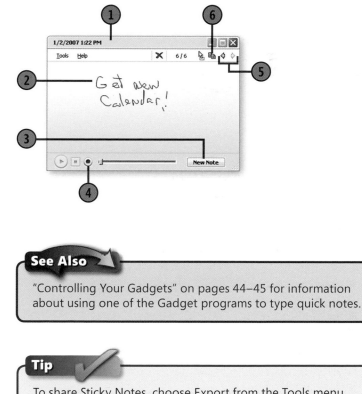

See Also

"Controlling Your Gadgets" on pages 44–45 for information about using one of the Gadget programs to type quick notes.

Tip

To share Sticky Notes, choose Export from the Tools menu, save the Sticky Notes file, and send it to someone else. To add other notes to your existing stack, choose Import from the Tools menu, and open the Sticky Notes file.

Writing and Drawing Notes

The Windows Journal is an extremely versatile tool that provides an ideal palette on which you can assemble diverse types of information. Although it's primarily for writing notes and making quick sketches with a stylus, you can modify the content, move it around, and even convert your hand-writing to text.

Write and Draw

① If the Journal isn't already running, click the Start button, type **jou** in the Search box of the Start menu, and click Windows Journal to start the program.

② Write a title for the note using your stylus or mouse.

③ If you want to use a different pen color or shape, click and choose your options from the Pen drop-down menu. To make additional changes, choose Pen Settings, and make your selections in the Pen And Highlighter Settings dialog box.

④ Write the content of your notes and draw the pictures using your stylus or mouse.

⑤ To highlight any material, click the Highlighter button, and drag the highlight over the desired items. To use a different highlight color or width, click the down arrow next to the Highlighter button. To return to writing or drawing, click the Pen button again.

⑥ To delete content, click the Eraser button, and drag the Eraser over the content you want to remove.

⑦ Click Save to save the note. Click Save periodically to save your most recent edits.

Tip

To always open a note with a specific template, pen color or shape, or to design your default page using line spacing and a background picture, choose Options from the Tools menu, and make the settings you want.

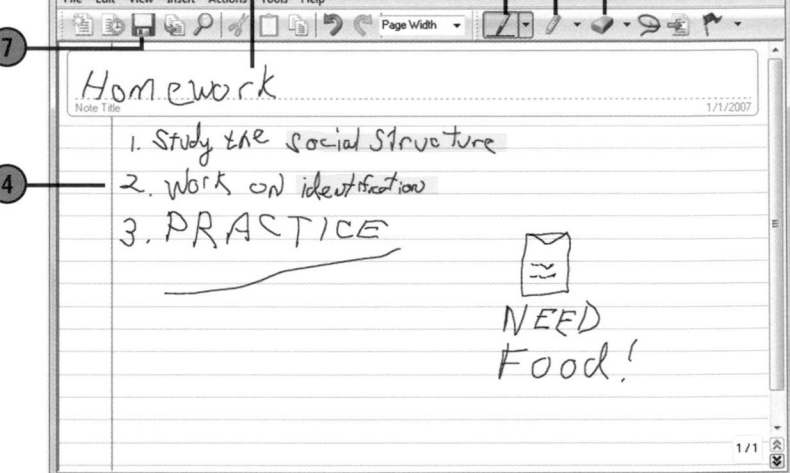

Tip

To use a different background—for example, music staffs, graph paper, or a monthly calendar, among others—choose New Note From Template from the File menu, and select the background you want from the list in the Open dialog box.

Modify and Use Your Content

(1) Click the Selection Tool, and drag the selection around the material you want to change.

(2) To modify the content, do any of the following:

• Drag it to a new location.

• Drag a sizing box to increase or decrease the size of the content.

• Click the Cut or Copy button to move or copy the content to the Windows Clipboard.

• Choose Format Ink from the Edit menu to change the color and thickness of the ink or to apply bold or italic formatting to the selection.

• Choose Convert Selection To E-Mail from the Actions menu to convert writing to text and then send the text in an e-mail message.

• Choose Convert Selection To Text from the Actions menu to convert the writing to text and then either copy the text to the Windows Clipboard or replace the selected writing with text.

• Point to Change Shape To on the Actions menu, and choose the shape you want the selected content to be converted to.

(3) Click the Pen button, and add more writing or drawings.

(4) Click any of the editing buttons to modify your document.

(5) Click Save.

(6) Click New Note to create a new note, or click the Close button to end your work in the Journal.

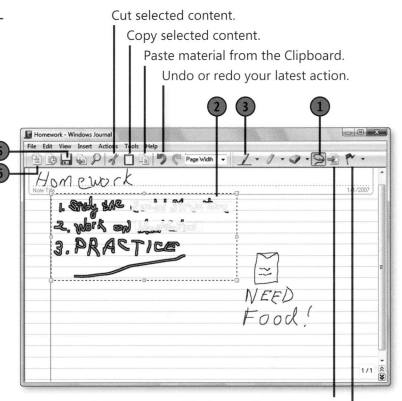

Cut selected content.
Copy selected content.
Paste material from the Clipboard.
Undo or redo your latest action.

Add or remove blank space in the Journal.
Add an identification flag.

Tip ✓

Whenever you choose to convert writing to text, a dialog box appears in which you can then correct the handwriting-recognition results. If the results are so bad that the correct text isn't offered as an alternative, use your physical keyboard or the On-Screen Keyboard in the Input Panel to enter the correct text.

Annotating a Document

One of the most useful features of the Windows Journal is the ability it gives you to import a document from another program and then annotate the document with written notes, pictures, and highlights. This feature makes the Journal one of our favorite tools, whether or not we use a stylus for input.

There are two ways to import a document: Either the Journal automatically opens the document in its default program and then uses a special printer driver, or you open the document in its program and then use the printer driver to send the content of the document to the Journal.

Make Your Comments

(1) If the Journal isn't already running, click the Start button, type **jou** in the Search box of the Start menu, and click Windows Journal to start the program.

(2) Click the Import button, select the file to be used, and click or tap the Import button in the Import dialog box. If you haven't already installed the Journal printer driver, do so when requested. If the Journal can't open the program for the type of file you want, open the file in its correct program, choose to print it with the Journal Note Printer, and save the print file as a note.

(3) Use the Journal tools to annotate the document. You can't, however, modify the actual content of the document.

(4) Save the annotated note.

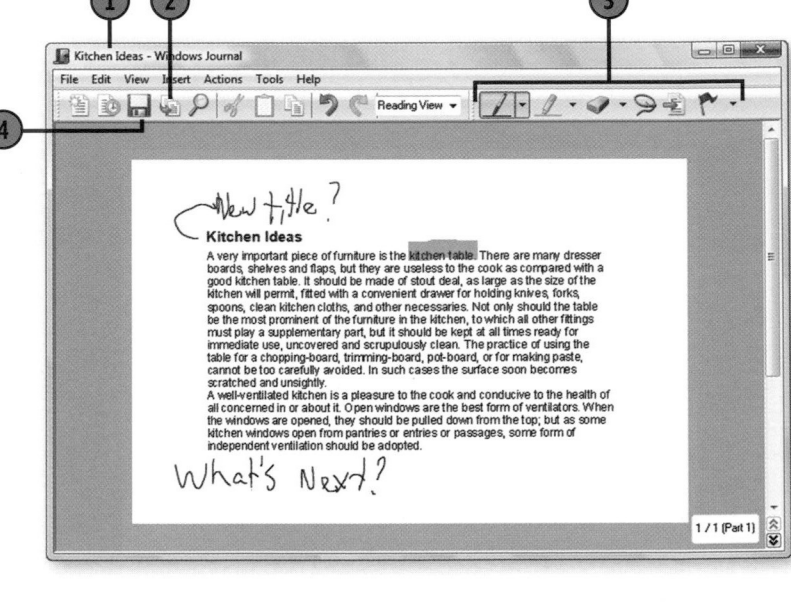

Sharing Your Journal Notes

Why keep all the creative information you've recorded in the Windows Journal to yourself? You have a variety of choices as to the way you share that content, and you can share it even if the person you're sharing it with doesn't have the Windows Journal installed on his or her computer.

E-Mail Your Note

1 With the Journal open and your note complete, choose Send To Mail Recipient from the File menu to display the Send To Mail Recipient dialog box.

2 Select the format you want to use to send the note:

- Journal Note to send the note as an attachment that can be opened only in Windows Journal. The recipient can then edit the received note.

- Web Page to send the note as a single-file Web page that can be opened in Internet Explorer or other Web browsers. The content, however, can't be edited.

- Black And White Image to send the note as a picture in the .tif format. The content can't be edited except as a graphic, and any color properties will be lost.

3 Click OK.

4 Add any content to your e-mail message, and then send it.

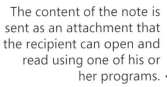

The content of the note is sent as an attachment that the recipient can open and read using one of his or her programs.

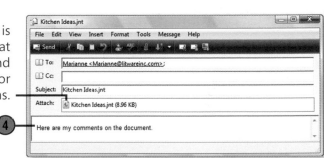

> **Tip** ✓
>
> To save a note in a format others can read without having the Windows Journal installed, choose Export As from the File menu, and, in the Save As Type list, save the note in a Web Archive (a single-file Web page) or as a Tagged Image File Format (.tif) to save the note as a black-and-white image.

Controlling Your Gadgets

Gadgets are nice little programs that sit quietly on your Desktop doing their own specific thing, usually without your having to do much to make them work.

Control the Gadget

1. Point to the gadget you want to control.

2. Click the Options button.

3. Make whatever settings you want.

4. Click OK.

5. Point to the gadget again, and control it using any controls that appear.

6. To move the gadget up or down the Sidebar, or to move it off the Sidebar, point to the gadget's handle, and drag the gadget into the position you want.

7. If you've added more gadgets than will fit in a single column, click the left or right arrow to see your additional gadgets.

Tip

Each gadget is an individual program that works in its own way. Therefore, the controls for using it, as well as its options, are different for each gadget.

Try This!

Right-click a gadget, point to Opacity on the shortcut menu that appears, and choose an opacity percentage from the submenu that appears. Right-click the gadget again, and choose Remove From Sidebar. Right-click the gadget again, and choose Attach To Sidebar.

See Also

"Controlling the Sidebar" on pages 46–47 for information about displaying the Sidebar if it isn't already displayed.

Add or Delete Gadgets

1. Click the Gadgets button to display the Gadgets window.

2. Double-click a gadget to add it to the Sidebar.

3. Click Get More Gadgets Online to see and download other gadgets from the Web.

4. Double-click any other gadgets you want to add, including any that you downloaded.

5. Close the Gadgets window when you've finished.

6. To remove a gadget, point to it and click the Delete button. The gadget is deleted from the Sidebar, but the file remains stored on your computer in case you want to restore it.

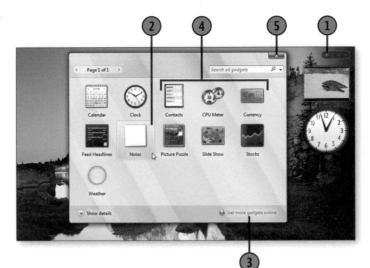

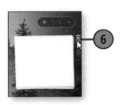

Tip

To see a list of all the gadgets on your Sidebar and who created them, right-click the Sidebar, and choose Properties from the shortcut menu to display the Windows Sidebar Properties dialog box.

Caution

Gadgets are individual programs, many of which haven't been fully tested or reviewed by Microsoft Therefore, it's a good idea to read any reviews and find out what you can about the source that's providing the gadget before you download it.

Try This!

Add the Notes gadget to your Sidebar. Click in the gadget, and type a note. Click the plus sign to create a new blank note, and type your information. Unlike the way you use the Sticky Notes program, you use the keyboard to type your notes in the Notes gadget instead of using a stylus or mouse. Each note will be saved until you delete it.

Controlling the Sidebar

The Windows Sidebar is a nifty section of your Desktop. You can store all sorts of gadgets on the Sidebar and can organize your gadgets so that they don't take up a lot of space on your Desktop. You can switch between showing and hiding the Sidebar and all its gadgets, move it to the other side of the Desktop, or display it on a different monitor if you're using dual monitors. If you don't want to use the Sidebar at all, you can simply turn it off instead of hiding it.

Display, Hide, or Exit the Sidebar

① If you want to use the Sidebar but you don't see either the Sidebar or the Sidebar icon in the notification area of the taskbar, click the Start button, type **sideb** in the Search box of the Start menu, and click Windows Sidebar to start the feature.

② If you want to hide the Sidebar and all its gadgets, right-click a blank area of the Sidebar, and choose Close Sidebar from the shortcut menu.

③ If the Sidebar isn't displayed but the Sidebar icon appears in the notification area of the taskbar, click the Sidebar icon if you want to display the Sidebar.

④ If you don't want to use the Sidebar at all, right-click the Sidebar icon, and choose Exit from the shortcut menu. If you want to use the Sidebar again, you'll need to start again it from the Start menu.

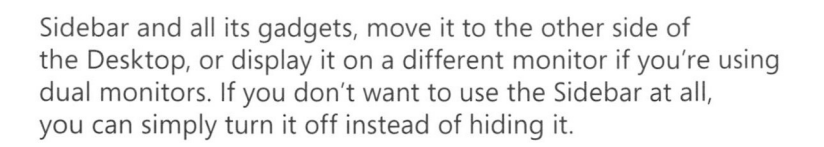

See Also

"Customize the Notification Area of the Taskbar" on page 263 for information about showing and hiding icons in the notification area of the taskbar.

Move the Sidebar

(1) Right-click the Sidebar icon on the taskbar, and choose Properties from the shortcut menu to display the Windows Sidebar Properties dialog box.

(2) Select this check box if you want the Sidebar to be on top of any open windows rather than having windows on top of the Sidebar.

(3) Clear this check box if you don't want the Sidebar to start every time you start Windows.

(4) Specify on which side of your Desktop you want the Sidebar to be displayed.

(5) If you have more than one monitor connected to your computer, click this button, and specify on which monitor you want the Sidebar to appear.

(6) Click OK.

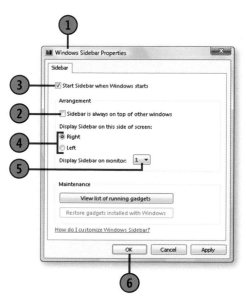

The Sidebar appears on the left side of screen and is set to be on top of other windows.

Running Commands

In Windows Vista, the command prompt is the place where you can execute command-line instructions. Most of the commands are the old standard MS-DOS commands, some are enhancements of the MS-DOS commands, and others are commands unique to Windows Vista. When you want or need to work from the command prompt, you can open a command-prompt window and execute all your tasks

there, including using the basic commands, starting a program, and even starting a program in a new window. Note that the command prompt is a powerful weapon that can disrupt your system, delete files, and create general havoc. Don't execute commands unless you know what they're designed for.

Run a Command

① Click the Start button, type **prompt** in the Search box of the Start menu, and click Command Prompt to open the Command Prompt window.

② At the prompt, type a command, including any switches and extra parameters, and press Enter.

③ Enter any additional commands you want to run.

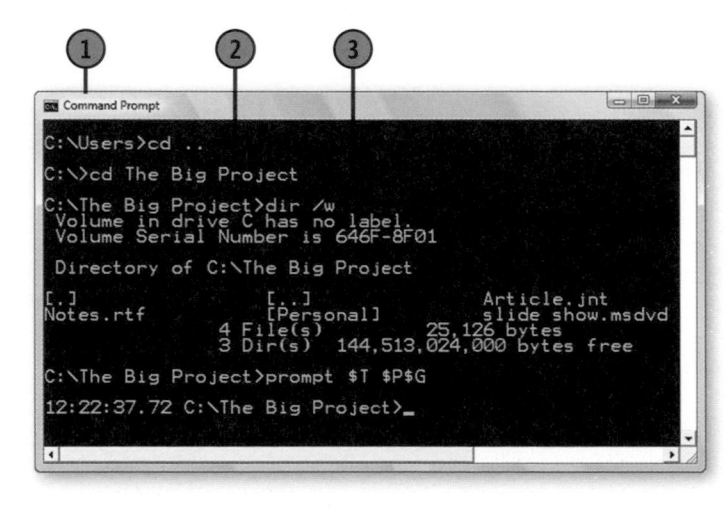

The Top 10 Command Prompt Commands

Command	Function
cd	Switches to the specified folder (or directory).
cls	Clears the screen.
copy	Copies the specified files or folders.
dir	Shows the contents of the current directory.
exit	Ends the session.
ipconfig	Displays network connection information.
ping	Tests network connection using IP address.
path	Displays or sets the path the command searches.
prompt	Changes the information displayed at the prompt.
rename	Renames the specified file or files if the wildcard characters ? or * are used.

Tip

Many commands have switches that allow the use of extra parameters, giving you much greater control of the command. A *switch* is the part of the command with the forward slash (/), followed by a letter, a number, or some other instruction. A *parameter* is an additional instruction you provide, such as the file name or drive letter.

Find a Command

1 At the command prompt, type **help** and press Enter.

2 Review the list of commands.

3 If the information scrolls off the screen, use the scroll bar or the scroll arrows so that you can see the entire list.

Tip

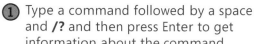

To change some of the settings for the Command Prompt window—the font, the cursor size, or the colors, for example—right-click the window's title bar, and choose Properties from the shortcut menu.

Try This!

At the command prompt, type **help > dosref.txt** and press Enter. Use Notepad or WordPad to open the file *dosref.txt* that's stored on your hard disk (it's the folder that was active when you typed the command). The > symbol redirected the output from the screen to the file. You now have a reference for the commands, which you can easily print out.

Get Information About a Command

1 Type a command followed by a space and **/?** and then press Enter to get information about the command.

2 Read the information.

3 If the information scrolls off the screen, use the scroll bar or the scroll arrows so that you can see the entire text.

Running Older Programs

Most programs work well with Windows Vista. Some older ones, however, are designed exclusively for earlier versions of Windows and won't work properly in Windows Vista. In most cases, Windows will try to run a program that doesn't work, using settings that should allow the program to run while at the same time protecting your system. However, in a few cases, you might need to change settings to get the program to work correctly.

Set the Compatibility

1. Locate the program you want to run, either on the Start menu or in a folder window.

2. Right-click the program, and choose Properties from the shortcut menu to display the program's Properties dialog box.

3. On the Compatibility tab, select this check box to run the program in Compatibility mode.

4. Specify the version of Windows for which the program was designed.

5. Select the check boxes for applying the appropriate restrictions to the display based on the program's documentation and updated notes from the manufacturer.

6. Select this check box if the program needs to access restricted content and you're sure the program will do no harm to your computer.

7. Click OK, and try running the program. If it still doesn't run, open the Properties dialog box again and change the settings. Continue experimenting until you get the program to work or until you're convinced the program can't run on your computer. (If changing the Compatibility mode or the display settings doesn't fix the problem, check with the manufacturer for updated drivers or other fixes.)

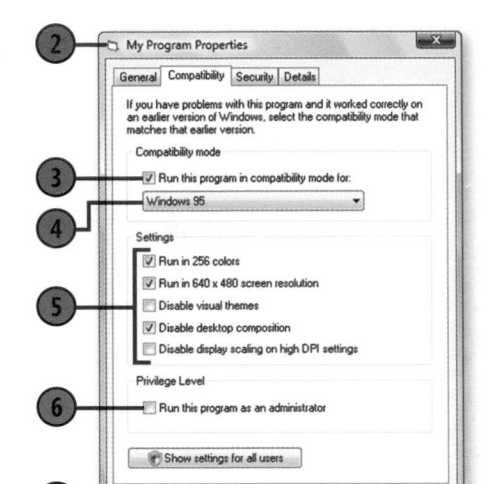

Caution

Running programs that weren't designed for recent versions of Windows can cause problems—for example, a program might start working and then lock up. Windows Vista will usually close the stopped program for you, but if it doesn't, click the Close button. If that doesn't work, right-click a blank spot on the taskbar, and choose Task Manager from the shortcut menu. On the Applications tab of the Task Manager dialog box, click the offending program, and then click End Task.

4

Communicating and Scheduling

The ability to communicate electronically is one of a computer's most used and most valued features. In this section, we'll discuss the tools that Windows Vista provides to enable you to reach out and connect with other people.

You can use Windows Mail to organize your e-mail and newsgroup messages, and to read and compose your e-mail even when you aren't connected to the Internet. You can format your messages with fonts and colors, and you can choose or create your own e-mail stationery. If you often send one message to several people, you can combine all their addresses into a *group* so that you don't have to enter each individual's address. You can enclose files, or *attachments,* with your e-mail, and if an attached file exceeds the size that your mail system can handle, you can *compress* the file to make it smaller.

Using the Windows Calendar, you can keep track of your own appointments and meetings, as well as those of your family members. You can also list the tasks you have to accomplish, set the priority for each, and specify when you want Windows Calendar to remind you about the task. With access to your coworkers' calendars, you can compare your schedule with your colleagues' schedules to see whether there are any conflicts before you propose a date and time for a meeting.

Sending E-Mail

Most of us can't imagine life without e-mail! You don't have to address an envelope or trek to the mailbox on a cold, rainy day. All you do is type a name, create a message, and click a Send button. Windows Mail and your mail server do the rest. What could be quicker or more convenient?

Create a Message

1. Click the Start button, and choose Windows Mail from the menu. Click Create Mail. If you want to send a formatted message with a background and coordinated fonts and bullets, click the down arrow next to the button, and click the stationery you want to use.

2. Type the recipient's name or enough of it to make it uniquely identifiable in your list of contacts. To add more names, type a semicolon (;), and then type all or part of another recipient's name. The names and addresses will be completed when you move to another part of the message.

3. Press the Tab key to move to the CC field, and type the names of the people who are to receive a copy of the message.

4. Press Tab to move to the Subject line, type a subject, and press Tab again to move into the message area.

5. Type your message. Use any of the formatting tools to format your message.

6. Do either of the following:

   • Click Send to send the message.

   • Choose Send Later from the File menu to leave the message in the Outbox until you're ready to send it.

7. When you've composed all the messages you want to send, click Send/Receive to send the messages in the Outbox to your mail server.

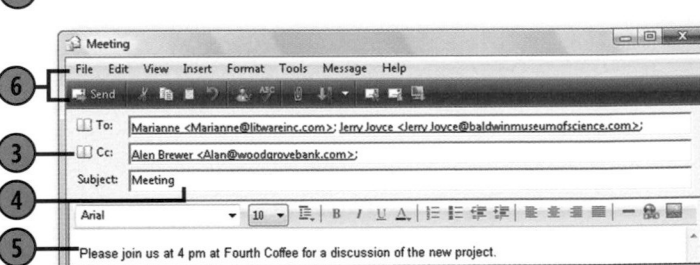

Tip

To send an e-mail to someone who isn't in your Contacts list without adding that person to the list, simply type his or her e-mail address on the To line.

See Also

"Setting Up Windows Mail" on pages 246–247 for information about setting up e-mail accounts in Windows Mail.

Saving and Sending a Draft Message

You can't always complete an e-mail message without being interrupted by someone or something. Or perhaps you want to mull over what you've said for a while and make a few changes to the wording before you send the message.

Fortunately, you can save your message in its incomplete form and then return to it when you're ready, finish it, and send it on its way.

Create a Draft

1. In Windows Mail, create a new message, address it, add a subject, and write your content.

2. Choose Save from the File menu.

3. If a message box appears, click OK.

4. Continue working on the message, choosing Save from the File menu occasionally. When you need to stop, click the Close button.

Tip

Even if you're able to complete a lengthy message in one sitting, you'll probably want to save it occasionally just as a precaution. If you close a partially completed message without sending it, Windows Mail will ask you whether you want to save a draft.

Send the Draft

1. Open the Drafts folder. If the Folder list isn't displayed, click the Folder List button to display the list.

2. Double-click the draft message to open it.

3. Complete the message, and click Send to send it. Note that it's automatically deleted from the Drafts folder.

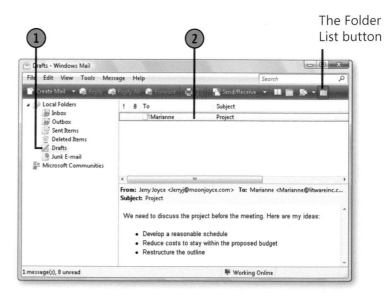

The Folder List button

Receiving and Reading E-Mail

Windows Mail lets you specify how frequently you want it to check for incoming e-mail, and it notifies you when you receive new mail. You can check your Inbox and see at a glance which messages have and haven't been read, or you can set the view to list unread messages only.

Read Your Messages

(1) Click the Inbox if it isn't the currently active folder.

(2) On the View menu, specify how you want to view your messages:

- Point to Current View, and choose the type of messages you want displayed.

- Point to Sort By, and choose the way you want the messages to be ordered.

- Choose Layout, specify whether and where you want the preview pane displayed, and click OK.

(3) Click a message header, and read the message in the preview pane.

(4) Double-click a message header to read the message in a separate window.

Try This!

On the Read tab of the Options dialog box, click the Fonts button. Click a different font in the Proportional Font list and a different font size in the Font Size list, and click OK. Close the Options dialog box, and take a look at the messages in the preview pane.

Tip

When you start Windows Mail, it checks for your mail, and it checks periodically thereafter while it's running. To receive mail immediately when you don't want to wait for the system to check your mailbox for you, click the Send/Receive button. To change the frequency with which Windows Mail checks for mail, choose Options from the Tools menu, and change the settings on the General tab.

Replying to or Forwarding a Message

When you receive an e-mail message that needs a reply or that you want to forward to someone else, all it takes is a click of a button to create a new message. But be careful when you use the Reply All button—your message could be received by a lot of people for whom it wasn't intended!

Reply to or Forward a Message

① Select the message header.

② Click the appropriate button:

- Reply to send your reply to the writer of the message only

- Reply All to send your reply to the writer of the message and to everyone listed in the original message's To and CC lines

- Forward to send a copy of the message to another recipient

③ Add names to or delete names from the To and CC lines.

④ Type your reply message or any note associated with the forwarded message.

⑤ Click Send.

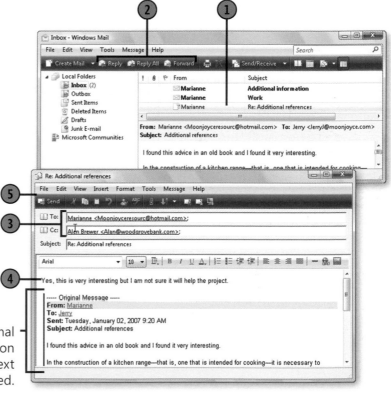

The original header information and message text are included.

Tip

When you reply to a message that has an attached file, the attachment isn't included with your reply. When you forward a message, though, the attachment is included so that the recipient can open or save it.

Tip

If the original message isn't included in the reply, choose Options from the Tools menu, and, on the Send tab, select the Include Message In Reply check box.

Designing Your Default Message

Why not let your computer do some of your work for you? When you design a default mail message, every new message that you start will look exactly the way you want, with all the elements in place—a specific background picture, your signature automatically inserted at the end of the message, a font that makes the message a little more "you," and so on.

Add a Signature

1. In Windows Mail, choose Options from the Tools menu, and click the Signatures tab of the Options dialog box.

2. Click New.

3. Type the signature you want to use as your default signature, or specify the text or HTML document that contains the signature.

4. Specify whether you want the signature added automatically to all outgoing messages and whether or not you want it included in replies and forwarded messages.

5. If you have more than one mail or news account, click Advanced.

6. Select the check boxes for the accounts that will use this signature, and then click OK.

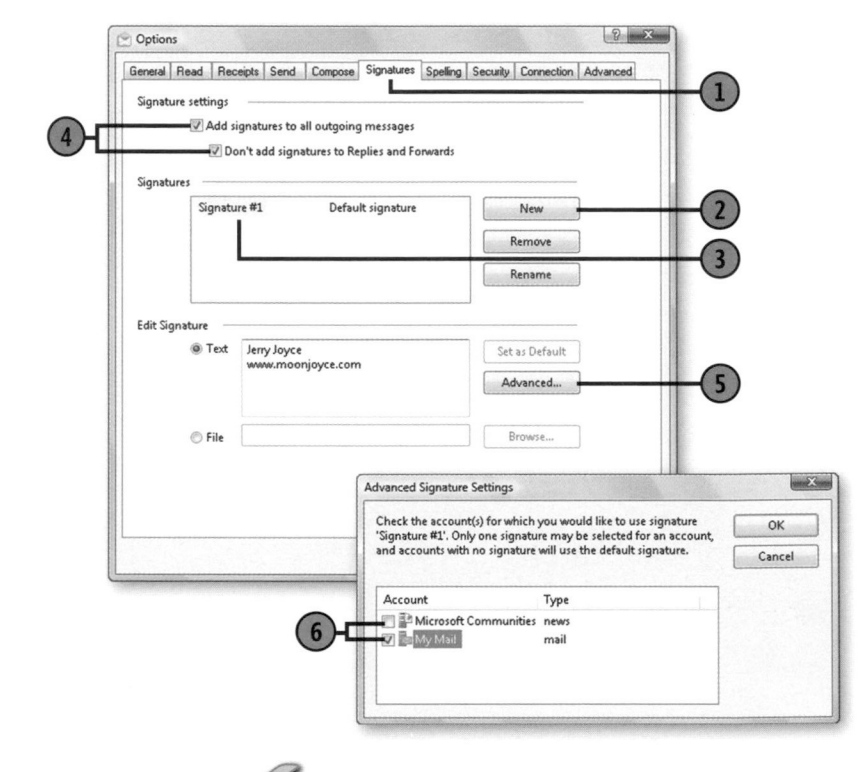

Tip

If your message is in HTML format, your signature file can be an HTML document too. If you enjoy experimenting with the HTML format, you can create anything from an attractive or ornate signature to a humorous or truly obnoxious one. The signature file, however, can't be any larger than 4 KB.

Specify Your Stationery

1 On the Compose tab of the Options dialog box, select this check box to use stationery.

2 Click Select.

3 In the list, click the stationery you want to use.

4 If you like what you see in the Preview pane, click OK.

5 Click Apply.

6 Click the Send tab, and click the HTML option for your mail format if it isn't already selected.

7 Click OK to close the Options dialog box.

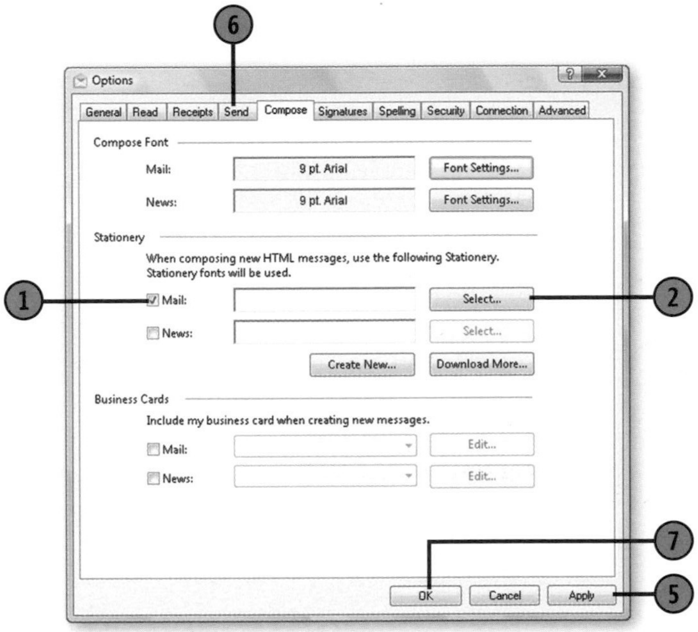

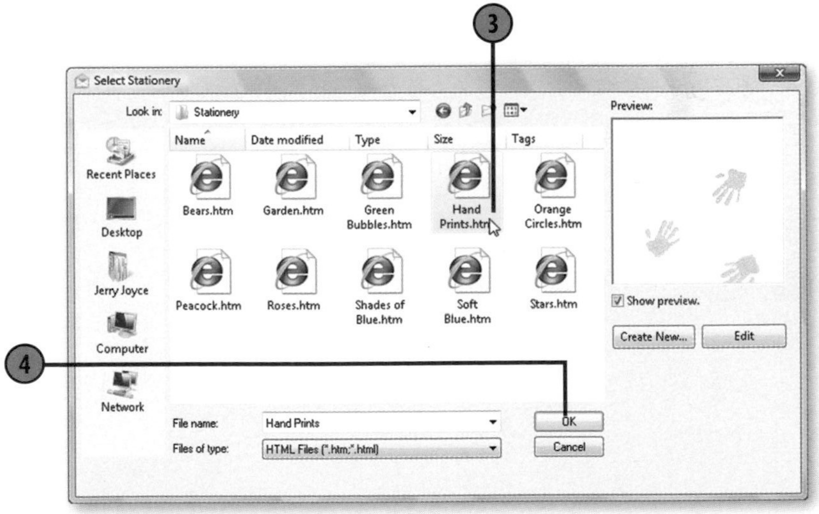

Caution

Although you can use stationery and other formatting in a news message, many newsgroups require or suggest that you use plain Text formatting to keep your messages to an easily manageable size.

Tip

To create your own e-mail stationery, click the Create New button on the Compose tab of the Options dialog box, and complete the Stationery Setup Wizard.

Adding Your Contacts

Your Contacts folder contains information about the people you communicate with. You use your Contacts list to quickly enter an e-mail address, look up a business or home address, jump to a Web site, place a phone call, and so on. You can even add an identifying picture to personalize the contact information. Each contact is contained in its own file, so you can access the contact information in multiple programs or directly from the Contacts folder.

Create a New Contact

1. In Windows Mail, click the Contacts button to display the Contacts folder.

2. Click New Contact to display the Properties dialog box.

3. On the various tabs of the Properties dialog box, enter the information you want to record. You can include as much or little as you want, but you'll need a unique name and an e-mail address if you intend to send e-mail to that contact.

4. To include an identifying picture, click here, choose Change Picture from the menu that appears, and use the Open dialog box to locate and select the picture you want. Click Open.

5. Click OK.

6. Close the Contacts folder when you've finished.

Tip

You can also open the Contacts folder by clicking the Start button, typing **contact** in the Search box, and clicking Windows Contacts on the Start menu.

Add an Address from a Message

(1) In the Windows Mail Inbox, right-click the message.

(2) Choose Add Sender To Contacts from the shortcut menu. If the command is grayed (unavailable), connect to the Internet or to your mail server, click the message to download it, and then right-click it and choose the command again.

(3) If you want to add the contact information for someone listed in the CC line of the message, double-click the message to open it in a separate window, and then right-click the name you want to add.

Tip ✓

To automatically add to your Contacts folder the addresses of all the people whose messages you reply to, choose Options from the Tools menu, and, on the Send tab, select the Automatically Put People I Reply To In My Contacts List check box.

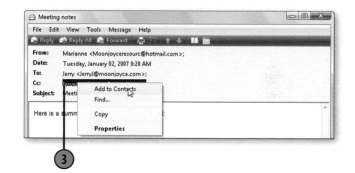

Creating a Contacts Group

If you frequently send one message to the same group of people, you can gather all their addresses into a *group,* and then all you need to do is enter the group name to send the message to all the individuals. It's a real time-saver.

Create a Group

1. In Windows Mail, click the Contacts button to display the Contacts folder.

2. In the Contacts folder, click New Contact Group to display the Properties dialog box.

3. On the Contact Group tab, type a descriptive name, or *alias,* for the group.

4. Click Add To Contact Group.

5. Click to select the name of someone you want to include in the group. Hold down the Ctrl key and continue clicking names until the contact group list is complete.

6. Click Add.

7. Type a name and an e-mail address for someone you want to add to the list but don't want to save as a contact, and then click Create For Group only.

8. Add any further information to the Contact Group Details tab.

9. Click OK.

Try This!

Create a group. Start a new e-mail message, and use the group name as the address in the To line. Send the message, and then look at that message in your Sent Items folder. Note that the address of each member of the group is listed.

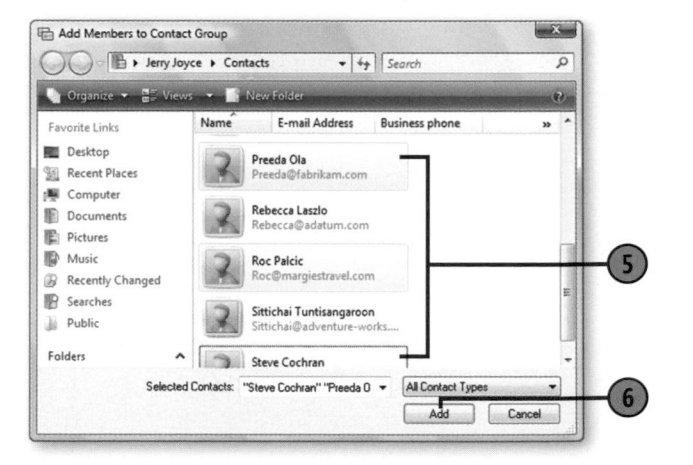

Transferring Files

In most cases, transferring files is a simple task; if you want to transfer a few small files, you can easily send them by e-mail. You can copy larger or more numerous files to a removable disc or a removable USB (Universal Serial Bus) memory device. On a network, you can simply designate the files as shared files and either move them to a Public or shared folder or post them to a SharePoint site. However, if you need to transfer a number of large files electronically but you don't have access to a network, there are several possible solutions. Listed below are additional methods for directly transferring files; you should find at least one among them that's appropriate for your situation. To find more information about any of these methods, look in the index of this book and/or search the Windows Vista Help And Support Center.

VPN: A Virtual Private Network connection creates a secure connection over the Internet between your computer and another network or computer.

Windows Live Messenger: You can send a file to or receive a file from any online contact. The recipient must agree to receive the file before you can send it. Although it isn't a part of Windows Vista, Windows Live Messenger is available for download.

FTP Transfer: You can use FTP (File Transfer Protocol) to transfer files to an FTP server over the Internet. In most cases, you'll be able to use Internet Explorer to connect and manage the files.

Ad Hoc Wireless Connection: You can create a temporary *ad hoc* connection between two or more computers in the same vicinity by using each computer's wireless network adapter. You can transfer files from Public and shared folders.

Windows Meeting Space: Creates a secure connection between computers so that files can be posted as handouts and can be automatically delivered to meeting participants.

Remote Assistance: When two computers are connected in a session, you can transfer files between the two computers over the secure connection.

Compressed (Zipped) Folders: Windows Vista provides the Compressed Folders feature, which reduces the size of the files it contains and keeps all the compressed files in one location. When you transfer a compressed folder, the receiving computer sees either a compressed folder (if the Compressed Folders feature is installed) or a ZIP-type file that can be opened using one of several third-party programs.

Windows Briefcase: The Windows Briefcase is a file-management tool that you can use for transferring files with computers that aren't running Windows Vista. The Briefcase helps you keep track of different versions of a file when the file has been edited on different computers. You copy files from your computer to the Briefcase and then transfer the entire Briefcase to another computer, where the files can be edited and saved back into the Briefcase. When you return the Briefcase to your computer, the original files on your computer can be updated automatically.

Sharing Contacts

A Contacts file can contain as little as a name and an e-mail address or it can be rich with information: home and work mailing addresses and phone numbers, notes about the family, birthdays and other significant dates, and even digital certificates for keeping your messages secure. Instead of all your friends and colleagues having to fill out their own set of contacts, you can exchange contact information by sending your electronic business card (*vCard*) and the vCards of mutual acquaintances to all your contacts, and in turn you can receive electronic business cards from others for your own use.

Send a Business Card

(1) In Windows Mail, click the Contacts button to display the Contacts folder.

(2) Right-click the contact you want to send, and choose Send Contact from the shortcut menu.

(3) Complete the e-mail message that appears, and send the message with the business card.

See Also

"Creating Trusted Contacts" on page 298 for information about creating and using a trusted contact.

Tip

When you send the contact information, it's sent using the vCard (.vcf) format. This format is recognized by many mail programs, including Windows Mail and Outlook. However, if you want to send the information in Windows Contact format (.contact), right-click the contact, point to Send To on the shortcut menu, and choose Mail Recipient. You'll want to use the .contact format to create a trusted contact for some of your secure communications.

The business card is included as an attachment to the message.

Receive a Business Card

(1) In the message that contains the personal business card that someone has sent you, click the icon for the card.

(2) If you're asked whether you want to open the file, click Open.

(3) Review the content of the card to determine whether or not you want to add this person to your list of contacts.

(4) If you want to include this person as a contact, click Add To My Contacts.

(5) In the Properties dialog box that appears, review or modify the contact information, and then click OK to create the contact.

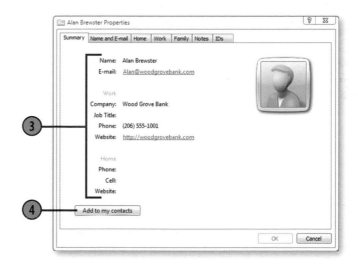

Tip ✓

To automatically include your business card with each outgoing message, in Windows Mail, choose Options from the Tools menu and, on the Compose tab, select the check box for including your business card, click the contact file you want to use in the drop-down list, and then click OK.

E-Mailing a File

A great way to share a file (or several files)—a Microsoft Word document, a picture, or even an entire Web page—is to include it as part of an e-mail message. The file is included as a separate part of the message—an *attachment*—that the recipient can save and open at any time.

Send a File by E-Mail

1. Use Windows Mail to create a message to your intended recipient, including the e-mail address, subject, and any accompanying text.

2. Click the Attach File To Message button.

3. Locate and select the file in the Open dialog box. If you want to send multiple files, hold down the Ctrl key as you select each file.

4. Click Open.

5. Click Send to send the message just as you'd send any other message.

Tip

Different mail systems can send or receive different sizes of attachments—some as small as 1 MB and others as large as 10 MB or more. If you need to transfer a large file or numerous files, try compressing the file or files, or use a different transferral method.

See Also

"Transferring Files" on page 61 for information about other ways to transfer files.

"Compressing Files" on pages 212–213 for information about using compressed folders.

Receive an Attachment

① Select a message you've received that contains an attachment.

② Click the Attachment icon.

③ If you want to open a file to view it or work on it, click the file's name. When you've finished working on the file, choose Save As from the File menu to save the file in the location you want.

④ To save the file or files for future work, choose Save Attachments, and use the Save Attachments dialog box to specify where you want to save the file or files. Select the files you want to save, and click Save.

Try This!

Double-click a message containing one or more attachments to open the message in a separate window. Right-click one of the attachments in the Attach line. Use any of the commands from the menu that appears.

Caution

Viruses are often distributed in attached files, so *don't* open an attachment from an unknown sender, and *do* make sure that you have a good anti-virus program installed on your computer.

Try This!

Open a folder window, and select one or more files. Right-click one of the files, point to Send To on the shortcut menu, and choose Mail Recipient from the submenu. In the e-mail message that appears, address the message, add any text you want, and send it.

E-Mailing Your Photos

We all want to share those wonderful pictures we've taken of our families, our friends, our pets, our gardens. Windows Vista makes it oh, so easy—just select the pictures and send them on their way. What's really useful is that Windows Vista gives you the ability to set the size of your pictures so that you can send several at a time without incurring the wrath of your e-mail service provider for overloading the system—or the eye-rolling of the recipient when the pictures take an hour to download! Also, if you size the pictures, they'll fit nicely on a screen when viewed.

Send Your Pictures

① Click the Start button, type **photo** in the Search box, and click Windows Photo Gallery to start the program.

② Click a picture you want to send. If you want to send other pictures, hold down the Ctrl key and click each picture.

③ Click E-Mail.

④ Select the size to which you want to compress the pictures.

⑤ Click Attach.

⑥ In the mail message that appears, address your message, modify the subject and text if necessary, and then click Send.

See Also

"Adding Photos to the Gallery" on page 113 for information about adding pictures to, and finding pictures in, Windows Photo Gallery.

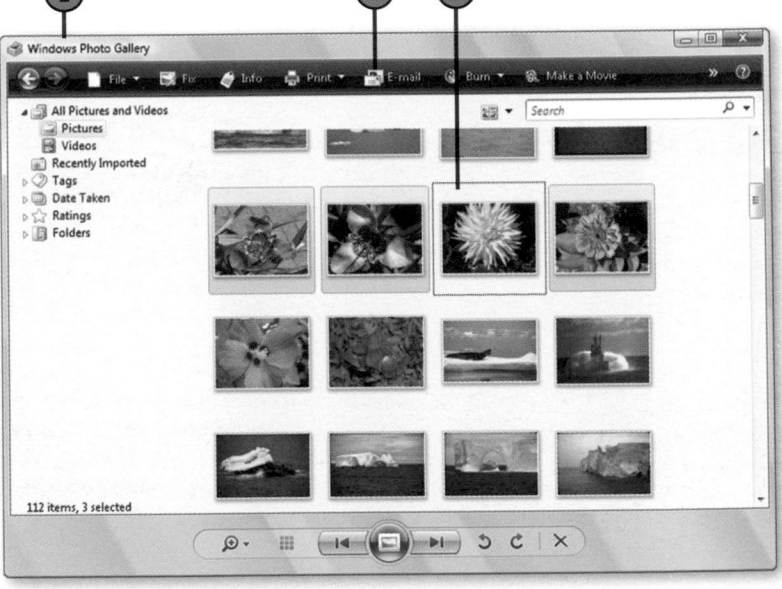

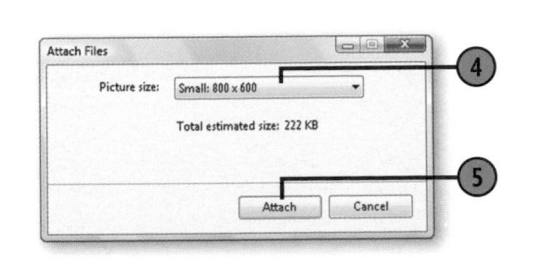

Organizing Your Messages

If there are Windows Mail messages of specific types or from specific people that you want to gather together, you can create additional folders and then move the items into those folders.

Organize!

① With Windows Mail running, point to Folder on the File menu, and choose New from the submenu to display the Create Folder dialog box.

② Type a name for the folder.

③ Click the folder in which you want this new folder to be located. If you want the new folder to be at the same level as your Inbox, click Local Folders.

④ Click OK.

⑤ Select the messages you want to move into that folder, and drag them onto the folder.

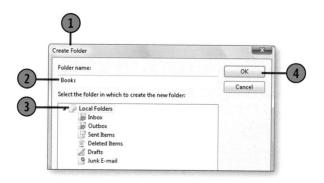

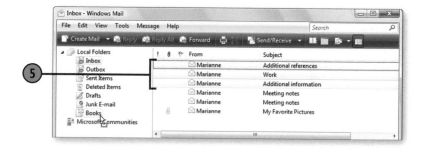

Tip

You can also organize your messages by sorting them alphabetically. To do so, click the title of a column at the top of the message pane (From or Subject, for example) to sort by that category. Click the title a second time to reverse the order of the sort.

See Also

"Managing Your Messages Automatically" on page 68 for information about using message rules to automatically place messages in different folders.

Managing Your Messages Automatically

Why not let Windows Mail do some of the work of organizing your e-mail messages? By creating *rules,* you can tell Windows Mail how you want your messages to be treated, based on subject, content, e-mail addresses, and various other factors.

Create Your Rules

① Point to Message Rules on the Tools menu, and choose Mail from the submenu to display the New Mail Rule dialog box.

② Select the check box for each identifying condition you want in your rule.

③ Select the check box for each action to be executed when the identifying conditions are met.

④ Click each link to provide the specific information required to execute the rule.

⑤ Type a name for the rule.

⑥ Click OK.

⑦ Verify the rule in the Message Rules dialog box, and then click OK.

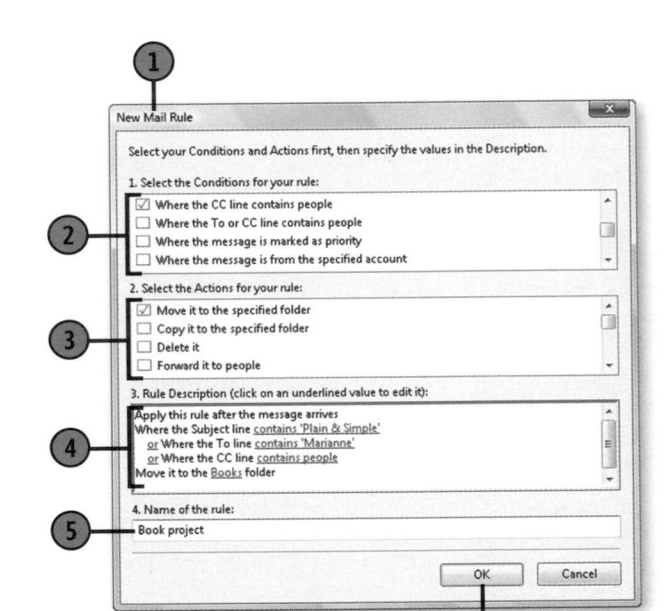

Tip

Create News rules to organize your newsgroups, and create a Block Senders list to have unwanted mail automatically deleted when it comes from a specified e-mail address or domain.

Tip

If a rule already exists, the Message Rules dialog box appears when you choose Message Rules from the Tools menu. Click New to display the New Mail Rules dialog box, or use the tools in the Message Rules dialog box to modify an existing rule or change the order in which the rules are enforced.

Tracking Your Schedule

The Windows Calendar is a great way to keep track of all your appointments, whether they're important business meetings, your child's soccer games, or coffee with friends.

With Windows Vista standing by to remind you of your appointments, you should never be late again!

Set an Appointment

1. Click the Start button, type **cale** in the Search box of the Start menu, and click Windows Calendar to start the program.

2. Click the day of the next appointment you want to record.

3. If the calendar doesn't show the Day view, click the View button until the Day view is displayed.

4. Click the time of your appointment, and type a label for the appointment.

5. Add any location information.

6. Specify the end of the meeting, or note whether it's an all-day meeting.

7. Click if you want to set up a series of meetings that repeat at set intervals.

8. Click to set how far in advance you want to be reminded of the meeting.

9. Add any notes about the meeting.

Click to change the month displayed.

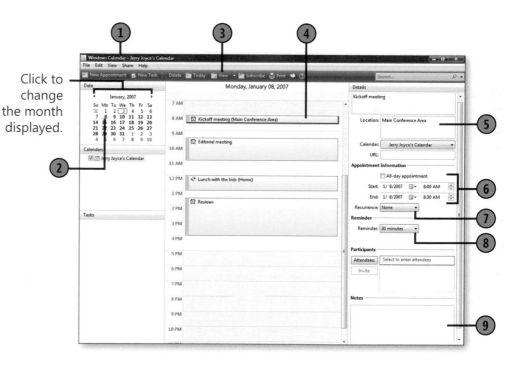

Tip

If you use more than one calendar, select the calendar and, if it's hosted on a Web site, enter the site's address when you set up the appointment time.

Tracking Your Tasks

You have a bunch of deadlines for getting your various projects completed, but you know how difficult it can be to remember the exact date for each one, especially if your deadlines are close together. Windows Vista can track those tasks so that you can quickly check to determine what needs to be done by what date. Then, once you've met your deadline, you can revel in the great satisfaction of checking off a completed task!

Track a Task

(1) If Windows Calendar isn't already running, start it from the Start menu.

(2) Select the calendar you want if you have more than one, and, if it's hosted on line, enter the Web-site address for the calendar.

(3) Click New Task, and type a label for the new task.

(4) Set the priority ranking of the task.

(5) Set the start and finish dates for the task.

(6) Click here, and then specify when you want to be reminded about the task.

(7) Type any notes about the task.

(8) When you've completed the task, select its check box. Smile!

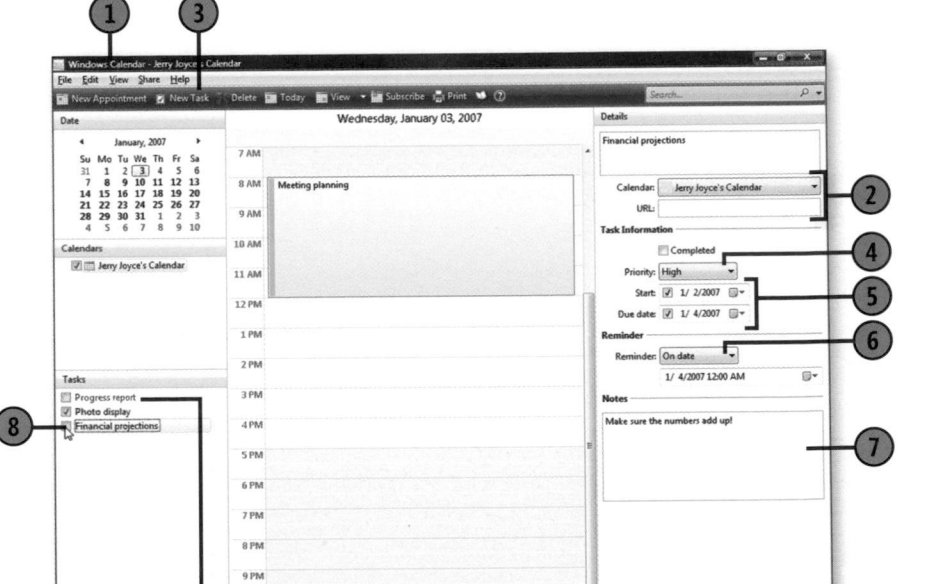

An overdue task is highlighted in color.

Tip

To change the length of time for which a completed task is displayed after you've completed it, the default time for a reminder to appear, or the color of overdue tasks, choose Options from the File menu.

Scheduling a Meeting

When you schedule a meeting, you can easily send the relevant information to all those who need to attend. When you e-mail the meeting invitation, a calendar file is enclosed with the e-mail. When the recipient opens this file—provided he or she has a calendar that supports the popular and common iCalendar format—all the information about the meeting is included and added to either the recipient's calendar or a new calendar.

Schedule a Meeting

1. Create the appointment for the meeting as you normally would.

2. Click Attendees.

3. In the Windows Calendar dialog box that appears, select the attendees, and then click To.

4. Click OK when you've finished.

5. Click Invite to create an e-mail that you'll send to each attendee and that will include the calendar file as an attachment. Modify the e-mail as necessary, and then send it.

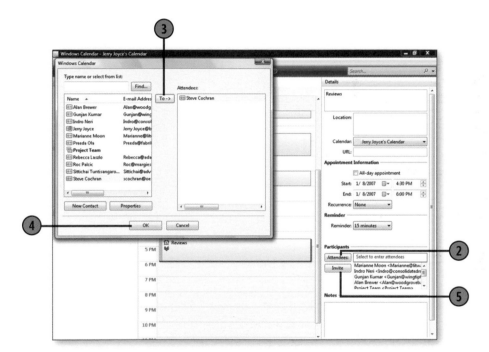

Tip

If you're inviting only one or two people, you can type their names in the box next to the Attendees list and then press Enter instead of clicking the button and selecting their names from the dialog box.

Tracking Multiple Schedules

You can record the schedules for several people and/or projects on separate calendars. Then you can compare the calendars to see whether there are any scheduling conflicts or, alternatively, when you might actually have a little free time.

Create Multiple Calendars

(1) If Windows Calendar isn't already running, start it from the Start menu. Choose New Calendar from th File menu to create a calendar for another person or project, and enter a descriptive name for the calendar.

(2) Clear the check boxes for all your other calendars, and verify that the check box for the calendar to which you want to add entries is selected.

(3) Choose an identifying color for calendar items.

(4) Create the appointments and tasks for that calendar.

(5) Repeat steps 1 through 4 for any additional calendars you want to create.

Create several calendars. Choose New Group from the File menu, and name the group. In the Calendars section, drag a calendar onto the new group. Drag additional calendars onto the new group. Use the check boxes to show or hide the entire group or the individual calendars within the group.

Compare Calendars

(1) Select the check box for each calendar you want to view, and clear the check boxes for the calendars you don't want to look at.

(2) Click a different day if you want to compare appointments for that day, or change the view to see more than one day.

(3) If you can't distinguish which calendar is associated with which appointments, click a calendar and change the color of the appointments. (Just make sure you don't select a color that's being used in another calendar.)

(4) If you want to see the details of an appointment, click the appointment, and then read the details in the Details pane.

(5) Examine the tasks that are listed. Each task is color coded, using the same color as the calendar color.

(6) When you've finished, clear the check boxes for the calendars you no longer want to view.

Sharing Schedules

There are two ways to share schedules with Windows Calendar outside of your computer. You can publish your calendar to a Web site to display your schedule, or you can subscribe to an existing calendar to receive schedules. When you publish a calendar, you're actually creating a copy of the calendar, which displays dates but can't be changed in any way. You can, however, set your calendar to update the published copy of your calendar whenever you make any scheduling changes.

Publish

① In Windows Calendar, click the calendar you want to publish, and then choose Publish from the Share menu to start the Publish Calendar Wizard.

② Use the proposed name of the calendar or enter a different one.

③ Type or paste in the address where this calendar is to be stored.

④ Select this check box if you want to automatically publish any changes to the calendar.

⑤ Specify which items from the calendar you want to include.

⑥ Click Publish.

⑦ To send an e-mail announcement with a link to the calendar, click Announce, and then complete and send the e-mail.

⑧ Click Finish.

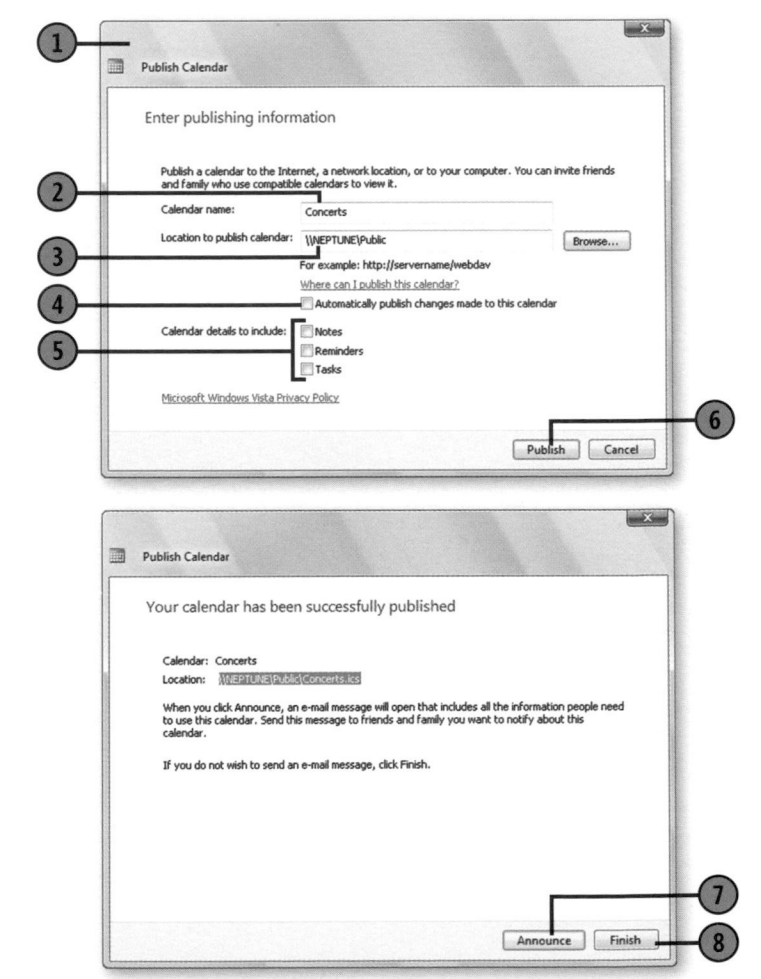

Subscribe

① In Windows Calendar, click Subscribe on the toolbar to display the Subscribe To A Calendar Wizard.

② Type the address and file name of the calendar you want to subscribe to.

③ Click Next.

④ Use the proposed name of the calendar, or enter a different one.

⑤ Click, and then choose from the drop-down menu how often you want to update the calendar from its source.

⑥ Specify which items from the calendar you want included.

⑦ Click Finish.

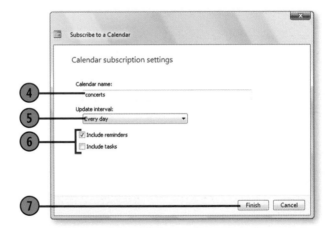

Tip ✓

Whether you publish your own calendar or subscribe to a calendar, you can change the settings by clicking the calendar in the Windows Calendar list and then making changes in the Details pane.

Tip ✓

You can publish a calendar to a Web site that accepts this type of calendar, or to a network share or public folder on a computer.

Tip ✓

You can also subscribe to an online calendar by visiting the Web site that hosts the calendar and then clicking the link to subscribe.

Subscribing to Newsgroups

With so many newsgroups available, you'll probably want to be selective about the ones you review. You can do so in Windows Mail by subscribing to the newsgroups you like. Those newsgroups will appear in the message pane when you select the news server, and they'll also appear on the Folders bar, if it's displayed, when you expand the listing for a news server. (Many newsgroups are now based on Web pages, so you can access them by using your Internet browser.)

Specify Your Newsgroups

1. With Windows Mail open and connected to the Internet, click the news server you want to access.

2. If you receive a notification that you're not subscribed to any newsgroups, specify whether you want to show the newsgroups with or without the Communities feature turned on.

3. If no dialog box appears, click the Newsgroups button.

4. If you have more than one news server, specify the one you want to use.

5. Double-click a newsgroup to subscribe to it. Repeat to subscribe to all the newsgroups you want to access.

6. Click OK.

Tip

The Communities feature is an enhancement to newsgroups; it allows you to rate other posts, add questions, show your profile, and more. To use these enhanced features, you need to sign in to the newsgroup using a .net passport.

See Also

"Setting Up Windows Mail" on pages 246–247 for information about setting up your news servers.

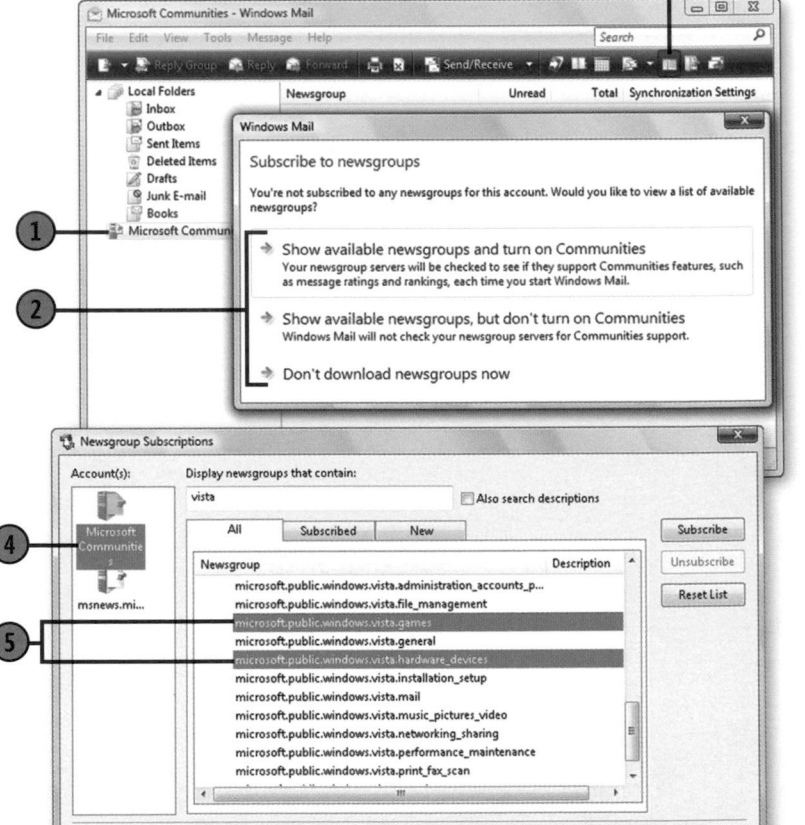

Reading and Writing the News

Reading and adding to the news—or the gossip, tirades, and misinformation that often pass for news in Internet newsgroups—is as simple as reading or sending your e-mail. All you need to do is specify a newsgroup and select a message, and then either read the message or click a button to respond to it.

Select a Message

① In the Folders list, expand the list under the news server if necessary, and click the newsgroup you want.

② Click a news message to display it. To open the message in a separate window, double-click the message.

③ Read the message.

④ Click the type of message you want to create:

- Write Message to create a new message under its own topic (to start a new *thread*)

- Reply Group to respond to the selected message and have your message added under that message (to add it to the thread)

- Reply to send an e-mail message to the author of the message only but not to add your message to the newsgroup

- Forward to send the message by e-mail to someone else

⑤ Compose your message. If you're posting a new message, select the type of message you want to create.

Tip

A "thread" is a series of messages: one person posts a message and others reply to the message and/or to the replies.

Caution

Unscrupulous people search through newsgroups to find valid e-mail addresses that they list and sell to spammers. To avoid extra junk mail, when you post a message, you can either use a fake e-mail address or a secondary account that you can easily purge of spam. When you use a fake e-mail address, people can't respond to your message by e-mail.

5

Exploring the Internet

Whether you call it the Internet, the Net, or the Web, and whether you use it for business, homework, research, communicating, or shopping, the Web is probably already your window on the world. With that insight in mind, one of the goals of Windows Vista's designers was to enable you to move between the Web and your own computer in an almost effortless fashion. Internet Explorer is designed specifically for this world, and it provides powerful features to make your explorations easy and safe.

When you start Internet Explorer, it takes you to your *home page* (or *home pages*)—usually a page or a group of pages that displays information you want to see every day. However, if you want to change your home page or pages to another page or group of pages, you can do so with a couple of mouse-clicks. You can keep several Web pages open, each on its own *tab*, and you can switch back and forth among them. If there's a page or group of pages you want to revisit, you can add it to your Favorites list, and Internet Explorer will create a shortcut to it for you. You can save a Web page and then send it to others, or copy part of the page and use it in a document. You can also subscribe to online feeds to automatically see new content on a site—updated news, schedules, or *blog* entries, for example.

What's Where in Internet Explorer?

Although you can use the Web browser of your choice in Windows, you might want to try the new and improved version of Internet Explorer that comes with Windows Vista—it's powerful, useful, and friendly. If you don't care for its new streamlined look, you can display the classic menus of previous versions by clicking the Tools button or pressing the Alt key.

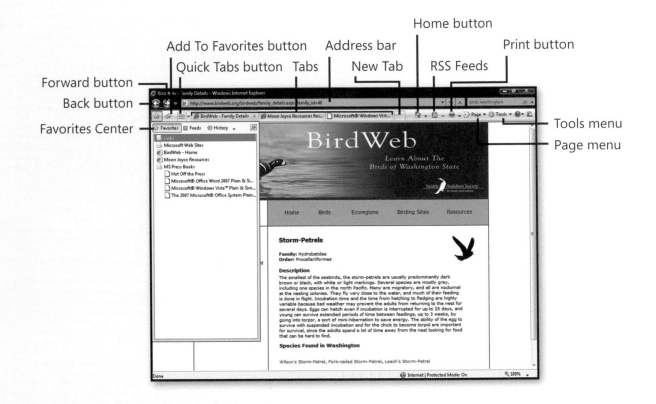

Home button

Add To Favorites button   Address bar   Print button

Quick Tabs button   Tabs   New Tab   RSS Feeds

Forward button

Back button

Favorites Center

Tools menu

Page menu

Finding a Web Page

You do most of your navigation on the Internet using the *hyperlinks* (also called *links* or *jumps*) that are located on Web pages and in search results. When you click a link, an Internet address is sent to your Web browser, which looks for the Web site and then displays the requested page. After you've located a Web page, you can explore further if you want. It's a bit like looking up a word in a dictionary and then looking up another word to expand your understanding of the first one.

Explore

① Connect to the Internet if you're not already connected, and start Internet Explorer if it isn't already running.

② From your current page, do any of the following:

- Click in the Search box, type names or keywords, and then press Enter to display on a new tab a listing of Web pages that contain the specific text.

- Click a relevant link on the page to go to a new page or site.

- Hold down the Ctrl key and click a link to open the Web page on a new tab, keeping the existing Web page open.

- Click the Forward or Back button to return to a previously visited site.

- Click the tab for an open Web page to view that page again.

- Open the Address bar drop-down list to specify and jump to a previously visited site, or type a new address to go to that site. Click the New Tab button first if you want the page to open on a new tab without replacing the existing page.

Back button   Address bar

Forward button   New Tab   Search box

Use a link to jump to another page.

Tip

If you start Internet Explorer from the Start menu or from the Quick Launch toolbar, Internet Explorer goes to the page you've designated as your home page. If you start Internet Explorer by clicking a link, choosing a menu command, clicking search results, or using an Internet address, Internet Explorer goes to that specific page and bypasses your home page.

Opening Multiple Web Pages

If you've ever wanted to jump back and forth between two or more Web pages, the new tabs in Internet Explorer now make it so simple. Just open the Web pages on their own tabs, and they'll be there until you close the page.

Specify the Web Page

① In Internet Explorer, click New Tab.

② Start typing the address of the Web site you want. If the address is displayed in a drop-down list, click the address. If it doesn't appear, type the entire address, and then press Enter.

Tip

To search the current Web page instead of the Internet, click the Search down arrow, choose Find On This Page from the drop-down menu, and use the Find dialog box to search for the text you want.

Use a Link

① Hold down the Ctrl key and click the link.

② Click the newly opened tab to view it.

Try This!

In Internet Explorer, search for something on the Internet. On the Search Results page that appears, hold down the Ctrl key as you click a result. View the information. Switch back to the Search Results page, hold down the Ctrl key, and click another result. Continue opening new tabs for results and closing tabs that aren't relevant to your search.

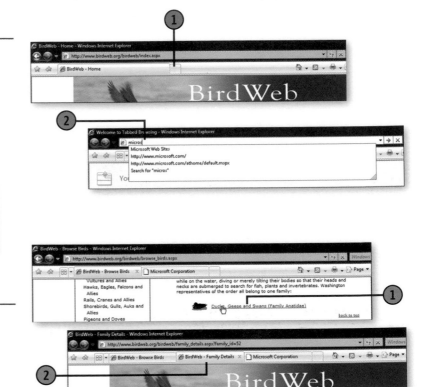

See Also

"Returning to Your Favorite Sites" on pages 84–85 for information about opening Web pages on their own tabs.

"Printing Web Pages" on page 189 for information about printing Web pages.

Viewing Multiple Web Pages

An important new feature in Internet Explorer is the ability it gives you to keep multiple Web pages open at the same time, each on its own tab. That way, you can leave a page open, open another page, and then easily and quickly move between pages.

View Different Web Pages

① In Internet Explorer, click a tab to view that Web page.

② Click the Quick Tabs button if you want to view all the open Web pages.

③ Click a Web page to switch to the tab for that Web page.

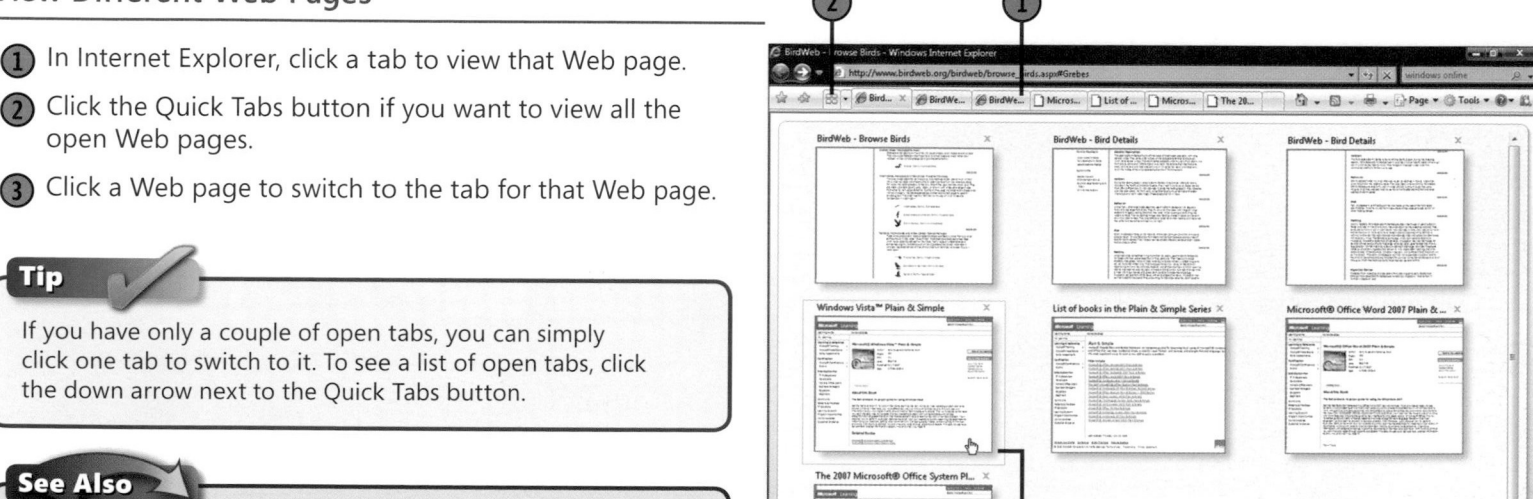

Tip

If you have only a couple of open tabs, you can simply click one tab to switch to it. To see a list of open tabs, click the down arrow next to the Quick Tabs button.

See Also

"Opening Multiple Web Pages" on the facing page for information about opening Web pages on new tabs.

Clean Up the Tabs

① With multiple Web pages open, right-click a tab, and, on the shortcut menu that appears, do either of the following:

• Choose Close to close the Web page and the tab that you clicked.

• Choose Close Other Tabs to close all the other Web pages and tabs except for the one you right-clicked.

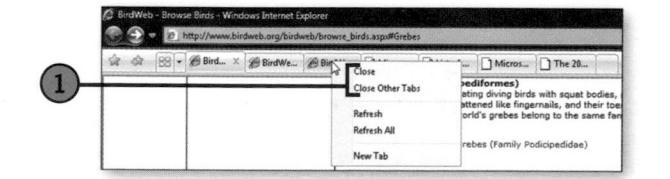

Returning to Your Favorite Sites

When you've found a good source of information or entertainment, you won't need to waste a lot of time searching for that site the next time you want to visit it. You can simply add the site to your Favorites list, and Internet Explorer will obligingly create a link to the site for you.

Save a Location

1. Go to the site whose location you want to save. If you want to save several sites as one tab group, open each site on a different tab.

2. Click the Add To Favorites button, and choose whether to save the active Web page to display the Add A Favorite dialog box, or to save the entire group of sites on different tabs to display the Favorites Center dialog box.

3. Type a name for the site, or use the proposed name, if any.

4. If you want to place the link in an existing folder in the Favorites Center, select the folder.

5. Click Add.

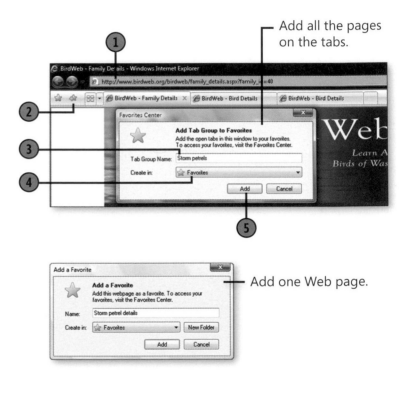

Add all the pages on the tabs.

Add one Web page.

Tip

If you don't want anyone who uses your computer to review the Internet sites you've visited recently, click the Tools button, and click Delete Browsing History. In the Delete Browsing History dialog box that appears, click the Delete History button.

Return to a Location

① Click the Favorites Center button.

② In the Favorites Center pane, click the Favorites button if it isn't already clicked.

③ If the link to the Web page you want to return to is visible, click the link.

④ If the Web-page link is contained in a folder and isn't visible, click the folder to display its contents.

⑤ If you want to open one of the Web pages listed, click the link. To open the Web page on a new tab, point to the link, and click the Open In New Tab button.

⑥ If you want to open all the Web pages in the folder on their own tabs, point to the folder, and click the Open In A Tab Group button.

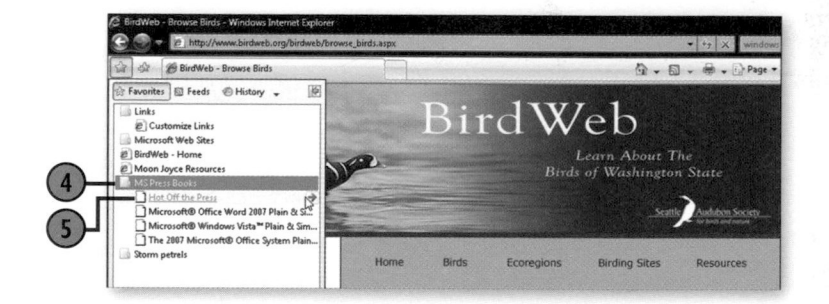

Tip

If you want to return to a site you recently visited but didn't save as a favorite, click the History button in the Favorites Center to see whether that site is listed there.

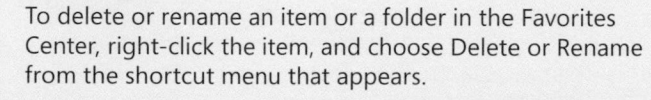

Tip

To delete or rename an item or a folder in the Favorites Center, right-click the item, and choose Delete or Rename from the shortcut menu that appears.

Going to a Specific Web Page

If someone has given you an Internet address that isn't in one of the usual forms—for example, a hyperlink in an online document, in an e-mail message, or in another Web page—you can easily specify the address. You don't even need to go to your default home page but can simply jump to the destination. To do so, you use the Address bar in Internet Explorer, on the Windows taskbar, or in any folder window.

Specify an Address

1. Click the current address on the Address bar to select the entire address.

2. Type or paste (press Ctrl+V to paste a copied address) the address you want to use to replace the currently selected address. (You don't need to type the *http://* part of the address.)

3. Click the Go button or press Enter to go to the site. If you want the site to open on a new tab, hold down the Alt key when you click Go or press Enter.

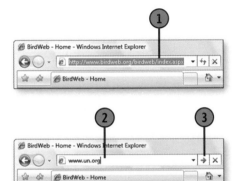

Try This!

Start typing an address for a Web page you visited recently. As you type, a list box might appear containing proposed addresses, as well as the names of Web sites you've previously visited. If the address or name you want is listed, use either the mouse to click the address or the Down arrow key to select the address, and then press Enter. If no proposed addresses ever appear, in Internet Explorer, choose Internet Options from the Tools menu, click AutoComplete on the Content tab, and select the Web Addresses check box. Click OK twice, and then try typing the address again.

Tip

You can use the Address bar for more than just accessing a Web page. You can also enter the address of a folder, a drive, or even another computer on your network.

Setting Your Home Page or Pages

When you start Internet Explorer, you automatically go right to your home page—a page that you might have customized or that contains the links and services you want. You can also set several pages as part of your home-page tab set. If you'd rather use a different home page, or if you want to reset the home page after a service or a program has changed it, you can designate a new home page with just a couple of mouse-clicks.

Set the Home Page or Pages

1. Use Internet Explorer to go to the page you want to use as your home page. If you want to designate additional pages as a new home-page tab set, open the other pages on their own tabs.

2. Click the Home button down arrow, and choose Add Or Change Home Page from the drop-down menu.

3. In the Add Or Change Home Page dialog box, select the option you want.

4. Click Yes.

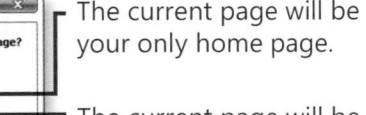

The current page will be your only home page.

The current page will be added to any other home pages and displayed on its own tab.

All the pages on the different tabs will become your new home-page tab set.

Tip ✓

To remove a page from your home-page tab set, click the Home button down arrow, point to Remove on the drop-down menu, and, on the submenu that appears, click the Web-page address you want to remove.

Tip ✓

Web-page content changes frequently, so what you see on some of the Web pages shown in this book might look a bit different from what you see when you access those same pages on line.

Finding Something on the Internet

To search for a specific item on the Internet—a list of sources where you can buy other *Plain & Simple* books, for example, or the menu and locator map for that new restaurant you want to try—you can search from almost anywhere in Windows Vista.

When the results are displayed, you can jump to the page that contains the information you're looking for, and, if it's not what you want, you can try another page.

Search for an Item

① In Internet Explorer, click the Search Options button, and select a search service if you want to use one other than your default service. If the service you want isn't listed, click Find More Providers, and then select the one you want from the Web page that appears.

② Click the Search box, type the search information, and press Enter to start the search. If you want the results to appear on a new tab, press Alt+Enter instead.

③ Click a link in the search results.

④ Conduct any other related actions or searches.

⑤ Close the Internet Explorer window when you've finished with the search results.

Tip

You must, of course, be connected to the Internet before you can search for anything on the Internet.

Tip

You can search from the Search box in any folder window or from the Start menu by clicking the See Other Options down arrow and choosing to search the Internet from the drop-down menu. However, you can use only the default search provider you chose in Internet Explorer.

Saving a Web Page

If a Web page contains important information that you know you'll want to refer to in the future, you can save the page on your computer. That way, even if the online Web page changes, you'll still have the original information. The way in which you save the page, however, affects which information will be available when you open it. After you've saved the Web page, you can send it to friends and colleagues if you want.

Save a Web Page

① Start Internet Explorer if it isn't already running, and connect to the Internet if you aren't already connected. Go to the Web page you want to save.

② Click the Page button, and choose Save As from the drop-down menu to display the Save Webpage dialog box.

③ If you don't want to save the document to the default folder, specify a different location, drive, or folder.

④ Type a name for the file, or use the proposed name.

⑤ Click Save As Type. In the drop-down list, specify how you want to save the Web page:

- Webpage Complete to save the formatted text and layout and to place all the linked resources, such as pictures, in a separate folder

- Web Archive, Single File to create a single archive file that contains all the elements of the Web page

- Webpage, HTML Only to save the formatted text and layout but none of the linked items, such as pictures

- Text File to save only the text

⑥ Click Save.

Tip

If you're planning to send a Web page to someone, save the page as a Web Archive so that the single file will contain all the elements of the Web page.

Caution

Sometimes, although certain items on a Web page appear to be text, they're actually graphics elements. This is usually the case when the designer of the page or site wanted to include some special formatting that couldn't be done with normal HTML formatting. If you save the page as either Web Page, HTML Only or Text File, the information that contains that special formatting won't be saved.

Controlling Pop-Up Windows

Argh! Doesn't it drive you crazy when you go to a Web site, only to face a relentless barrage of pop-up windows that try to sell you a bunch of stuff you don't want? With Windows Vista, you can tell Internet Explorer to whack those pop-up windows. However, if there are certain pop-up windows you want to look at, you can tell Internet Explorer to display them.

Set the Pop-Up Blocker

1. In Internet Explorer, click the Tools button, point to Pop-Up Blocker on the drop-down menu, and click Pop-Up Blocker Settings to display the Pop-Up Blocker Settings dialog box. If the Pop-Up Blocker Settings command is grayed (unavailable), first choose Turn On Pop-Up Blocker from the menu.

2. If you want to allow pop-ups from a specific Web site, type or paste the address of the Web site, and then click Add.

3. Select the notification options you want.

4. Select the level of filtering you want:

   • High to block all pop-ups

   • Medium to block pop-ups except when you click a link to open a pop-up window or when the Web site you're visiting is in the Internet Explorer Local Intranet or the Trusted Sites security zone

   • Low to allow most pop-ups

5. Click Close.

Tip

Visit a site before you add it to the Allowed Sites list to verify that it's the correct site. That way, when you start typing the address of a Web site to put it on your Allowed list, the Auto-Complete list appears with recently visited sites, so you can just click the site you want and thereby avoid misspellings.

Control the Pop-Up Windows

(1) In a Web site where a pop-up has been blocked, click the Information bar.

(2) Specify the action you want from the menu:

- Temporarily Allow Pop-Ups to allow pop-ups from this Web site during this one visit

- Always Allow Pop-Ups From This Site to add this site to your list of exceptions and to always permit pop-ups from this site

- Settings to turn off the Pop-Up Blocker, to hide the Information bar, to manually add the addresses of sites that you'll allow to show pop-ups, or to change the level (High, Medium, or Low) of the filtering of pop-ups

- More Information to find out even more details about working with the Information bar

Tip

The Pop-Up Blocker can block all pop-up windows or only those from sites you don't trust, depending on your settings. Blocking pop-ups is more than just a convenience; miscreants can use pop-ups to run malicious code or to steal your personal information.

Caution

The Information bar appears when a security problem is encountered—when a Web page tries to download a file or an ActiveX control, for example. To maintain security, make sure the Information bar isn't turned off, and pay attention to the messages it contains.

See Also

"Maintaining High Security" on page 292 for information about protecting yourself and your computer from the e-mail scams known as *phishing*.

Reading RSS Feeds

RSS feeds provide information, often from news Web sites or *blogs* (Web logs), that is available for a one-time download or by subscription. When you subscribe, updated information is periodically sent to your computer. And okay, here's yet another abbreviation to add to your list: RSS stands for Really Simple Syndication.

Get Your Feed

① In Internet Explorer, go to the Web site that has the RSS feed you want.

② Click the RSS button. The button is available only when there are available RSS feeds on that Web site.

③ On the Web page that appears, review the page to make sure you want to subscribe to this feed, and, if so, click to subscribe to the RSS feed or feeds that you want.

④ In the Internet Explorer dialog box that appears, make any changes you want to the name or location of the RSS feed.

⑤ Click Subscribe.

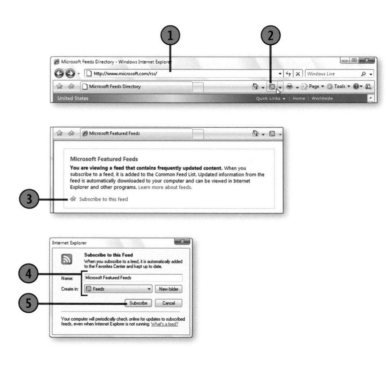

Tip

Not all Web sites that provide RSS feeds use the same methodology, so sometimes the RSS button won't be available. In those cases, follow the directions on the Web site to subscribe to the RSS feed.

Read Your Feed

① Click the Favorites Center button to display the Favorites Center.

② Click the Feeds button if it isn't already selected.

③ Click the feed you want to view.

④ Use the Search In Feed box or other tools to find the material you want in the feed.

⑤ Read the information.

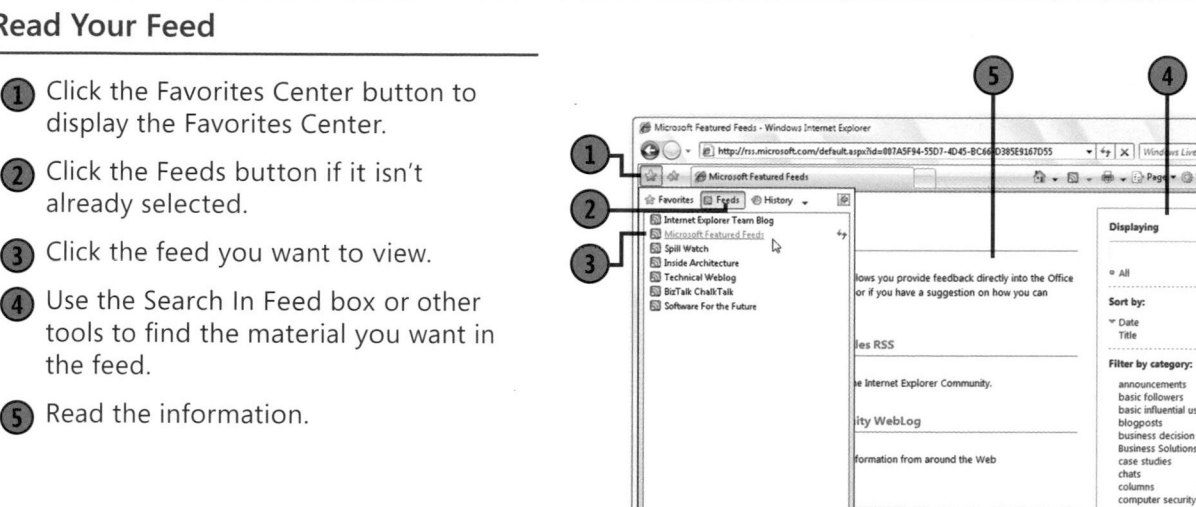

Click to change default settings, including the frequency of automatically updating your feeds.

Open the Favorites Center and click the Feeds button. Point to an RSS feed and click the Refresh This Feed button. Now click the feed. Note that only the latest information is shown.

Tip

Internet Explorer is only one of many different RSS readers. You can also use an RSS gadget in the Windows Sidebar, or in a different program. The list of RSS feeds you subscribe to in Internet Explorer should be available in any other RSS feed readers you use.

Transferring Your Settings

If you use more than one computer or more than one type of browser to explore the Internet, you don't need to duplicate your list of favorite Web sites, nor do you need to duplicate the registrations, sign-ins, and customizations for Web sites that usually keep that information stored as "cookies" (small data files) on your computer. Instead, you can export your list of favorite sites and cookies from one computer or program and import them into the other computer.

Save the Information

1 With Internet Explorer running, on the computer that contains the items you want to transfer, choose Import And Export from the File menu to start the Import/Export Wizard. If the menus aren't displayed, press the Alt key to display them.

2 Step through the wizard, specifying

- That you want to export your Favorites.

- The folder you want to export.

- The location in which you want to save the file containing the information.

3 Use the wizard again to export the cookies if you want to transfer them too, and a third time to export your RSS feeds, if you so desire.

4 Transfer the files to a location that will be accessible by the other computer, such as a shared folder or removable storage—a disk or USB storage device, for example.

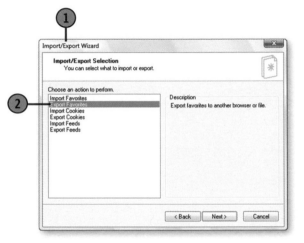

See Also

"Setting Internet Explorer Security" on page 293 for information about controlling cookies.

Tip

If you have more than one Internet browser on your computer, you can use the Import/Export Wizard to transfer Favorites (bookmarks) and cookie information directly among the browsers.

Transfer the Information

① With Internet Explorer running, on the computer to which you want to transfer the information, choose Import And Export from the File menu to start the Import/Export Wizard. If the menus aren't displayed, press the Alt key.

② Step through the wizard, specifying

- That you want to import Favorites information.

- The location of the file containing the information you previously exported.

- The destination folder.

③ Repeat the wizard to import cookies and RSS feeds if you previously exported them.

Tip

When you press the Alt key to display the menus, they're displayed only temporarily; they'll hide again after you've used a menu command or executed another action, such as clicking a tab. To display the menus all the time, click the Tools button, and choose Menu Bar from the drop-down menu.

Copying Material from a Web Page

Sometimes, although you might want to save one or two items from a Web page, you have no use for the entire page. It's a simple matter to save only the parts of the page you want.

Save a Picture

① Right-click the picture, and choose Save Picture As from the shortcut menu that appears.

② In the Save Picture dialog box that appears, save the picture in the folder and the format you want, using a descriptive file name.

Save Some Text

① Click at the beginning of the text you want to copy. You won't see an insertion point, but Internet Explorer is smart—it knows where you clicked.

② Drag the mouse over the text you want to copy.

③ Press Ctrl+C to copy the text.

④ Switch to a word processing program such as WordPad, paste the text (press Ctrl+V), and save the document.

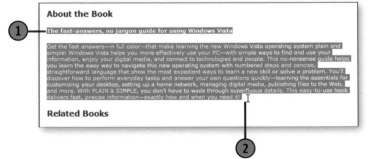

Tip

If you try to copy text from a Web page but can't select only the content you want, here's what to do. Select what you want, along with any other material that simultaneously becomes selected, copy it, and paste it into your word processing program. In that program, delete the superfluous content, and save the document. Not all Web pages let you copy their content.

Caution

When you copy material from a Web page, make sure that you're not violating any copyrights.

6 Playing Games

As the saying goes, "All work and no play makes Jack—or Jacqueline—a dull boy (or girl)!" Because we know that you, our readers, are anything but dull, this section of the book is all about playing games and having fun!

Whether you want to take a few minutes to work off some energy with a quick game of Minesweeper or FreeCell, challenge yourself with the constantly changing layout and effects of Ink-Ball, lose yourself for an hour in a game of Solitaire, or invite a friend or colleague to join you in a game of Chess Titans, Windows Vista is ready to play! If you're a devotee of the traditional Mah-jongg game, there's an intriguing one-player version called Mahjong Titans that you'll want to try.

There are even some games that small children can play, either by themselves or with your help. They'll be learning about colors and shapes as they create fantastic confections in the Comfy Cakes game, strengthening their visual memory as they match tile patterns in the Purble Pairs game, and playing a guessing game in Purble Shop. Our young tester got the hang of all three games with a minimum of assistance from us, and she enthusiastically challenged herself by increasing the difficulty level.

So without further ado...let the games begin!

Playing Chess Titans

Chess Titans is a great way to learn and practice your chess game. You can play against the computer or against an actual human opponent, in which case you and your opponent have to take turns using the same computer. When you play against the computer, you can choose the level of difficulty you want. You use the same rules and strategies in Chess Titans as you do when you're playing on a regular chess board.

Play Chess Titans

 Choose Chess Titans from the Games folder of the Start menu, and choose either New Game Against Computer or New Game Against Human.

 If you're playing against the computer, choose Options from the Game menu, and set the level of difficulty you want. Make any other settings, and click OK.

③ Click the chess piece you want to move.

④ Click the square you want to move the piece into. Squares into which you can legally move your piece are highlighted.

⑤ Wait for either the computer or your human opponent to move.

⑥ Repeat steps 2 through 4 until a King is in check. If your King is in check, move a piece to remove the King from check, if possible.

⑦ Continue playing until a King is checkmated or until someone quits by choosing Resign from the Game menu.

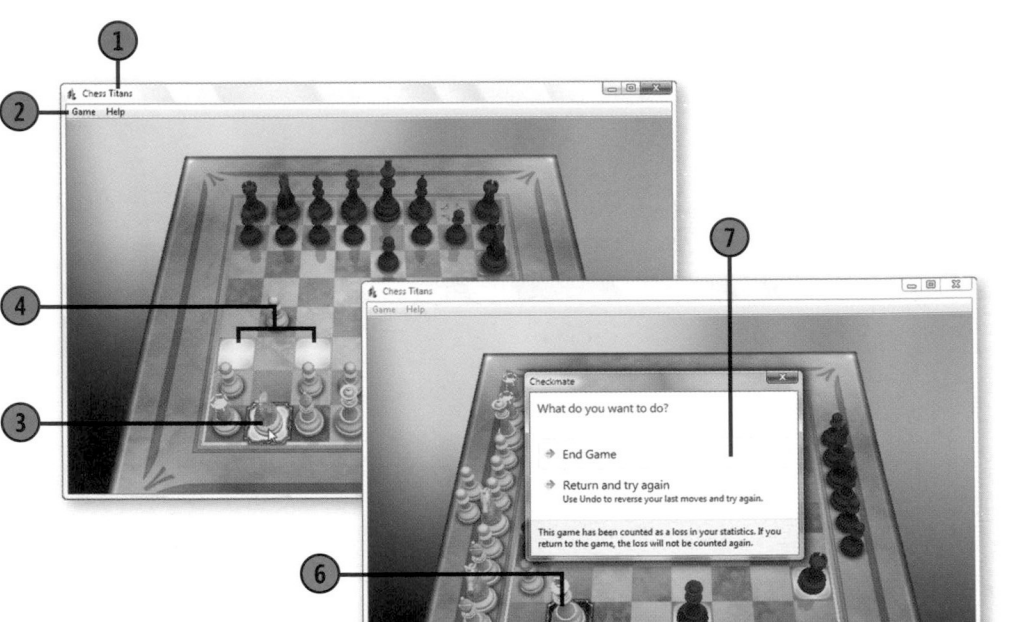

The square is red when the King is in check.

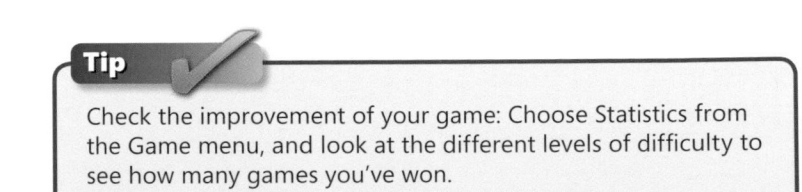

Tip

Check the improvement of your game: Choose Statistics from the Game menu, and look at the different levels of difficulty to see how many games you've won.

Playing FreeCell

FreeCell—a modified version of Solitaire—is a game you play by yourself. The entire deck is dealt, and, as in Solitaire, you arrange the cards by stacking them in descending order, alternating the red and black cards. Unlike the way you play Solitaire, the sequence of cards can begin anywhere in the stack. You can move a single card onto another card to add to the sequence of cards, or into one of the free cells at the top, or into a blank column after the column has been emptied of cards. You win by stacking all the cards by suit in ascending order.

Play FreeCell

① Choose FreeCell from the Games folder of the Start menu.

② When possible, move an Ace to the top of the window and stack the cards by suit in ascending order (FreeCell might do this for you automatically).

③ Click to select the card you want to move.

④ Click another card to move the selected card on top of it. (The cards must be stacked in alternating colors in descending numeric order.)

⑤ Continue stacking the cards, including moving cards into or from a free cell. You can also move one card or a series of cards into an empty column.

⑥ Repeat steps 2 through 5 until all the cards are stacked by suit.

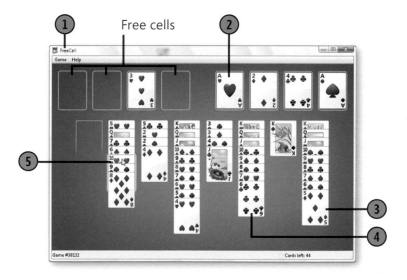

Free cells

 Tip

To replay a specific game, note the game number on the status bar. When you're ready to replay the game, choose Select Game from the Game menu, enter the game number, and click OK.

Tip

Try to free the Ace cards early in the game and to keep as many free cells and empty columns as possible.

Tip

If there are enough available free cells, you can move an entire series of cards from one column into another.

Playing Hearts

You play Hearts against three hands controlled by the computer. The objective is to score the *fewest* points. For each trick you win, you're awarded 1 point for each heart and 13 points for the Queen of Spades. You must use the same suit that's played first unless you're void of that suit. You take the trick if you've played the highest card of the suit played.

Play Hearts

1. Choose Hearts from the Games folder of the Start menu.

2. Click the cards to be passed, and click the Pass button.

3. The Two of Clubs is automatically played to start the game. If you don't have the Two of Clubs, wait for your turn, and then click the card you want to play. Continue playing until the hand is completed

4. Note the score, and click Play Next Hand. Continue playing hands until the first player scores 100 or more points. The lowest score wins.

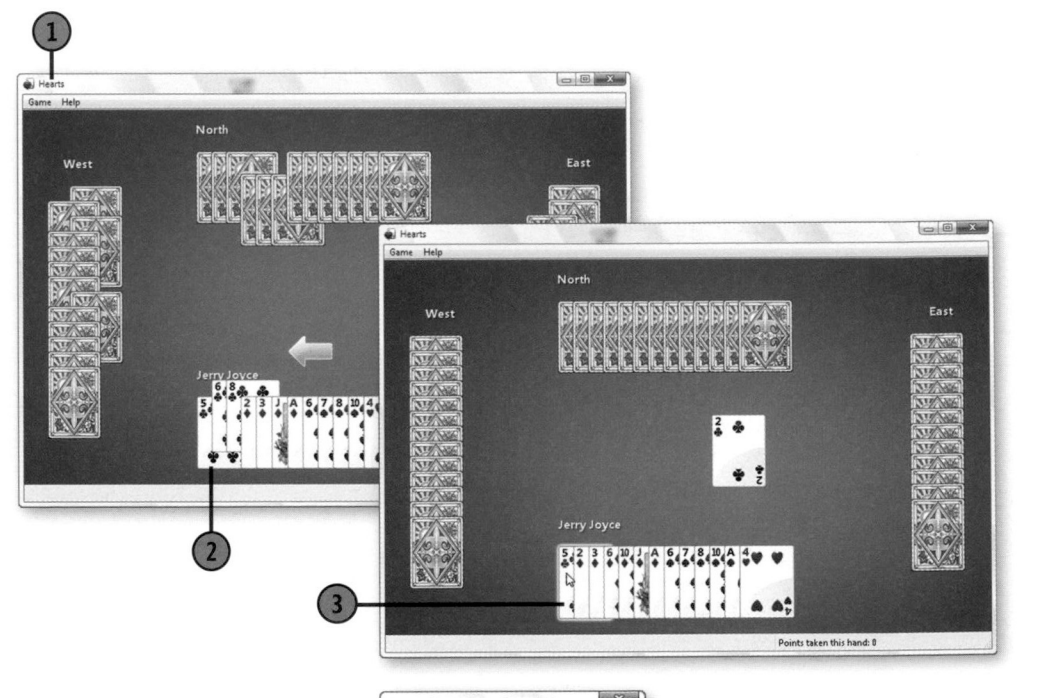

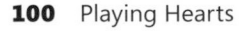

Tip

Another scoring option is to "shoot the moon," whereby you collect all the points in one hand. If you succeed, each of the other players receives 26 points, and you receive 0 (zero) points for the hand.

Playing InkBall

Although InkBall is designed to be played with a stylus on a Tablet PC, you can play it with a mouse or a stylus with a digitizing pad on any computer. The game's objective is simple: Get the bouncing colored balls into holes of the same color by drawing lines that act as temporary barriers to redirect the balls. You must do this before the time runs out or a ball goes into a hole of the wrong color. However, what makes the game not so simple is the fact that the layout and the effects change each time a new set of balls is released, so you'll need to play around a bit to find all the different variations.

Play InkBall

 Click the Start button, type **ink** in the Search box, and click InkBall to start a game.

② To specify the difficulty level of the game, choose the level you want from the Difficulty menu.

③ Draw lines with a stylus, or with the mouse by holding down the left mouse button, to redirect a ball either toward a hole of the same color or away from a hole of a different color. The line disappears once a ball has touched it. Use the table below to see which color balls you should concentrate on.

④ You can continue playing as long as you don't get a ball of one color into a hole of a different color, or until you run out of time. However, because the gray balls and the gray holes are neutral, a gray ball can go into a hole of any color, and a ball of any color can go into a gray hole without ending the game.

Ball	Points
Gray	0
Red	200
Blue	400
Green	800
Gold	1600
Any color into a gray hole	0

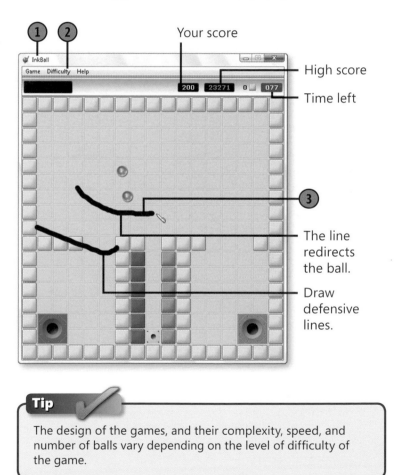

Your score

High score

Time left

The line redirects the ball.

Draw defensive lines.

Tip

The design of the games, and their complexity, speed, and number of balls vary depending on the level of difficulty of the game.

Playing Mahjong Titans

Mahjong Titans is a single-player version of the traditional Mah-jongg game. The object is to remove all the tiles by selecting matching tiles that are free to be removed. To be free, they must have either their left or right side unimpeded by another tile. The tiles have both classes and numbers, except for the special tiles depicting flowers, dragons, seasons, and winds. The tiles must match exactly, except for the flowers and seasons tiles; any season tile can match any other season tile, and any flower tile can match any other flower tile.

Play Mahjong Titans

① Choose Mahjong Titans from the Games folder of the Start menu, and select the game pattern to play to start the game.

② Locate two matching tiles that are free, click the first tile, and then click the second tile.

③ If you're stuck, do either of the following, and then click the highlighted matching pair of tiles:

- Press the H key to have the game highlight a matching pair.

- Right-click a tile, and, if a match is free, the matching tile will be highlighted.

④ Continue clicking free matching tiles until all the tiles are removed (you win) or there are no more available matches (you lose). To get bonus points, remove tiles of the same class and/or same class and number in consecutive turns, or remove sets of seasons or sets of flowers in consecutive turns.

> **Tip** ✓
>
> If you find it difficult to judge the height of each stack of tiles, try changing the appearance of the tiles and background by pressing the F7 key.

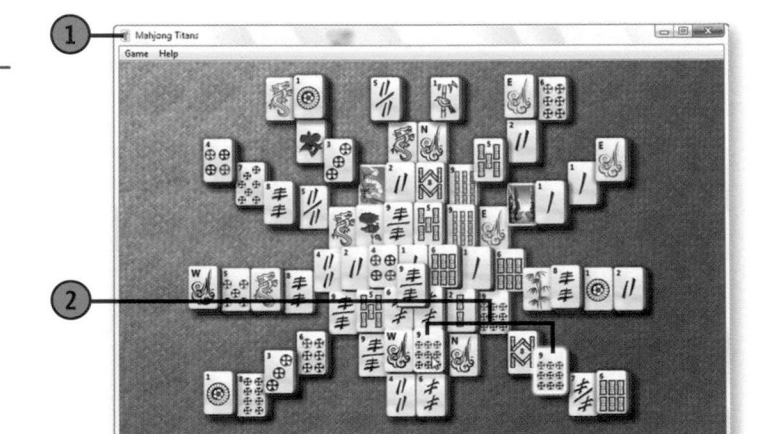

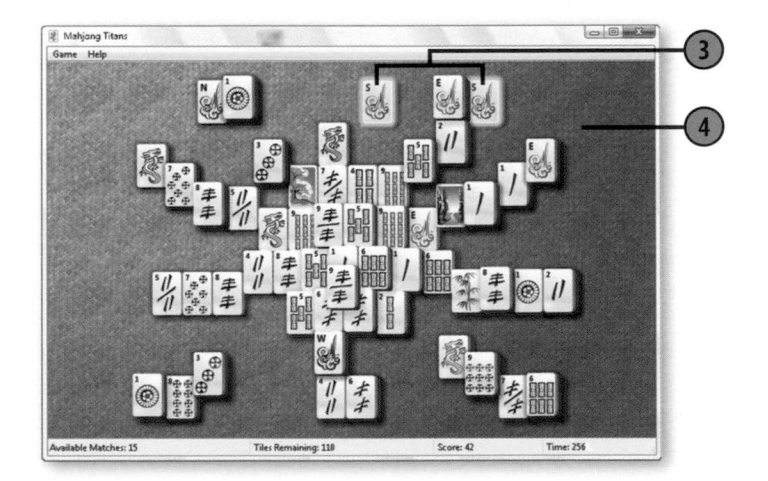

Playing Minesweeper

Minesweeper is a game you play against the computer. The goal is to uncover, in the shortest possible time, all the squares that don't contain mines. If you uncover a square that contains a mine, you lose. The key is to use the numbers in the uncovered squares to determine which adjacent squares contain the mines.

Play Minesweeper

① Choose Minesweeper from the Games folder of the Start menu. If this is the first time you've played this game, click the difficulty level you want to try.

② Click a square to uncover it and to uncover any adjacent squares that don't have mines next to them. You might need to click more squares before you can use the numbers of adjacent mines to determine mine locations.

③ Right-click to mark a square that you believe contains a mine. If you're not sure, right-click the square a second time to mark it as a possible mine.

④ Click a square that you believe doesn't contain a mine. Continue finding unmined squares and marking squares that contain mines until you've revealed all the unmined squares.

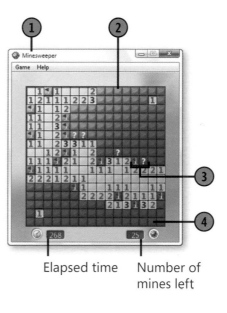

Elapsed time   Number of mines left

Tip ✓

The number in a square represents the total number of mines in adjacent squares—directly above, below, diagonal to, or to the left or right of the numbered square. Use several exposed numbers to figure out where the mines are.

Tip ✓

If the game is too easy or too difficult, choose a different level of difficulty for the game from the Game menu. The greater the level of difficulty, the more squares and mines the game contains.

Playing Purble Place

Here's a game for the very young set. It's designed to teach colors and shapes, and perhaps hook kids very early on computers—in the unlikely event they're not hooked already! Purble Place contains three games: Comfy Cakes, in which you (or a child) assemble a cake to match the shape, color, and patterns of the specified design; Purble Pairs, in which you turn over two tiles at a time and try to match symbols; and Purble Shop, in which you add eyes, nose, mouth, and other accoutrements to a figure, and then try to guess which features are on the mystery Purble behind the curtain.

Play Comfy Cakes

1. Choose Purble Place from the Games folder of the Start menu, and click the Comfy Cakes Factory, or choose it from the Game menu, to start the Comfy Cakes game. If this is the first time you're playing, choose the level of difficulty you want from the Select Difficulty dialog box that appears.

2. Look at the cake you're trying to create.

3. Click the correct pan shape.

4. As the cake moves along the assembly line, click the correct ingredients, and then move forward or backward to add ingredients and layers. To create a second layer, add a cake pan on top of the existing layer.

5. If a piece of cake paper enters the assembly line, start creating another cake while you're still working on the first one.

6. Move the completed cake to the end of the assembly line for packaging and credit for completing a cake.

7. Continue assembling cakes until you've either completed the cake order or made three incorrect cakes.

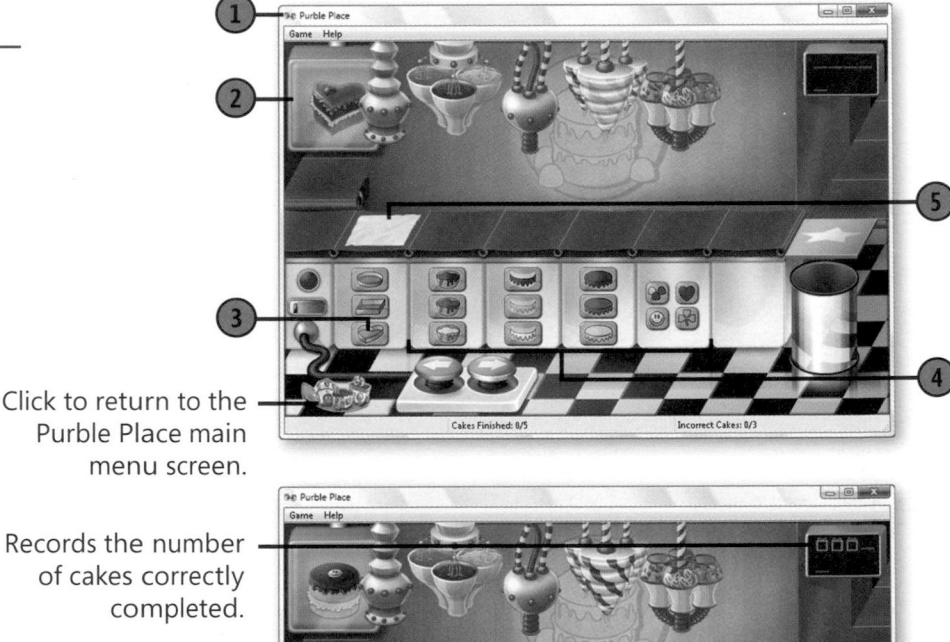

Click to return to the Purble Place main menu screen.

Records the number of cakes correctly completed.

Use the buttons to move forward or backward.

Play Purble Shop

① Choose Purble Place from the Games folder of the Start menu if the game isn't already running. Click the Purble Shop or choose it from the Game menu, and, if asked, specify the level of difficulty you want.

② Click a dashing accoutrement, a set of eyes, a nose, and a mouth.

③ Click to see whether your selection matches the Purble behind the curtain.

④ For items that aren't correct, select different features, and click the button. Continue selecting features until you've selected all the correct features for the mystery Purble, or until you've run out of guesses.

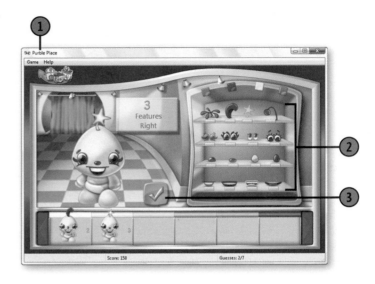

Play Purble Pairs

① Choose Purble Place from the Games folder of the Start menu if the game isn't already running. Click the Purble School or choose Purble Pairs from the Game menu, and, if asked, specify the level of difficulty you want.

② Click one tile and then a second tile. If the tiles don't match, remember the location of each.

③ Click a tile, and, using your memory, click a tile that matches.

④ If you want to take a quick look at all the items on the tiles, click a Sneak Peek token. Then continue trying to match two tiles until all the tiles have been matched.

Time remaining

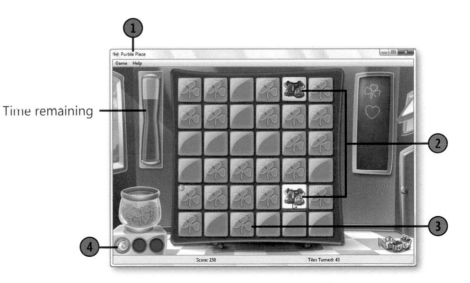

Playing Solitaire

Solitaire is a classic card game that, as its name implies, you play by yourself. The object is to reveal all the cards that are turned face down and eventually to arrange all the cards in four piles, with each pile being a single suit stacked in ascending order from Ace through King.

Play Solitaire

1. Choose Solitaire from the Games folder of the Start menu.

2. Use the mouse to drag one card on top of another card. (The cards must be stacked in descending numeric order, alternating the red and black cards.)

3. Drag any Ace cards into the top row. If there are any other cards for that suit in the pile, stack them in ascending numeric order.

4. Move an entire series of cards onto a card to continue the series.

5. If you can't see a play, press the H key to see a suggested move.

6. If you can't make a play, click the stack to turn the cards over. Drag the top card on top of a face-up card if the top card has the correct number and suit.

7. If all the cards have been moved from a row, move a King, if one is available, and any cards that are stacked on it, into the empty spot.

8. Continue moving the cards until you've moved all the cards stacked by suit on top of the Aces.

> **See Also**
>
> "Playing FreeCell" on page 99 and "Playing Spider Solitaire" on page 107 for information about other Solitaire card games

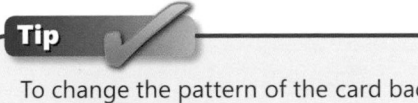

> **Tip**
>
> To change the pattern of the card backs, choose Change Appearance from the Game menu.

> **Tip**
>
> To change the way a game is played—the number of cards drawn at one time, whether or not the game is timed, or the method of scoring—choose Options from the Game menu.

Playing Spider Solitaire

Spider Solitaire is yet another version of Solitaire. Unlike the way you play other Solitaire games, the object is to stack the cards by suit in one column in descending order. When a series from King to Ace is complete, the cards are removed. The level of difficulty is determined by how many suits are used (one, two, or four).

Play Spider Solitaire

① Choose Spider Solitaire from the Games folder of the Start menu. If this is the first time you've played this game, click the difficulty level you want to use.

② Use the mouse to drag one card on top of another card. You can stack the cards in descending numeric order regardless of suit, but it's best to stack by suit.

③ Drag a group of sequential cards of the same suit onto another card. (Only cards of the same suit can be moved as a group.)

④ If there's an empty column, move a card or a sequence of cards into the column.

⑤ If no moves are available, click the stacked cards to deal another round. (You can't deal if there's an empty column.) Continue playing until all the cards have been removed or until all the cards have been dealt and there are no longer any moves available.

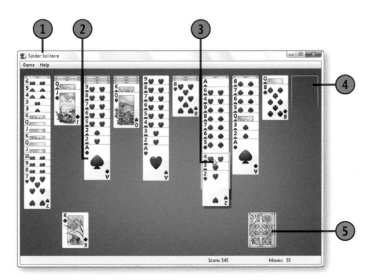

Tip

To display possible moves, press the M key. Press it again to see another possible move.

Tip

To change the difficulty level of the game, choose Options from the Game menu.

Controlling All Your Games

Windows Vista comes with a few games, but if you want, you can easily install more games. To easily access and control these games, the Games Explorer gathers all the games and information about the games into one window. From that window, you can see how well a game will run on your system, the rating for the game, and how to access online Web pages and forums about the game.

Control Your Games

1. Click the Start button, type **games** in the Search box of the Start menu, and choose Games Explorer to display the Games Explorer window.

2. Select a game.

3. Read the ratings that are required and recommended for the game, as well as the rating of your computer. (Note that this information isn't available for all games.)

4. If you don't see any up-to-date information about the game, click Options, and, in the Set Up Games Folder Options dialog box that appears, select the check box for downloading information. Click OK.

5. If you need to adjust any of your computer's hardware or firewall settings, click Tools, and select the item you need to change.

6. Click to go on line for information and forums about your game.

7. Click to set up or change any parental controls to restrict the games that you'll allow to be played on this computer based on their ratings.

8. Click a game, and then click Play to play the game. To start the game using a saved game or a different option, click the Play down arrow, and choose the way you want to start the game.

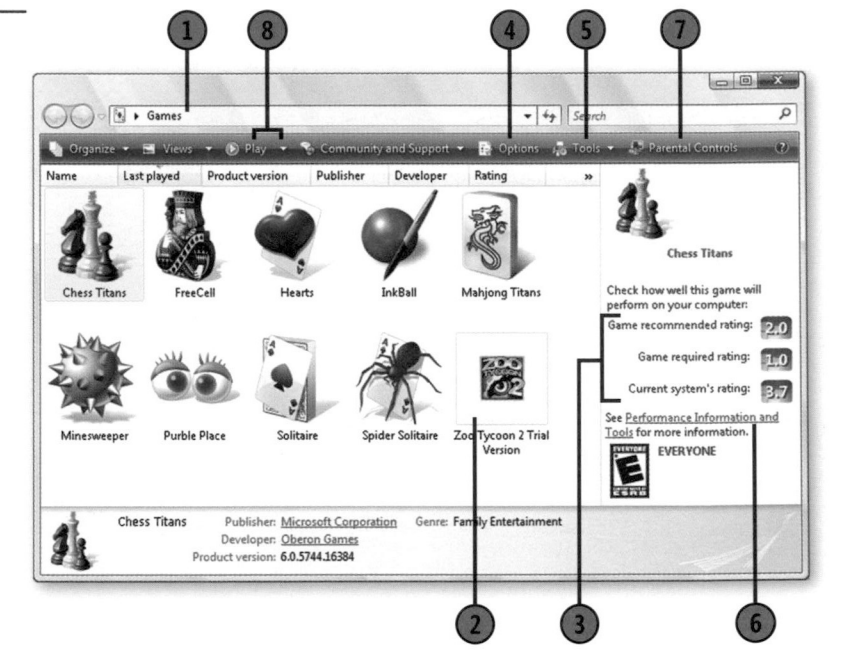

 **See Also**

"Restricting Access to Web Content" on pages 288–289 and "Restricting Access to the Computer" on pages 290–291 for information about setting up parental controls.

7

Working with Pictures

We all love pictures, whether they're photographs that record the significant events in our lives, candid shots of people, pets, and places, or pictures we've drawn ourselves. And, of course, one of the things we love to do with our pictures is to share them with other people. Whether you want to send your pictures via e-mail to far-flung friends and relatives, add them to your Web page, or lend some color to your documents with an original drawing or two, Windows Vista provides all the tools you need for professional-looking results.

The Windows Photo Gallery is your best friend when you're working with your pictures—it helps you sort and organize them so that you can find them easily, and you can even add captions, titles, and sequential numbering. You can use a wizard to move your digital camera pictures onto your computer, and then you can edit the pictures to improve them if necessary—cropping them, removing "red eye," and so on. You can create a dynamic slide show, with zooming, panning, and transitions as you move from one picture to another, and you can even include a video clip and a soundtrack.

You can create your own drawings or edit existing ones in the Paint program, using Paint's tools to create the special effects you want. Even if you're not a great artist, it can be a lot of fun!

Viewing Your Photos

It's easy to become overwhelmed by the proliferation of pictures on your computer, especially when they're stored in a variety of locations. We've found that the best way to access and sort all those pictures and to organize them so that you can easily locate them is to use the Windows Photo Gallery. The Photo Gallery automatically includes all the pictures and photographs that are stored in your Pictures folder, as well as any that are contained in subfolders.

Browse Your Photos

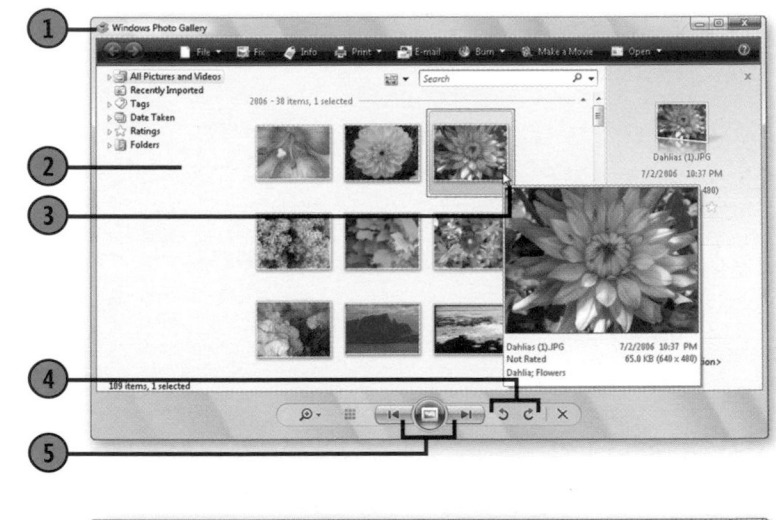

① Click the Start button, type **photo** in the Search box, and click Windows Photo Gallery to start the Photo Gallery.

② Scroll through the photos, noting that they're grouped by date.

③ Point to a photo to see an enlarged version of it, along with other details.

④ To rotate a photo, click to select it, and then click the Rotate Clockwise or the Rotate Counterclockwise button.

⑤ To view the other photos in sequence, click the Next Image button (or press the Right arrow key); or to view the pictures in reverse order, click the Previous Image button (or press the Left arrow key).

⑥ To view a photo in detail, double-click it.

⑦ Use the controls to change the magnification (zoom) of the image, to see additional photos, or to rotate the photo.

⑧ Click the Back To Gallery button when you've finished.

Find Your Photos

① Click the type of category you want to use to classify the photos, if the list isn't already expanded.

② Click the category you want to use. If necessary, click any subcategories to expand them, and then select the category you want.

③ View the photos in that category.

④ If you want to find a specific photo within the selected category, click in the Search box, and start typing a name, file type, or tag (classification) for the photo.

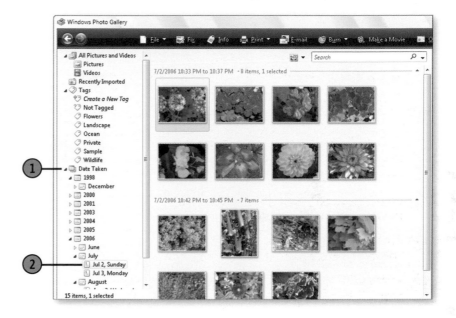

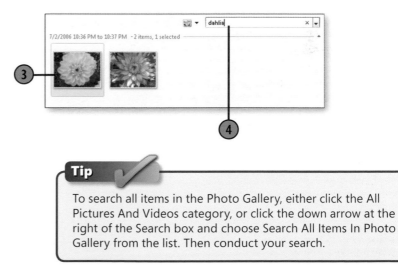

Try This!

Click the Views button next to the Search box, and choose a different view of your photos. Click the button again, and choose a different way to group and then sort the photos. Click the button again, and choose to show the table of contents. If the Info pane is open, click Close to close it. Use the Zoom Control to change the size of your photos. Now use the Views button to restore grouping and sorting, the Info button to display the Info pane, and the Reset Thumbnails To Default Size button to undo your zooming.

Tip

To search all items in the Photo Gallery, either click the All Pictures And Videos category, or click the down arrow at the right of the Search box and choose Search All Items In Photo Gallery from the list. Then conduct your search.

Viewing a Photo Slide Show

Instead of clicking through a static view of your photos, you can view them in a dynamic slide show that can include zooming, panning, and transitions. If you have any videos in the Photo Gallery, you can also include them.

View the Show

1. Start Windows Photo Gallery, and select a category, tag, rating, or folder to display only the photos you want in your slide show.

2. Click the Play Slide Show button.

3. Move your mouse to display the slide-show controls.

4. Click Themes, and select the slide-show style you want. If the controls don't appear, Photo Gallery is running in Basic mode due to the limitations of your computer's graphics display, and so you can't use the advanced controls. If this is the case, right-click the slide show, and control it using the commands on the shortcut menu that appears.

5. Click the Settings button to set the speed of the show, to specify whether you want the photos to be shown in order or at random, and to specify whether the show is to be played in a continuous loop or as a single show.

6. When you've finished viewing the show, move the mouse if the controls aren't visible, and click Exit or press the Esc key.

Adding Photos to the Gallery

Windows Photo Gallery automatically includes the photos in your Pictures folder, but you might have photos stored in other locations that you'd like to include in the Photo Gallery.

You can either copy a photo or folder to your Pictures folder and thus to the Photo Gallery, or let the Gallery know where the folder containing the photos is located.

Copy a Photo or a Folder

① With Photo Gallery open, open the folder that contains the folder or photo you want to add.

② Drag the folder or photo onto the Gallery. The folder or photo is copied to your Pictures folder and added to the Gallery.

See Also

"Viewing Photos Stored in Different Locations" on page 115 for information about viewing photos that aren't in the Photo Gallery.

Include a Folder on Your Computer or Network

① Click the File button, and choose Add Folders To Gallery from the drop-down menu to display the Add Folders To Gallery dialog box.

② Specify the location of the folder.

③ Click OK.

Importing Photos from Your Camera or Removable Media

Many digital cameras come with their own software for down-loading your photos and managing them on your computer. However, Windows Vista makes it so simple to download and organize the photos from your camera that you might want to try both systems to see which one you like best. Windows also uses the same method to transfer photos from a CD, a DVD memory card, or a USB storage device. However, the way Windows handles this task depends on how you have your AutoPlay settings configured for the device or the type of media you're using.

Import Your Photos

(1) Connect or insert the device you're using, and, if necessary, turn it on. If the AutoPlay dialog box appears, click Import Pictures, and then click OK. If nothing happens, in the Windows Photo Gallery, choose Import From Camera Or Scanner from the File menu, select your device in the Import Pictures And Videos Wizard, and click Import.

(2) In the Importing Pictures And Videos dialog box that appears, click Options.

(3) In the Import Settings dialog box that appears, select the location, the folder, and the file-naming method you want for your photos.

(4) Make any other changes you want to the way your photos are imported.

(5) Click OK.

(6) Type a tag for the pictures.

(7) Click Import.

See Also

"Scanning a Picture" on page 191 for information about scanning photos and other pictures.

"Set the AutoPlay" on page 271 for information about adjusting the AutoPlay settings.

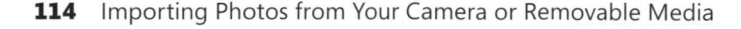

Viewing Photos Stored in Different Locations

Windows Vista provides a variety of ways to view your photos and other pictures so that you can decide which ones to keep, copy, print, or send to friends. Although the Windows Photo Gallery is a superb way to organize and view your photos, you might want to look at some photos that you haven't yet included in the Gallery—those on a removable USB memory device, for example.

View Your Photos

1 In the folder that contains the photos, click the down arrow at the right of the Views button, and drag the slider to Extra Large Icons.

2 Click a photo that you want to see in detail.

3 Click the down arrow at the right of the Preview, Edit, or Open button (whichever is shown), and choose Windows Photo Gallery from the list. If none of these buttons is shown, right-click the photo, and choose Preview from the shortcut menu.

4 View the photo, and use the tools in the viewer just as you use them in the Windows Photo Gallery.

See Also

"Labeling and Tagging Your Photos" on pages 116–117 and "Managing Your Photos" on pages 122–123 for information about organizing and viewing photos using the Windows Photo Gallery.

"Printing Your Photographs" on page 188 for information about printing your photos.

"Setting Your Default Programs" on pages 240–241 for information about setting a program that opens by default for a specific type of file.

Labeling and Tagging Your Photos

Most photo file formats allow you to store extra data, called *metadata,* in the photo file. The camera often stores information such as the date the photo was taken, the camera model, the resolution, and so on. You can add other information: tags to classify the subject matter, captions to add more information about the photo, and your rating of the photo. You can then use these tags and ratings to find or sort your photos.

Add a Tag

① If it isn't already running, start Windows Photo Gallery from the Start menu. If the Info pane isn't shown, click the Info button to display it.

② Use the categories or folders to show the photos to which you want to add tags.

③ Click a photo to select it. Hold down the Ctrl key and keep clicking additional photos until you've selected all the photos to which you want to add the same tag.

④ Click Add Tags, and do either of the following:

• Click a tag in the list.

• Type a new tag, and press Enter.

⑤ Repeat step 4 to add more tags to the selected photos, or repeat steps 2 through 4 to add tags to other photos.

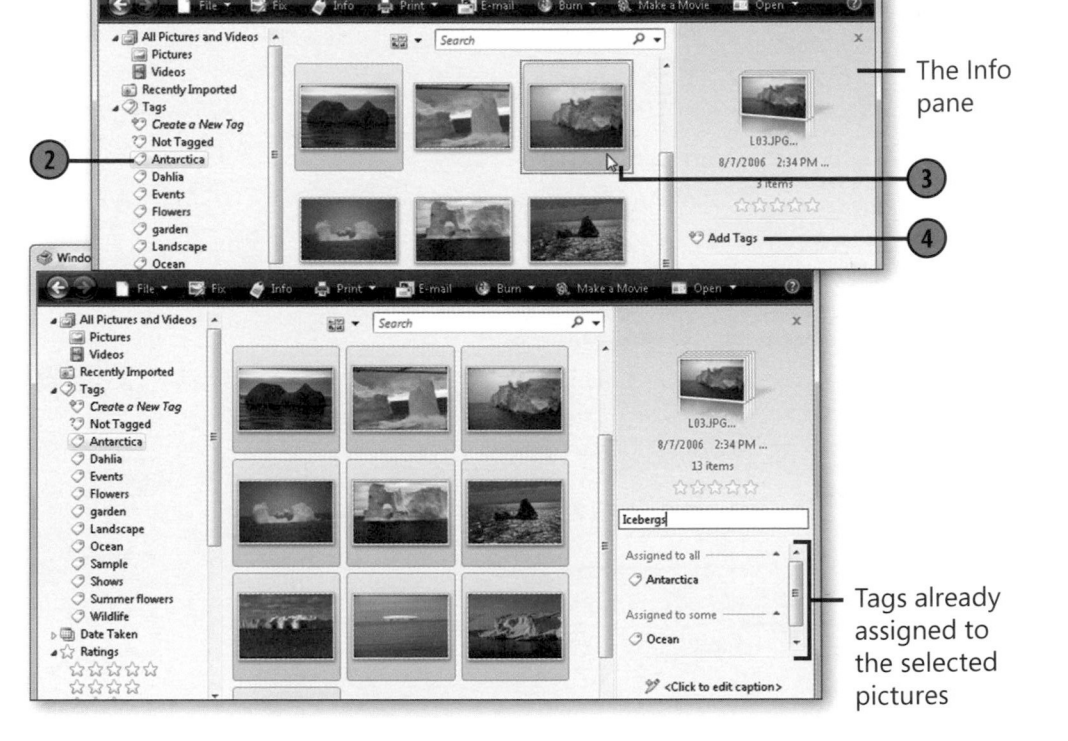

The Info pane

Tags already assigned to the selected pictures

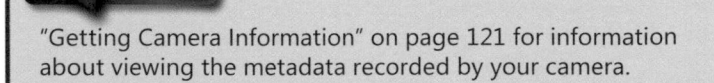

See Also

"Getting Camera Information" on page 121 for information about viewing the metadata recorded by your camera.

Add a Caption

1. Select the photo or photos to which you want to add a caption or a title.

2. Click the Click To Edit Caption text box at the bottom of the Info pane, type the caption, and press Enter.

Rate a Photo

1. Select the photo or photos you want to rate.

2. Click the number of stars (0 worst, 5 best) that you want to assign to the photo.

Tip

To remove the rating from a photo, right-click it in the Photo Gallery, and choose Clear Rating from the shortcut menu.

Try This!

Add a tag, a caption, and a rating for a photo. From the Start menu, open the folder (the Pictures folder, for example) that contains the picture file, and select the file. Note that for most types of photos and pictures (except bitmap files), the information you added about the file is shown in the Details pane, and that you can edit this information or add new information.

Editing Your Photos

Often, on closer inspection, the photo that looked so perfect in the camera seems to have a few flaws: The lighting or the color is slightly off, the subject isn't framed quite right or has those disconcerting red eyes, or the photo is under- or over-exposed. You can adjust these problems using the tools in Windows Photo Gallery, and, if you don't like what you did, you can easily revert to a copy of the original photo.

Adjust the Exposure and Color

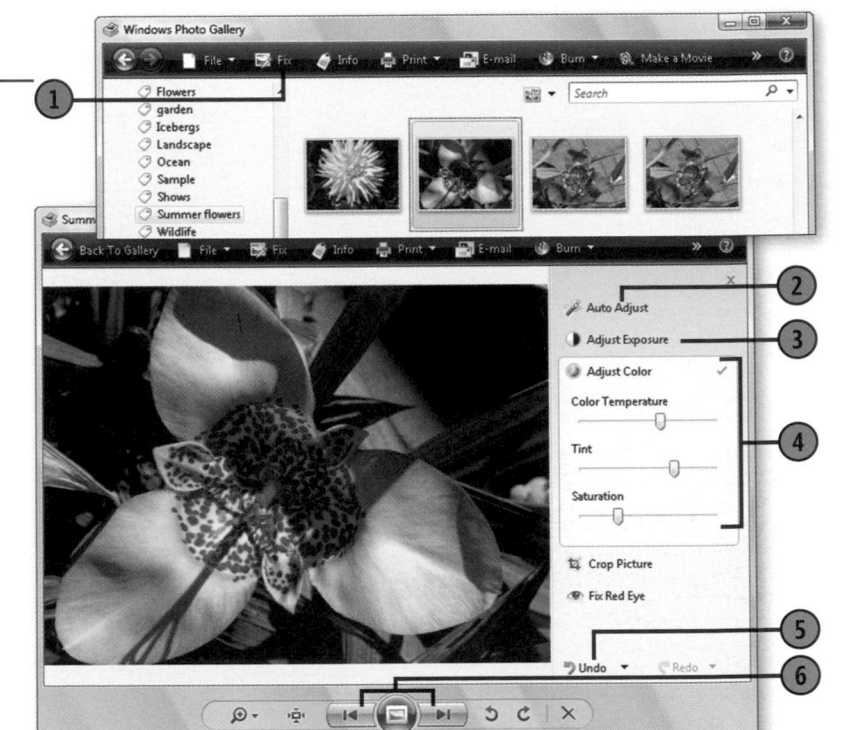

1 In Windows Photo Gallery, click the photo you want to edit to select it, and then click the Fix button.

2 Click Auto Adjust if you want to let the computer adjust the brightness, contrast, and color.

3 Click Adjust Exposure, and use the sliders to change the brightness and contrast.

4 Click Adjust Color, and use the sliders to change the Color Temperature (the percentages of red and blue), the Tint (the shadings of the colors), and/or the Saturation (the intensity of the colors).

5 If you don't like one of your changes, click the Undo button. To undo a series of changes, click the down arrow next to the Undo button, and choose from the series of items that you can undo.

6 To edit another photo, use the Next or the Previous button to display additional photos.

 **Tip**

Windows Photo Gallery editing does only the most basic photo-editing tasks. If you have a more powerful editing program installed on your computer, select the photo to be edited, click the Open button, and choose the program you want to use from the drop-down list.

Tip

Changes are automatically saved as you work, but a copy of the original file is kept in the Photo Gallery. To undo all your editing, click the File button in the editing window, and choose Revert To Original from the drop-down menu.

Crop a Photo

1 Click Crop Picture to specify which part of the photo you want to keep while the remaining parts are discarded.

2 Click Proportion, and select the finished size you want for the photo.

3 Use the mouse to drag the frame to include what you want to keep. If the frame is oriented incorrectly, click Rotate Frame.

4 When the photo is cropped exactly the way you want, click Apply.

Remove "Red Eye"

1 In a photo in which someone has those lovely red eyes caused by the camera flash, use the Zoom Control to enlarge and clearly pinpoint the red eyes, and click Fix Red Eye.

2 Drag a rectangle over the red part of the eye. Repeat for any other red eyes.

3 Click Back To Gallery to return to the Photo Gallery.

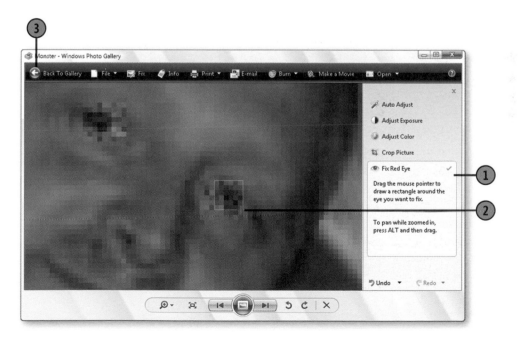

Sharing Your Photos

If you've taken some photos that you're especially proud of, you usually can't wait to share them with family, friends, or colleagues. Windows Vista and Windows Photo Gallery provide several easy ways to share those great photos.

Printing: Windows provides you with an easy-to-use printing wizard when you're ready to print your photos. Alternatively, via the Internet, you can send the photos to a photo service. You can also copy your photos to a USB storage device and then take the device to your local camera shop for printing. To quickly copy the photos, with the USB device attached to your computer, select the photos you want to print, right-click one of the selected pictures, point to Send To on the shortcut menu, and choose your USB device. All your selected pictures will be copied to the device.

E-Mail: Not only can you conveniently send photos via e-mail directly from the Windows Photo Gallery, but you can specify the size of the photos and thus the size of the files. Be kind, though! Sending small files creates happy recipients—no one likes to wait while large files download, and it's torture for people who have slow Internet connections.

On Your Computer: If other people have access to your computer using their own accounts, you can make your photos available to them by placing them in the Public Pictures folder. You can also share your photos by displaying them as a screen-saver slide show, as a custom slide show that you run from the Windows Photo Gallery, as a slide show in Windows Media Center, or as a static Desktop background.

Network Sharing: If your computer is on a network, you can place your photos in a public folder (the Public Pictures folder, for example); share the folder that contains the pictures; or simply share the individual files you want people to see. You can also share your photos as a slide show in Windows Media Player by sharing your Windows Media Library with other people on your network.

CD/DVD Storage: Whether you plan to send a collection of photos to other people or just store the photos for your own use, you can easily move all your photo files onto a CD or DVD and thereby free up some space on your computer.

Video DVD: Using the Windows DVD Maker, you can create a DVD with an animated slide show of your photos, complete with panning, zooming, and professional-looking transitions between photos. You can even include a soundtrack and video clips.

Multimedia Video Movie: Using Windows Movie Maker, you can take full control of the photos in a slide show, whether you use the AutoMovie feature to create a quick movie with default settings, or build your movie piece by piece: inserting the photos you want, setting customized display durations and transitions, adding music or a narration, and adding video clips. When the movie is completed, you can choose the methods you want to use to save and distribute it.

SideShow Display: If you have an auxiliary display, such as a *wireless photo frame* or a *smartphone* that works with the Windows SideShow feature, you can display your photos away from your computer.

There are, of course, many other ways you can share your photos that aren't directly supported by Windows Vista. These include posting photos on your Web site, your Web community spaces, or your blog. You'll need to check on how to do these from the providers of the services.

Getting Camera Information

Often, to capture a moment, you'll take a photo really fast, with no time to set up, and, to your amazement, it's a masterpiece! Or you set up slowly and methodically, with the perfect lighting and framing, and the photo is a disaster.

What happened? Now you can review your camera settings for a particular photo and perhaps understand why it's so perfect or so disappointing.

Get the Information

① In Windows Photo Gallery, click the photo to select it.

② Click the File button, and choose Properties from the drop-down menu (or press Alt+Enter) to display the Properties dialog box.

③ On the Details tab of the Properties dialog box, view the settings that you used.

④ Click OK when you've finished.

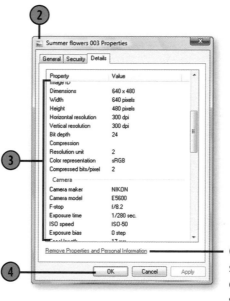

Click if you don't want to share this information with others when you send or share the photo.

> **Tip** ✓
>
> You'll usually find that not all of the properties on the Details tab are completed. For those properties, you complete the field by pointing to the empty area where the information should be, and then, if a text box appears, you can enter the information.

Managing Your Photos

The Windows Photo Gallery does an excellent job of managing your photos, but every so often you might want to do a bit of extra management—for example, renaming a series of photos or copying some photos to a Word document. You can go directly to the folder where the photo is stored and do whatever file management you want.

Rename Your Photos

1 In Windows Photo Gallery, click the photo to select it. If you want to rename a series of photos with the same name and then number them consecutively, select all the photos you want to rename.

2 Click the File button, and choose Rename from the drop-down menu.

3 Type the new name for the photo or series of photos, and then press Enter. Photo Gallery will automatically number the series of photos.

See Also

"Recovering a Deleted Item" on page 208 for information about restoring photos that you deleted.

Caution

Be aware that when you delete a photo from either the Photo Gallery or a folder, the photo is automatically deleted from the other location. Therefore, if you delete a photo from the Photo Gallery, it's also deleted from its folder and removed from your computer.

Copy Your Photos

 Select the photo or photos you want to copy.

 Click the File button, and choose Copy from the drop-down menu to copy the photo or photos to the Clipboard so that you can paste them into a different program or folder.

Caution

Some programs—Paint, for example—don't allow you to paste multiple pictures, so you should copy only a single file if you want to paste it. You'll need to check or experiment with your application to see whether it will allow you to paste multiple pictures at the same time.

Manage the File

 Right-click the photo you want to manage, and choose Open File Location from the shortcut menu.

 In the folder window that appears, conduct whatever management you want, just as you would with any other file.

8

Working with Multimedia

In Windows Vista, the term "multimedia" covers a lot of ground, depending on which version of Windows Vista is installed on your computer. The multimedia tools include Movie Maker, Photo Gallery, and Media Player. If you have either the Home Premium or the Ultimate version of Windows, you also have DVD Burner and Media Center. If you like playing around with multimedia, this section of the book is for you!

You can create a slide show on a DVD, complete with a soundtrack, panning, and zooming. You can download complete videos or video clips from your camera onto your computer and burn a DVD. You can use Media Player to play music or videos from the playlists you create, and you can copy music onto your computer's hard disk instead of inserting individual CDs. You can share your music or video collections over your network, or listen to or watch your media while you're on the move by synchronizing them with a portable device. With Media Center, you can watch TV or movies, burn or play CDs and DVDs, listen to the radio, and create a Media Library. Last but not least, you can produce movies that can include narration, a soundtrack, transitions between clips, and various special effects. You can even add titles and credits to give your movie a really professional look, and then publish it to glowing reviews!

Creating a Multimedia Slide Show

A great way to display your photographs is to create a slide show on a DVD. You can enliven the photos with panning and zooming, and you can even add a musical soundtrack and videos to animate your show. You can also play a slide show using Windows Media Center, provided it's set up on your computer.

Assemble a DVD Slide Show

(1) Click the Start button, type **photo** in the Search box, and click Windows Photo Gallery to start the program.

(2) Select the photos that you want for the slide show.

(3) Click Burn, and choose Video DVD from the drop-down menu.

(4) If you want to add photos from other locations, click Add Items. In the Add Items To DVD dialog box that appears, locate and select the photos, and click Add.

(5) Click a photo, and use the Move Up or Move Down button to position the photo. Continue selecting and arranging the photos until they're in the order you want.

(6) Type a name for the slide show.

(7) Click Options if you want to customize when the DVD menu appears or if you want to change the screen's aspect ratio for wide-screen viewing.

(8) Click Next.

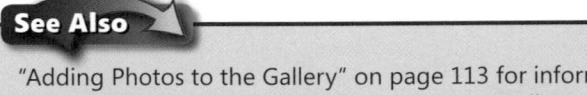

See Also

"Adding Photos to the Gallery" on page 113 for information about adding photos to the Windows Photo Gallery.

Create the Slide Show

1. Select the menu style you want.

2. Click the Menu Text or the Customize Menu button if you want to modify the menu or add background video or music to it.

3. Click Slide Show.

4. Click Add Music to add music files for the audio background.

5. Select the options you want for the slide show.

6. Click Change Slide Show.

7. Click Preview to view your slide show, and then click OK.

8. With a recordable DVD in the DVD drive, click Burn to create your DVD slide show.

Tip

To save the project if you're not going to complete it in one session, click the File button, and choose Save.

See Also

"Viewing a Photo Slide Show" on page 112 for information about creating a slide show in which you can vary the length of display, incorporate video, and use professional-looking transitions between photos.

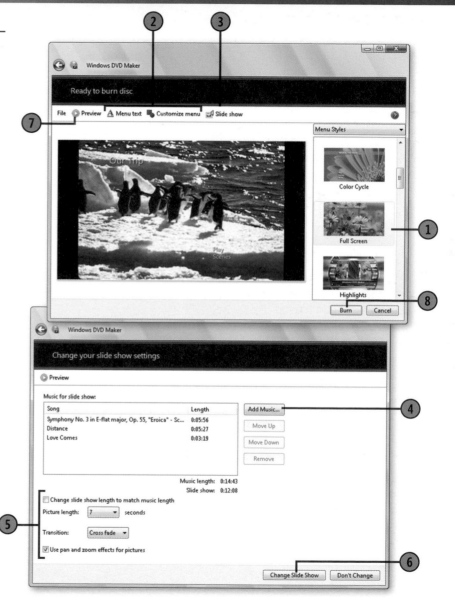

Playing with Multimedia

Windows Vista gives you a choice of tools that can deter-mine the way you manage and play your multimedia. These tools include Windows Photo Gallery, Windows Movie Maker, Windows Media Player, Windows Media Center, Windows DVD Burner, and the Windows Import Video Wizard. Each has its specific uses, and it's your choice as to which tools you use and how you use them. Note that Media Center and DVD Burner are available only in the Windows Vista Home Premium and Windows Vista Ultimate versions. Of course, you'll need the proper equipment—a DVD reader to watch DVD movies, a DVD burner to create your own DVDs, and lots of computer memory, disk space, and video power to enjoy all the features.

Windows Photo Gallery is mainly used to organize and preview your photos, but it also gives you access to your videos. You just double-click a video file to play the video directly in Photo Gallery, using a simple viewer. You can also use Windows DVD Maker directly from Photo Gallery to create an animated slide show or a video, complete with clips, transitions, and a title, and then burn it onto a DVD.

Windows Movie Maker is a video-editing program. You use it to edit and rearrange existing video files; to eliminate extraneous materials; and to add effects such as transitions between scenes, video transformations (recoloring, for exam-ple), and a narration or a soundtrack. Movie Maker also makes it easy to share your finished videos with others through e-mails, video CDs, or DVDs, or right from your computer.

Windows Media Player is a multipurpose program that you use to organize and play your multimedia, including video files, streaming video from the Internet, DVDs,

music files, and music CDs. You can also purchase and down-load music files from the Internet. You can organize what you want to hear using playlists, coordinate your music with visual displays, record your own music CDs, transfer music to a por-table device, and share your media library with other computers on your network.

Windows Media Center is an entire environment that's designed to bring the vast multimedia computer world into your living room. Media Center uses all your computer's power to maximize your experience as you watch television, record shows, play DVDs, listen to the radio and CDs—and you can do it all with a remote control, your mouse, or your keyboard!

Windows DVD Maker is a program that enables you to quickly create video DVDs using photos and/or videos. You can set the title and menu text and can choose from a variety of themes for the opening of the video DVD. You can also use DVD Maker to create a DVD directly from video recordings on a video camera.

Windows Import Video Wizard is a tool you use to import video from an .avi-format (also called Mini-DV) video camera. With this wizard, you can transfer an entire video recording, or selected sections of it, onto your computer or onto a DVD, or you can capture the live feed from the camera as a video on your computer. To use the wizard, you need to have the camera attached to your computer with an IEEE 1394 (also called a Firewire or i.LINK) cable and port. You can also use a USB 2 connection if the camera supports USB streaming (a USB Video Class camera).

Creating a Video DVD

If you have a video that you want to share with others, and you don't need to edit it or add titles, transitions, or a soundtrack—or if you've already done so in another program—you can create a video DVD, complete with an opening menu and a visual layout scheme.

Create the DVD

1. With a recordable DVD disc in your DVD Burner, click the Start button, start Photo Gallery, select the videos you want to include on the DVD, and click Burn. Choose Video DVD from the drop-down menu to start Windows DVD Maker. If your video files aren't included in Photo Gallery, start Windows DVD Burner from the Start menu, and then add the videos.

2. If there are additional videos you want to include, click Add Items, locate and select the videos, and click Add. Drag the videos up or down to set the order of play.

3. Click Options to customize the video play-back, the video aspect ratio, the video format, or the DVD writing speed.

4. Type a name for the video DVD.

5. Click Next.

6. Click the menu style you want.

7. Click Menu Text to modify the font and the menu text, and to add any notes. Click Change Text when you've finished.

8. Click Preview to make sure the video appears as you want it. Click OK.

9. Click Burn to create the DVD.

Downloading a Video from a Camera

With the digital video camera attached to your computer, you can transfer the recorded video to your computer in one of three formats, described below.

Download the Entire Video

1. With your camera attached to the computer, turn the camera on, and then set it to play the recorded video.

2. In the Import Video Wizard that appears, type a name for the video, and specify the location where you want the video file to be stored.

3. Click Format, and select the format you want:

   - Audio Video Interleaved (Single File) to copy the video using the .avi standard

   - Windows Media Video (Single File) to transform the video into the .wmv standard

   - Windows Media Video (One File Per Scene) to transform the video into the .wmv standard, dividing the video into separate files where the wizard believes the scenes change.

4. Click Next.

5. Select this option to import the entire videotape.

6. Click Next, and wait while the videotape is being rewound.

7. If you want to stop the recording before the entire tape has been transferred, click Stop.

8. Click Finish when the video has been transferred.

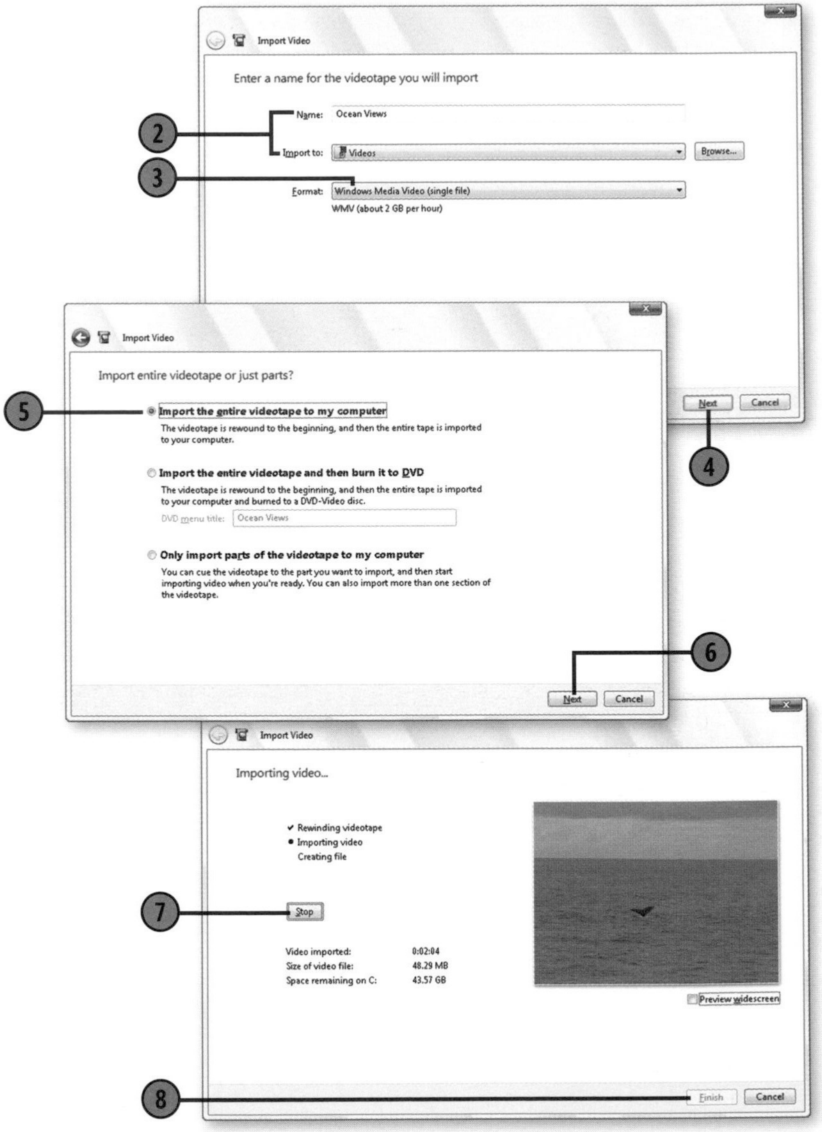

Downloading Video Clips from a Camera

Sometimes, rather than putting an entire video on your computer, you'll want to use only the best shots or the most interesting sections. To save the time and disk space that it takes to transfer the entire video and then edit it, you can go through the video on your camera and select which parts you want to download.

Download the Clips

(1) With the camera attached to your computer, turn the camera on and set it to play the recorded video. In the Import Video Wizard that appears, type a name for the video, select the location where you want to store the video file, and select the video format you want. Click Next.

(2) Select this option to import parts of the videotape.

(3) Click Next.

(4) Use the controls to move through the video until you locate the part you want to record. Use the Next Frame and Previous Frame controls to find the exact location where you want to start the recording.

(5) Click Start Video Import, and watch your clip.

(6) Click Stop Video Import when you reach the spot where you want to stop the importing.

(7) Repeat steps 4 through 6 until you've imported all the clips you want, and click Finish.

Downloading Video to a DVD

One way you can share the very large files you create when you download a video from your camera is to burn the video to a DVD. Using the Video Import Wizard, you can tell Windows to download your video and to create a DVD at the same time.

Transfer to a DVD

1. With a blank recordable DVD in you DVD burner and with the camera attached to your computer, turn the camera on and set it to play the recorded video. In the Import Video Wizard that appears, type a name for the video, select the location where you want to store the video file, and select the video format you want. Click Next.

2. Select this option to download the video and burn it to a DVD.

3. Click Next.

4. Wait for the video to be rewound and downloaded.

5. If you want to end the transfer before the entire tape has been transferred, click Stop.

6. Wait for the DVD to be completed, and then remove it and make sure that the content of the DVD is the way you want it.

> **Tip**
>
> The video files created in the download remain on your hard disk after Windows has created the DVD. If you don't want to keep those files on your computer because they take up so much disk space, make sure that the DVD is fully readable, and then delete the files from your hard disk.

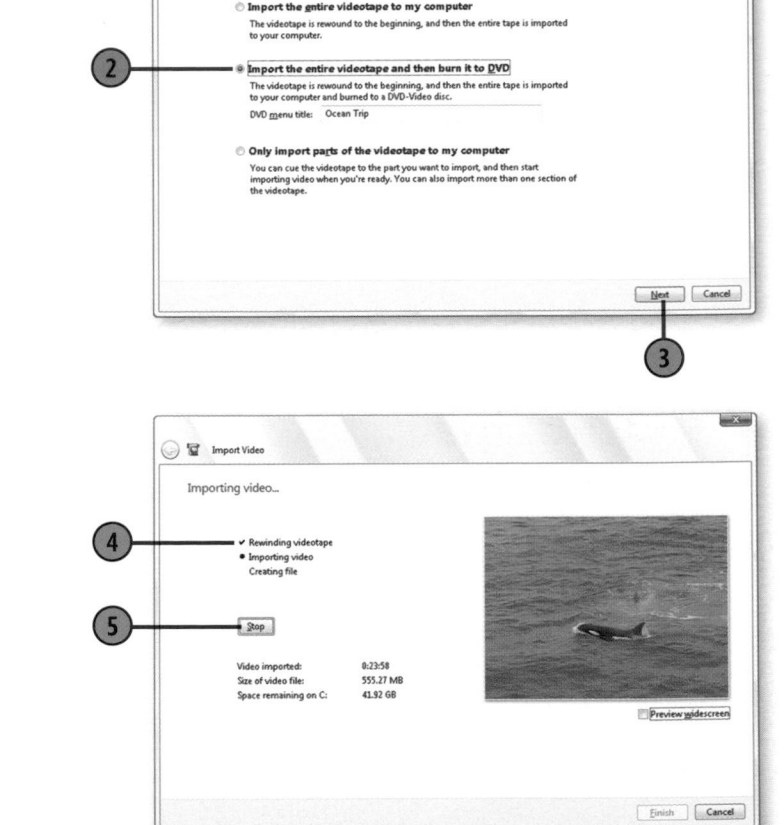

Recording a Video from a Camera

With the proper connection, you can record a live feed from your video camera directly onto your computer, creating a video file (or files) in the format of your choice.

Record Your Video

1 With the camera attached to your computer, turn the camera on, and, if necessary, set it to the Record Video mode, but don't start recording yet. In the Import Video Wizard that appears, type a name for the video, specify the location where you want to store the video file, and select the video format you want. Click Next.

2 Click Start Video Import to start recording the feed.

3 Click Stop Video Import to pause the recording.

4 Repeat steps 2 and 3 until you've completed the recording.

5 Click Finish, and view your video in the Photo Gallery window that appears.

Tip

If you choose the Windows Media Video (One File Per Scene) format, Windows creates a new file each time you click Start Video Import. If you use either of the other formats, all of your video will be contained in a single file.

Arranging Your Media with Playlists

When you've amassed a large number of media files, it can be difficult to keep track of them and even more difficult to figure out how to organize them. Media Player comes to your rescue with two tools that can relieve your frustration:

Playlists to help you go through your files and decide which items you want to group together; and Auto Playlists, with which Media Player assembles various playlists depending on the criteria you specify.

Create a Playlist

① With Media Player running, point to Library, click the down arrow, and choose Create Playlist from the drop-down menu.

② Type a descriptive name for the playlist, and press Enter.

③ Drag an item you want in the playlist from the Library to the playlist.

④ Continue adding files from the Library to your playlist.

⑤ Drag a file up or down in the list to change the order of play.

⑥ Click Save Playlist to create the playlist.

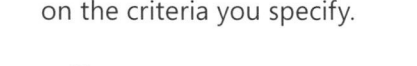

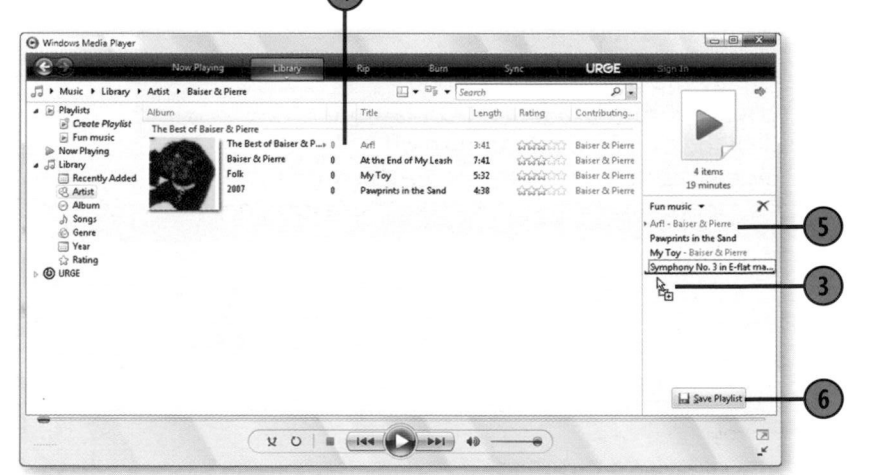

Tip

To add any media file in the Library to a playlist, right-click the file, and choose to add it to the playlist you want. If you don't see the playlist you want, point to Add To, choose Additional Playlists, and then select the playlist in the Add To Playlist dialog box.

Create an Auto Playlist

1 Point to Library, click the down arrow, and choose Create Auto Playlist from the drop-down menu to display the New Auto Playlist dialog box.

2 Type a name for the playlist.

3 Click to specify the criteria you want to use to assemble the playlist.

4 Click each underlined item to specify conditions for that criterion.

5 Click to add other criteria.

6 Click to add limitations to the criteria you've added to the list.

7 If you added an item that you've now decided you don't want to use, click the item, and then click Remove.

8 Click OK to create your list.

New Auto Playlist

Select the criteria that you want to change in the auto playlist. The auto playlist is updated automatically each time you open it.

Auto Playlist name: Driving home music

Create an auto playlist that includes the following:
♪ Music in my library
  ▼ Genre Is Jazz
  ✚ [Click here to add criteria]
And also include:
♪ Music in my library
  ▼ My rating Is At Least 4 Stars
  ✚ [Click here to add criteria]
And also include:
  ✚ [Click here to add criteria]
And apply the following restrictions to the auto playlist:
  ✚ [Click here to add criteria]

Remove   OK   Cancel   Help

Tip

If you no longer want a playlist, right-click it in the Navigation pane, and choose Delete from the shortcut menu.

Tip

After you've created an auto playlist, it's included in the list of all your playlists, so make sure that you use a descriptive name to remind yourself about the parameters you used to create the auto playlist.

Try This!

In the Navigation pane, right-click a playlist, and choose Edit In List Pane from the shortcut menu. Drag the music up or down to change the play order. Locate some music you want to listen to that isn't in your playlist, and drag the music onto the List pane. Right-click a piece of music in the playlist, and choose Remove From List from the shortcut menu. When you've finished modifying the playlist, click Save Playlist.

Copying CD Music

Instead of inserting a CD into your computer every time you want to hear a particular song or piece of music, you can *rip* (copy) individual tunes or entire CDs onto your computer's hard disk, after which you can play the saved music in any order you like. When you copy the music, you can set the file type for compatibility and the bit rate for balancing file size and quality, or you can just set the defaults and forget about the individual settings.

Rip from a CD

① Place the music CD in its drive. If the AutoPlay dialog box appears, choose to play the CD using Media Player.

② Click Rip to select the Rip tab if it isn't already selected.

③ Clear the check boxes for any tracks you don't want to copy.

④ Click Rip to display the Rip drop-down menu, and make any file-format or bit-rate settings you want.

⑤ Click Start Rip, and wait for the selected tracks to be copied.

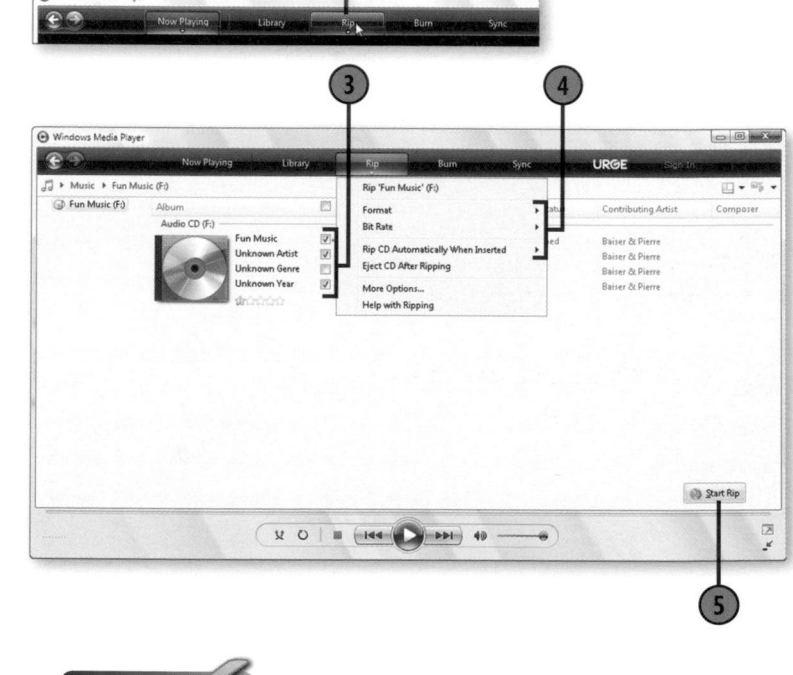

> **See Also**
>
> "Set the Autoplay" on page 271 for information about setting what action is automatically taken when you insert a music CD.

> **Tip**
>
> Before you rip any music, check the file-type requirements with any portable or external device you want to use so that you'll save the music in a compatible format.

> **Tip**
>
> To create your own default settings, such as the file location and file type, click Rip, choose More Options from the drop-down menu, and make your changes on the Rip tab of the Options dialog box.

Create a Music CD

① Make sure you have a blank CD in your CD drive. Click Burn.

② Use the Navigation pane to locate what you want to copy, and then select the music genre, album, playlist, or track that contains the music you want to copy.

③ Drag the tracks onto the Burn List.

④ Move through additional categories to locate the other tracks you want to copy, and drag them onto the Burn List.

⑤ Drag items up or down on the Burn List to specify the order in which you want the tracks to be placed on the CD.

⑥ Click Start Burn, and wait for the tracks to be copied onto your CD.

See Also

"Automatically Synchronizing Media with a Portable Device" on pages 148–149 and "Manually Synchronizing Media with a Portable Device" on page 150 for information about copying music to a portable device.

Tip

If you have any problems while you're recording, or if you want to reduce the bit rate for the files so that you can squeeze more tracks onto a CD, click Burn, and choose More Options from the drop-down menu. On the Burn tab of the Options dialog box, reduce the recording speed to try to fix any recording problems, or modify the bit rate to change the file size.

Controlling Video Playback

Watching video with Windows Media Player, whether it's streaming video from the Web or video files on your computer, is fairly straightforward. All you need to do is click the link on the Web page for the streaming video or choose the video from your Media Library, and then watch it on the Now Playing tab of Windows Media Player. However, you can also control the speed of the video playback and can even examine it frame by frame.

Adjust the Playback

1. With your video playing, click the Now Playing down arrow, point to Enhancements, and choose Video Settings from the drop-down menu.

2. Use the sliders to adjust the hue, brightness, saturation, and contrast of the video.

3. Click Select Video Zoom Settings to specify the size of the video image.

4. Keep clicking the Next Enhancement or the Previous Enhancement button until the Play Speed Settings controls are displayed.

5. Drag the slider to set the speed of the playback. The green area shows the range of available speeds.

6. Click the Next Frame button to pause the video. Then click the Previous Frame or the Next Frame button to move the image backward or forward by single frames.

7. Click the Next Enhancement or the Previous Enhancement button, and use the other enhancements to adjust the sound.

Playing a Music CD

Playing a CD is as simple as putting the CD into the drive and waiting for Windows Media Player—provided it's your default player—to start playing the music. Otherwise, you can start the CD manually.

Play a Music CD

① Insert the CD into your computer's drive, and wait for Windows Media Player to start. If it doesn't start, start it from the Start menu, and, on the Library tab, click the CD, and then double-click the album to start it.

② Click the Now Playing tab if it isn't already selected.

③ If the information, tools, and appearance you want aren't displayed, click Now Playing again to display the drop-down menu, and do any of the following:

- To see information about the album that isn't displayed, choose Show List Pane.

- To display tools for controlling the sound and the playback, point to Enhancements, and choose the type of enhancement you want to control the sound.

- To display the album art or to include geometric representations of the music, point to Visualizations, choose the type of visualization you want, and, if a sub-menu appears, choose the visualization you want.

④ Use the tools to adjust the playback. Click the Next Enhancement or the Previous Enhancement button to display other tools.

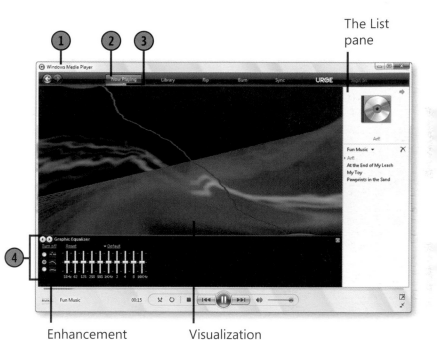

The List pane

Enhancement   Visualization

Tip

If you don't see the album art or the names of the music tracks, click Now Playing, and choose More Options from the drop-down menu. On the Security and the Privacy tabs of the Options dialog box, make changes so that you can receive information from the Internet. Click OK, and, if necessary, connect to the Internet to download the information.

Playing a DVD

When you play a DVD movie with Windows Media Player, whether it's a commercial video or one you created yourself, you can view it in full screen and still have access to the play controls, or you can show it in the Media Player window, with access to even more controls.

Play the DVD

① Insert the DVD into your computer's DVD drive. If the DVD doesn't start, start Media Player from the Start menu, and, on the Library tab, click the DVD, and then double-click the disc to start it. If you're not in Full Screen mode, press Alt+Enter.

② Move the mouse to display the controls.

③ Click DVD, and change any settings you want:

- Audio And Language Tracks
- Lyrics, Captions, And Subtitles
- Menus
- Camera Angles

④ Use the controls to stop, pause, go to the previous or the next scene, or adjust the volume.

⑤ Drag the slider if you want to jump forward or backward in the DVD.

⑥ If you want to use additional controls, click Exit Full Screen Mode, and use the enhancements available in the Full mode.

See Also

"Changing the Way a CD Starts" on page 271 for information about setting the default program when a CD or other type of disc is inserted.

"Restricting Access to Web Content" on pages 288–289 for information about enabling parental controls for specific users.

"Preventing Access While Using Media Player" on page 295 for information about locking your screen in Full Screen mode when a video is playing.

Changing Media Player's Shape

Windows Media Player can assume a variety of shapes, so you can use it however you like—in Full mode, for example, to let it take over your computer, or in Mini Player mode so that you can keep on working. Of course, some shapes aren't appropriate for all types of media, but you can play around with the shapes to see which is best for you.

Switch Modes

1 With Windows Media Player running, do any of the following:

- Press Alt+Enter to switch to Full Screen mode.

- In Full Screen mode, press Esc or click the Exit Full Screen Mode button to return to the previous mode.

- In Full mode, click the View Full Screen button to switch to Full Screen mode, or click the Switch To Compact Mode button to switch to Mini Player mode.

- In Mini Player mode, click the View Full Screen Mode button to switch to Full Screen mode, or click the Return To Full Mode button to switch to Full mode.

- Press Ctrl+2 to switch to Skins mode.

- In Skins mode, click the Switch To Full Mode button.

- In Mini Player or Skins mode, click the Minimize button to reduce the player to a Media Player toolbar on the taskbar. If the toolbar player isn't shown, right-click the taskbar, point to Toolbars, and click Windows Media Player.

See Also

"Playing a DVD" on the facing page for information about using Full Screen mode.

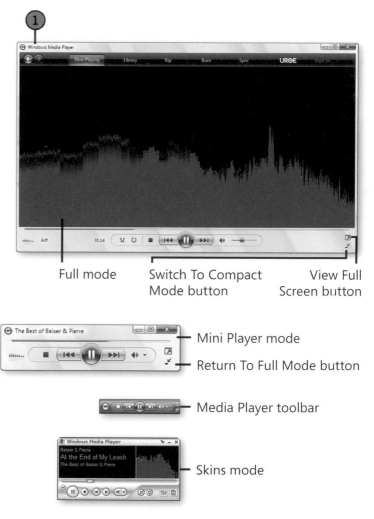

Full mode   Switch To Compact   View Full
            Mode button   Screen button

Mini Player mode

Return To Full Mode button

Media Player toolbar

Skins mode

Downloading Music

When you want to purchase and download music, you'll find that Windows Media Player has direct links to many online stores. Initially, the default provider is Urge, but you can choose from a variety of other providers.

Get Your Music

1. If you want to use Urge, click the Urge button, and, on the Web page that appears, follow the instructions for signing up, sampling music, and downloading the items you want.

2. If you want to use a service other than Urge, point to Urge (or to Online Stores if you didn't set up Urge as your default service when you set up Media Player), click the down arrow, and choose Browse All Online Stores.

3. Double-click the store you want to use as your default store, and follow the directions for signing up and downloading the music you want.

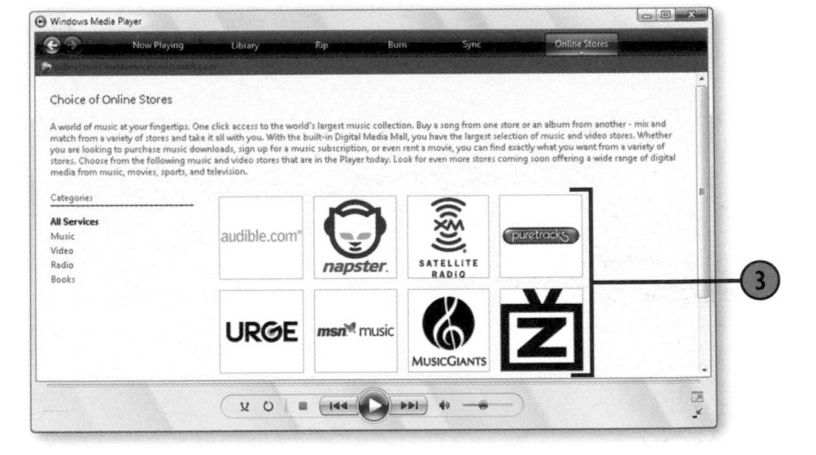

Tip

Because the Online Stores information is a live Web page, you might see different stores from the ones shown here.

Sharing Media on Your Network

With so many households having more than one computer or more than one user on a computer, media collections can become scattered and inaccessible. By sharing your media collections among users and across your network, you can play your music, your videos, or whatever other media you want on one computer, regardless of where the media are stored.

Set Up Sharing

1 With Windows Media Player running, click the Library down arrow, and choose Media Sharing from the drop-down menu to display the Media Sharing dialog box.

2 Select the items you want to share.

3 Click OK, and confirm that you want to share the media.

4 Specify with whom you want to share the media, and click Allow or Deny. Repeat for any other devices—another computer, an Xbox 360 console, or any other compatible extender on your network.

5 Click Settings to set the defaults for the names used to identify the shared media source and the types of media being shared.

6 If you want to make custom settings of types of shared media, select the device, and then click Customize.

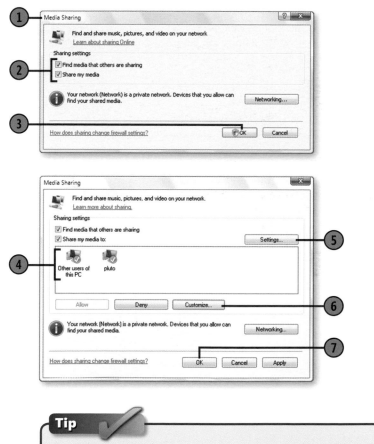

Tip

To share media, all the computers must be running Windows Vista and must have Media Player set up.

Automatically Synchronizing Media with a Portable Device

If you prefer to listen to your music or watch your videos while you're on the go instead of sitting at your computer, provided you have a compatible device, you can have Media Player automatically synchronize the content in your Media Library with the content on your portable device. When the files are transferred, they're automatically converted to the format required by the portable device.

Set Up the Synchronization

1. In Windows Media Player, with your portable device attached to the computer and properly set up, click the Sync tab if it isn't already selected. Click the Sync tab again, point to the name of the device on the drop-down menu, and choose Set Up Sync from the submenu to display the Device Setup dialog box.

2. Specify whether you want to automatically synchronize the device when it's connected to your computer.

3. If you chose automatic sync, you can now add, delete, or create new playlists to set the list of items you want to be included in the sync. Drag the playlists up or down to set the priority of synchronizing if all the items you want won't fit on your device.

4. Select this option if you want to automatically replace the existing files on the device with different files from your playlists.

5. Click Finish, and wait for the files to be synchronized.

6. After the files have been synchronized, click the device's name to expand the list, and then click Sync Results to verify that the files you want on the device have been synchronized.

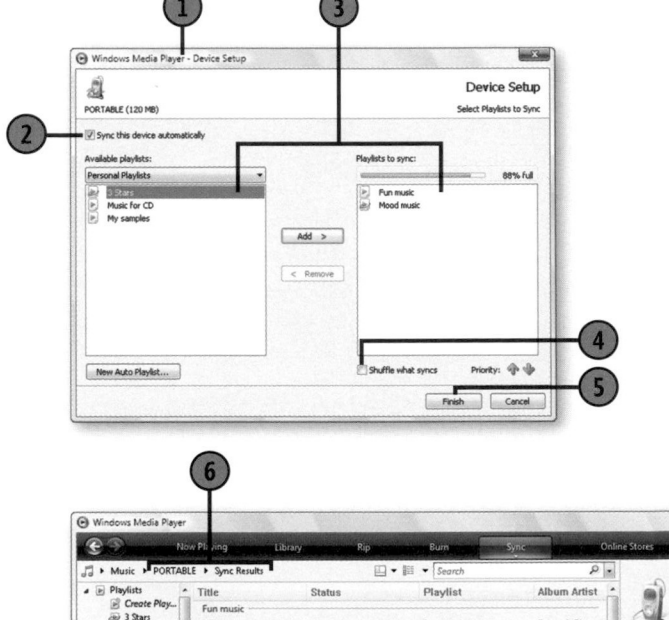

Control the Synchronization Settings

(1) Click the Sync tab down arrow, point to the device on the drop-down menu, and choose Advanced Options from the submenu to display the Properties dialog box for the device.

(2) Select this option if you want the synchronization to occur when the device is connected.

(3) Use the slider if you want to prevent the synchronization from filling up the entire device.

(4) Click the Quality tab, and specify whether you want the files to be converted automatically or by using your settings.

(5) Click OK.

Tip

To turn off automatic synchronization, click the down arrow below the Sync tab, point to the device, and choose Set Up Sync from the submenu. Clear the Sync This Device Automatically check box, and click OK.

Tip

Use Shuffle mode if the quantity of media in your library is too large to fit on your device and you want access to different materials each time you synchronize.

Try This!

Click the Start button, type **sync** in the Search box, and click Sync Center. In the Sync Center window that appears, click the tasks that are listed to see the status of your device and a history of its synchronizations. Note that the Sync Center shows all the devices that have been set up for synchronizing, including smart phones and other devices.

Tip

In addition to dedicated portable music or video players, you can synchronize with a removable memory device such as a USB flash memory device that you can then use with a different computer or device.

Manually Synchronizing Media with a Portable Device

You can take total control over which playlists or files are synchronized with your portable device by specifying them and manually synchronizing them with the device. If you have too many files in your library to fit on the device, you can easily replace the existing files on the device with different files from your library.

Add Items to the Device

1. On the Sync tab, locate the playlist or the file you want to add.

2. Drag it onto the Sync List pane. Repeat for other playlists or files.

3. When all the playlists and files have been added, click Start Sync.

See Also

"Automatically Synchronizing Media with a Portable Device" on pages 148–149 for information about stopping an automatic synchronization.

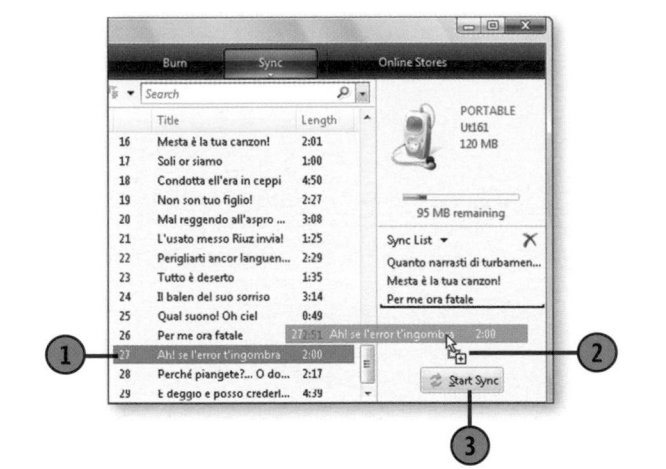

Add Random Items to the Device

1. If there are unwanted items in the Sync List, click Sync List, and choose Clear List from the drop-down menu.

2. Click Shuffle Music, and wait for the files on the device to be deleted and different files transferred.

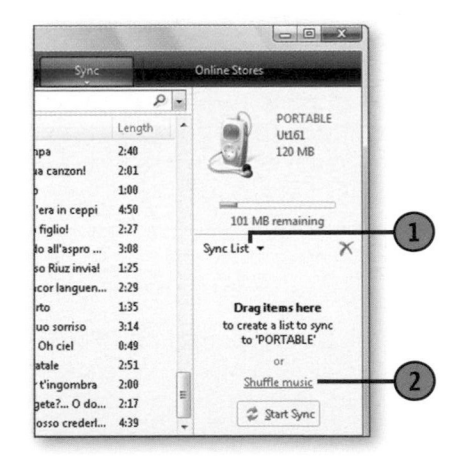

Watching Windows Media Center

Media Center is a specialized tool that's designed to run primarily on a computer that's customized with TV and radio cards or connectors, and that has a very large amount of disk storage space, a large high-resolution display, and a remote control. However, with some—or even none—of these features on your computer, you can still use parts of Media Center.

Control Media Center

1 If Media Center isn't running, start it from the Start menu. If a Setup Wizard starts, complete it to configure your system.

2 Scroll through the menus using either the mouse or the arrow keys on your keyboard or remote control. Click an item or press Enter when the item you want is selected.

3 Move the mouse to display the controls, and then use the controls with the mouse to change channels, fast-forward, and so on; or use the arrow keys and the numeric keypad on your keyboard or remote control to control the play.

4 To return to the previous page, click the Back button or press the Back key on your remote control or the Backspace key on your keyboard.

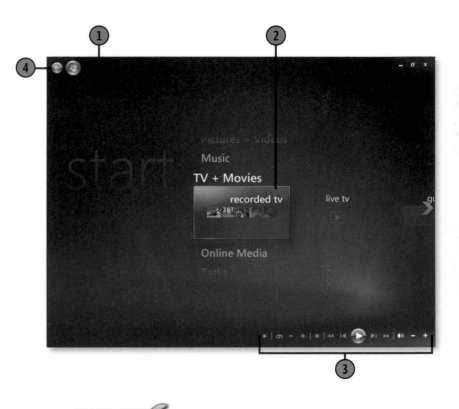

Tip ✔

If you're using a fully equipped Media Center computer, follow the directions for using the remote control and any specialized keyboard that came with the system.

Tip ✔

You can control all the functions of Media Player from the keyboard. To find the extensive list of keyboard shortcuts, search Windows Help for Media Center keys.

Creating an AutoMovie

If you have one or more video files that you want to turn into a movie, why not let Windows Movie Maker do the work so that you don't have to? With AutoMovie, the video file is split into clips and the transitions are automatically inserted between the clips. You can also add special video effects to the entire movie.

Create a Movie

① Start Windows Movie Maker from the Start menu.

② Click Collections, and select the collection containing the video file or files you want for your movie. If you want only certain video files to be used, select the files.

③ Click AutoMovie.

④ Select the movie style you want.

⑤ Click, and enter the title of your movie.

⑥ Click, and add audio or background music from a file.

⑦ Click, and wait for Movie Maker to create your movie.

⑧ Make any changes to the movie on the Storyboard and Timeline, save the project, and publish your movie.

See Also

"Preparing to Produce a Movie" on pages 156–157 for information about creating a collection, including files in the collection, and editing the files.

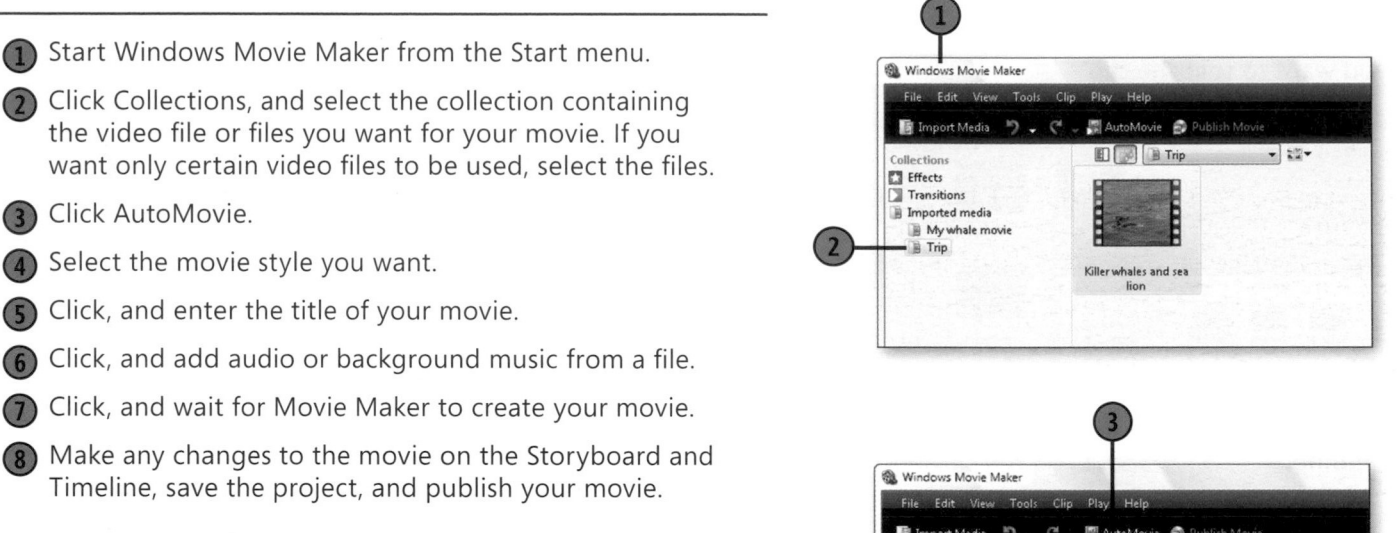

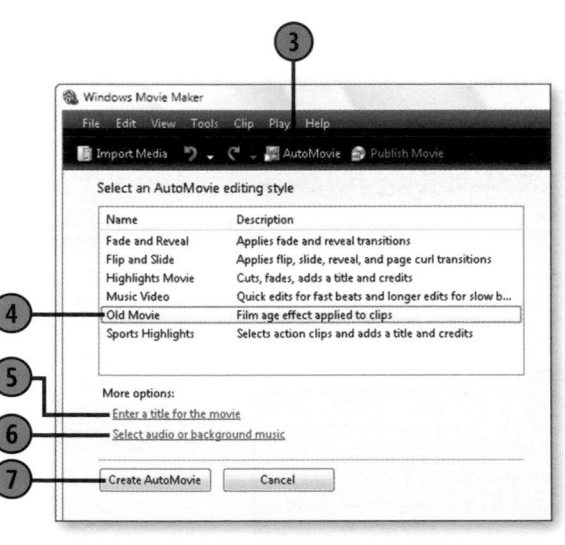

Creating a Custom Movie

When you create a movie with Movie Maker, you have full control of the production process. You decide which clips to use and the order you want them in; you choose the transition styles and the timing used between clips; and you add any other effects, soundtrack, or narration you want.

Set Up the Movie

1 Start Movie Maker from the Start menu. If the Collections pane isn't displayed, click the Show Or Hide Collections button.

2 Select the collection that contains the video clips you want to use.

3 Select the first video clip to be shown in the movie.

4 Drag the clip onto the first frame of the Storyboard. If the Storyboard isn't displayed, choose Storyboard from the View menu.

5 Select and drag additional video clips onto the Storyboard to design your movie. If you want to, you can use clips from different collections. If necessary, drag the clips around on the Storyboard to rearrange the order in which you want them to be played.

6 Add transitions, video effects, and a soundtrack or a narration to your movie. Save the project and the movie to the location you want.

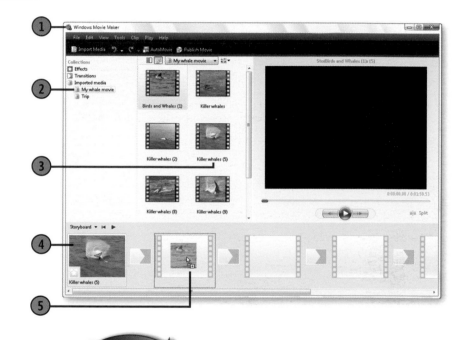

See Also

"Preparing to Produce a Movie" on pages 156–157 for information about creating collections and editing video clips.

"Adding Transitions to Your Movie" on page 160 for information about adding transitions.

"Using Video Effects" on page 161 for Information about adding video effects.

"Adding Audio to Your Movie" on pages 164–165 for information about adding narration or a soundtrack to your movie.

Adding Transitions to Your Movie

Most movies consist of multiple scenes. With each scene on a different video clip, you can add smooth transitions between scenes, just as the professionals do. For example, as you switch scenes, you can create the effect of turning a page, or you can have the current scene flip away and the next scene flip in. It's simple to do with Movie Maker's built-in transitions.

Add the Transitions

①With Movie Maker running and your current project open, make sure that all your video clips are arranged on the Storyboard exactly as you want them. If the Storyboard isn't displayed, choose Storyboard from the View menu.

②Choose Transitions from the Location drop-down list to display all the available video transitions.

③Select a transition you might want to use.

④Click the Play button to preview the transition.

⑤If the transition is what you want, drag it onto the Transition box between the clips.

⑥Repeat steps 3 through 5 to add more transitions.

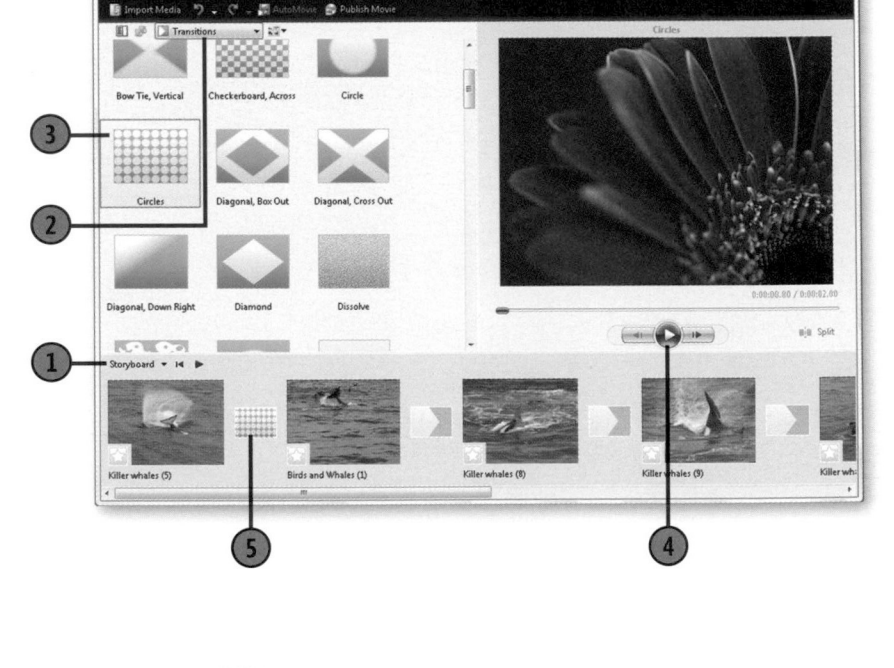

See Also

"Preparing to Produce a Movie" on pages 156–157 for information about separating your scenes into different clips.

Using Video Effects

If you want something more interesting than just a plain old movie, you can get really creative with some special video effects. You can make your movie look like an old film, or you can add color effects that make it look as though it was filmed on another planet or in an alternate universe. All you have to do is add the effects you want while you're composing your movie in Movie Maker.

Add the Effects

1. With Movie Maker running and your current project open, make sure that all your video clips are arranged on the Storyboard exactly as you want them. If the Storyboard isn't displayed, choose Storyboard from the View menu.

2. Choose Effects from the Location drop-down list to display all the available video effects.

3. Click the effect you want to use.

4. Click the Play button to preview the effect.

5. If you like the effect, drag it onto the Video Effects box of the video clip to which you want to apply it.

6. Repeat steps 3 through 5 to add more video effects to other clips.

Try This!

Right-click the Video Effects box on a clip on the Storyboard, and choose Effects from the shortcut menu. In the dialog box that appears, add two or more effects, and click OK. Play the clip to see how the effects work. If necessary, repeat the process and remove any effects you don't want.

Adding Titles and Credits

What's a movie without a title and credits? You might not need to acknowledge the gaffer, the best boy, the drivers and caterers, and so on, but you can easily add a title, along with such credits as directing, filming, and writing.

Add the Title

① With your movie fully assembled in Movie Maker, choose Titles And Credits from the Tools menu to display the Titles And Credits options.

② Choose where you want to add the title. If you want the title to precede a clip or to be on a clip, select the appropriate clip before you click the title option you want.

③ Type the first line of the title.

④ If you want a second line of text, click in this area, and type the text.

⑤ Click to change the title animation, and select the animation you want for a one- or a two-line title.

⑥ Click to change the title font, color, and alignment, and specify whether you want to use large or small text.

⑦ Click to add the title.

⑧ Repeat steps 1 through 7 to add any other titles to your movie.

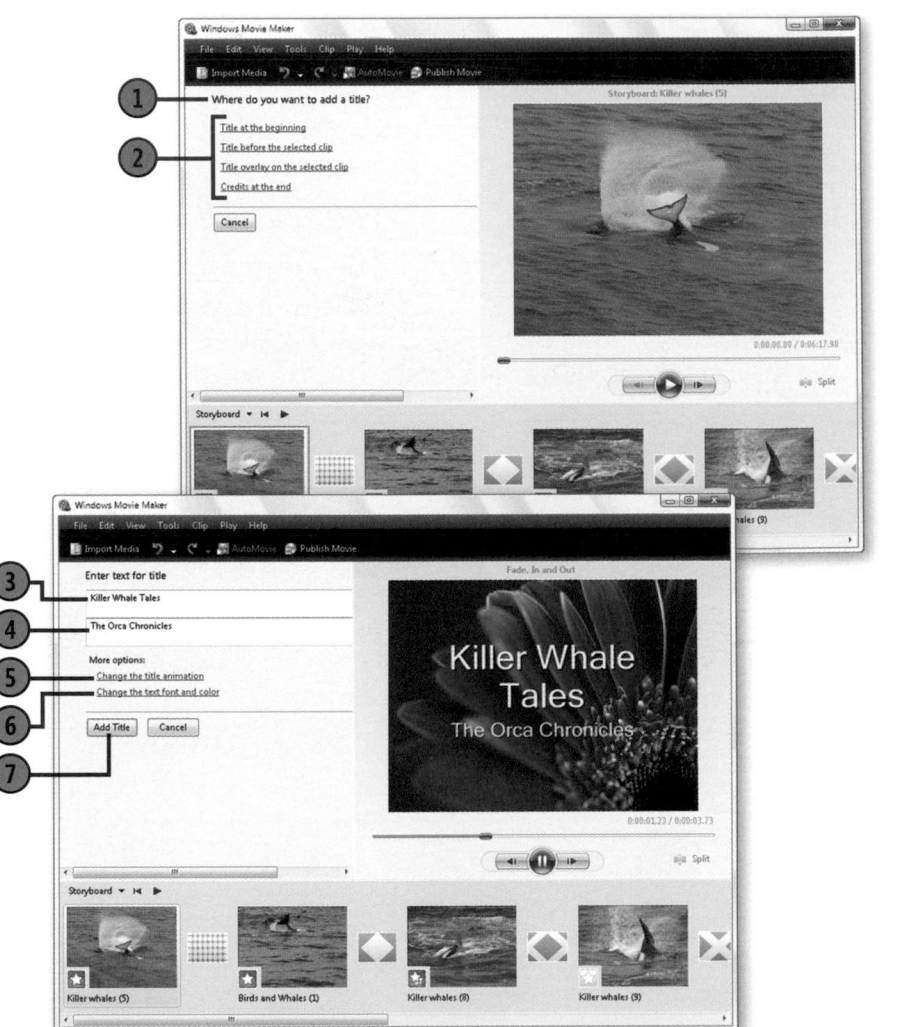

Add the Credits

1. Choose Titles And Credits from the Tools menu if the Titles And Credits options aren't displayed.

2. Click Credits At The End.

3. Type **Credits** or any other title you want at the beginning of the credits. Press Tab to move to the next line.

4. Type the title of the specific credit, and press Tab to move to the next box.

5. Type the name of the person, company, or organization that receives the credit, and press Tab to move to the next line.

6. Repeat steps 4 and 5 until all the credits are complete.

7. Click to change the animation or the font and color for the credits.

8. Click to add the credits to the movie.

Tip

If you want to include extra information (metadata) about the movie, including the title, author, copyright, or comments, choose Project Properties from the File menu, and complete the information in the Project Properties dialog box.

Tip

To edit an existing title or credit, double-click the clip containing the title or credit on the Storyboard or on the Timeline. If the title is on an existing video clip, double-click the title in the Title Overlay section of the Timeline. Make your changes, and then click Done.

Adding Audio to Your Movie

When you record a movie with Movie Maker, any existing audio from your video clips will be included. You can also add a narration or a music soundtrack that will be integrated with the audio. If you didn't record an audio track when you originally recorded the video, however, and you want to add one now, or if you want to add a narration or a musical soundtrack to an existing movie, it's a simple process. A narration can either merge with the existing audio for the movie or completely replace it, whereas a soundtrack is always merged with any existing audio for the movie.

Create a Narration

1. Start Movie Maker, open your project (or save the project you're currently working on), and make sure that the video clips and transitions are ordered correctly.

2. Choose Timeline from the View menu if the Timeline isn't already displayed.

3. Click in the Timeline at the point where you want the narration to start. You can narrate only in locations where you haven't already inserted a narration or a soundtrack.

4. Choose Narrate Timeline from the Tools menu.

5. Check the options for your recording. If the options aren't visible, click Show Options in the Narrate Timeline area to display the options. Make whatever changes you want.

6. Set the microphone Input level. Speak into your microphone, and use the slider to determine the proper sound level.

7. Click Start Narration. Watch your movie in the preview and on the Timeline as you record your narration. When you've finished, click Stop Narration, and save the file when prompted to do so. The narration will automatically be placed on the Audio/Music portion of the Timeline. Click Close.

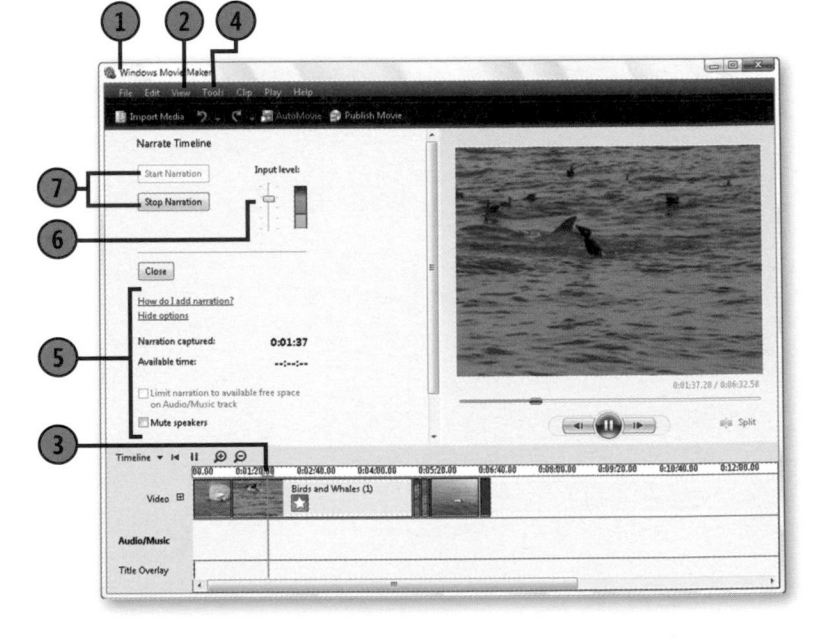

Tip

The Audio line on the Timeline shows the audio that's incorporated into your video clip. The Audio/Music line shows the narration or the soundtrack. Items on the Audio/Music line can be cropped, moved, or deleted to customize your movie.

Add a Soundtrack

 Create or import the audio files that you want to use for your soundtrack.

② If the Audio line for the Video section isn't shown, click the plus sign in the Video section to display the line so that you can see the existing audio.

③ Drag a sound clip onto the Audio/Music line at the location (that is, the time) where you want the clip to be played during the movie. Add and position any other sound clips.

④ Click the Rewind Timeline button.

⑤ Click the Play Timeline button to preview your entire movie with the narration or soundtrack in place.

⑥ Click an audio clip, and press Ctrl+U (or choose Audio Levels from the Tools menu), choose Volume from the menu, and then use the Audio Clip Volume dialog box to adjust the volume of that clip. Repeat for audio clips in both the Audio and the Audio/Music lines to get the correct sound levels.

⑦ Save your project.

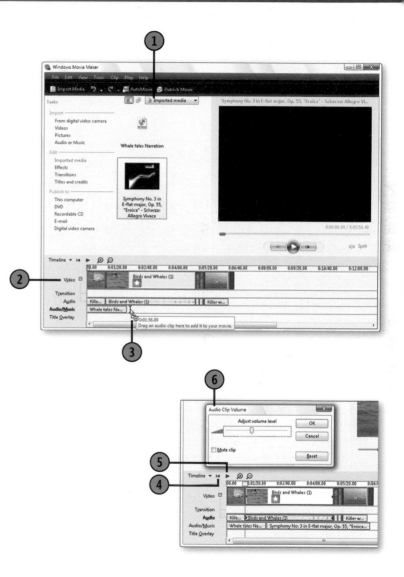

Adding Slides to Your Movie

Your movie doesn't have to be all action. You can add digital pictures—photographs from a digital camera, for example—to your video clips to create title slides, or add still photographs to supplement the video clips. Or you can create a movie file using your still pictures and some music to produce a slide show with an accompanying soundtrack as part of the movie. You can also edit pictures or create them from scratch to add title slides for your movie.

Add Slides

1. Start Movie Maker from the Start menu.

2. Click the Show Or Hide Collections button if the Collections pane isn't displayed. Import the photos or other pictures for the slide show into the Collections folder you want to use.

3. Choose Options from the Tools menu to display the Options dialog box, and, on the Advanced tab, specify the length of time you want each picture to be displayed. Click OK.

4. Drag the pictures onto the Storyboard in the sequence in which you want them displayed. Add any transitions and/or video effects. Use the Timeline view to add any audio or to modify the length of time an individual picture is displayed.

5. Save the project, and, after reviewing and editing the slide show, publish your movie.

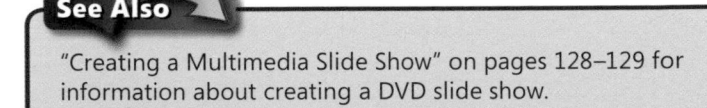

See Also

"Creating a Multimedia Slide Show" on pages 128–129 for information about creating a DVD slide show.

Editing Your Movie Layout

When you've assembled all the components of your movie, you'll probably want to tweak it by changing the order of the clips, perhaps trimming off part of a clip at the beginning or end of the movie, or even overlapping clips for special effects.

Tweak Your Clips

1 With Movie Maker running and all your clips placed on the Storyboard, choose Timeline from the View menu to show the clips by time.

2 Click Zoom Timeline In until you can easily see the clips and their beginnings or endings.

3 To move a clip, click it and drag it to a new location.

4 To trim a clip, play the movie until you locate the point at which you want to trim the clip, click the clip you want to trim, and drag either the beginning border to the right or the ending border to the left.

5 To overlay portions of two clips, select a clip, and then drag a portion of it to the left over the ending of the previous clip.

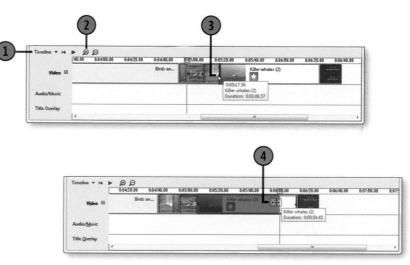

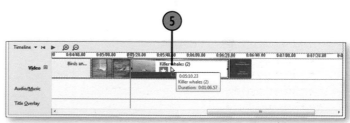

See Also

"Preparing to Produce a Movie" on pages 156–157 for information about importing media into a Collections folder.

Try This!

Instead of trimming a clip, drag a border to extend the clip over another clip. Right-click another clip, and choose Fade In from the shortcut menu. Right-click another clip, and choose Fade Out from the shortcut menu. Play the movie to see how these changes affect the transitions between the clips.

Publishing Your Movie

Now that you've created your movie, the next step is, of course, to show it! The Publish Movie Wizard helps you figure out how to distribute your movie and what settings you should use.

Publish It

(1) With Windows Movie Maker running, the project open, and your movie completed, click the Publish Movie button to start the Publish Movie Wizard.

(2) To specify the way you want to publish the movie, choose one of the following:

- This Computer to specify the file name, location, video compression, and type of video format, and to publish the video file to your computer

- DVD to start Windows DVD Maker and create a DVD

- Recordable CD to name the file and the CD, and to record the movie in DV-AVI or Windows Media format to a CD

- E-Mail to create a file in Windows Media format small enough to fit into an e-mail, and to attach the file to an e-mail message

- Digital Video Camera to upload the movie in the DV-AVI format to your digital video camera

(3) Click Next, and step through the wizard to publish your movie.

Publish Movie

Where do you want to publish your movie?

This computer
Publish for playback on your computer

DVD
Publish for playback on your DVD player or computer

Recordable CD
Publish for playback on your computer or device that supports WMV files

E-mail
Send as an e-mail attachment using your default e-mail program

Digital video camera
Record to a tape in your DV camera

How do I publish a movie?

[Next] [Cancel]

Tip

To change the video format (NTSC or PAL), the aspect ratio for screen dimensions, and the maximum size of an e-mailed video, choose Options from the Tools menu, and make your changes on the Advanced tab of the Options dialog box.

9

Using Voice and Sounds

If the sound your computer emits to signal an event—the logon or logoff sound, for example—is an earsplitting assault, relief in the form of adjusting the volume is just a click or two away with Windows Vista's volume control. And, if you can't stand the startup sound, you can simply turn it *off!* You can also use the Volume control to keep your music and other sounds muted so that you don't disturb other people.

If you'd like to verbally command your computer instead of typing and using the mouse, try Windows Vista's powerful speech-recognition program. It's important to go through the tutorial so that the program can recognize your voice and the way you pronounce words, and so that you learn the correct commands. Be patient! It might take a bit of trial and error, but you'll know it was time well spent when you can dictate letters or long documents without touching the keyboard! Instead of saving your fingers, perhaps you want to save your eyes by using the Narrator program, which actually reads aloud to you. Using your sound system, Narrator can describe items on your screen and can read blocks of text to you. But what if you can't—or don't want to—hear any sounds from your computer? You can set it to give you visual clues, including flashes and captions, instead.

Controlling the Volume

Although a computer blaring loud music can be fun when you're relaxing or having a party, it's *not* a good idea when you're working on a notebook computer around other people in a crowded room or office. Fortunately, you can adjust the sound levels for your system and for each of your applications.

You can also turn off the Windows startup sound if you don't want to announce to everyone in the room that you just turned on your computer. If your computer has more than one output device, you can specify which one is the default device while you're setting the volume levels for each device.

Set the Defaults

1 Click the Start button, type **sound** in the Search box of the Start menu, and click Sound to display the Sound dialog box.

2 On the Playback tab, double-click a device to display its Properties dialog box. Make any device-specific settings that you want to be the default settings for that device, including volume levels and enhancements, and click OK. Repeat for each device. (The settings that you can make in the Properties dialog box vary for different devices because of the different features of individual devices.)

3 Click the device that you want to set as the default device, and click Set Default.

4 On the Sounds tab of the Sound dialog box, clear this check box if you never want to hear the Windows startup sound when you turn on your computer, or select the check box if you do want to hear the sound.

5 Click OK.

Set the Master Volume Level

1 Click the Volume icon in the notification area of the taskbar.

2 Do either of the following:

- Drag the slider to adjust the volume.
- Click the Mute button to mute the sound or to turn off muting.

3 Click outside the Volume Control to close it.

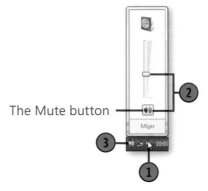

The Mute button

See Also

"Associating a Sound with an Event" on pages 180–181 for information about modifying which Windows sounds are used for specific events.

"Customizing the Taskbar" on pages 262–263 for information about displaying the Volume icon if it isn't already displayed on the taskbar.

Set the Volume for Events and Programs

1 Click the Volume icon on the taskbar, and click Mixer to display the Volume Mixer dialog box.

2 Click Device, and specify which device you want to set the sound levels for if you have more than one device.

3 Adjust the volume for the device.

4 Adjust the volume for the event sounds used with Windows.

5 Adjust the sound level for each running program.

6 Close the Volume Mixer dialog box when you've finished.

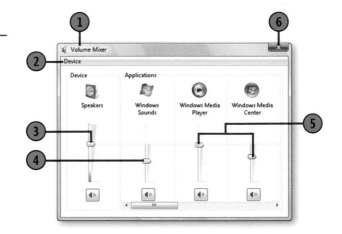

Directing Your Computer with Voice Commands

Windows Vista includes a powerful speech-recognition program that makes it possible for you to use your voice to command the computer. Although speech recognition is designed primarily for people who have difficulty using the keyboard and/or the mouse, the ability to direct Windows and your other programs with your voice has a certain authoritative appeal. And, as with the mouse or the keyboard, there are numerous ways to accomplish any specific task.

Start Speech Recognition

①　Start Windows Speech Recognition from the Start menu if it isn't already running. If it's running but sleeping, say "Start listening."

②　Use the commands that you learned in the tutorial or from Help. If you can't remember a command, say "What can I say?" to display Windows Help And Support, which lists all the commands you can use.

③　If you want to access something in a window but can't figure out how, say "Show numbers." Say the number for the item, and then say "OK."

Visual feedback for the spoken command

See Also

"Dictating Text" on pages 174–175 for information about using the Alternates Panel if a command isn't clearly understood.

Use the Commands

To do this	Say this
Start a program	"Start," and then the name of the program.
Open the Start menu	"Start."
Open a menu in a program or window	The name of the menu.
Activate a toolbar button	The name of the button.
Activate a link	The name of the link.
Click an item	"Click," and then the name of the item.
Use the equivalent of keystrokes	"Press," and then the name of the key or the name of the keyboard shortcut.
Switch to a program	"Switch to," and then the name of the program.
Scroll in a window	"Scroll down" or "Scroll up."
Scroll a specific number of lines	"Scroll," and then the number of lines.
Move the speech-recognition program out of the way	"Move speech recognition."
Work without using speech recognition	"Stop listening."

Tip

You must go through a full setup process prior to using the speech-recognition program for the first time, including setting up your microphone and stepping through a tutorial that teaches you the basics of using speech recognition.

Caution

Don't skip the tutorial! As you work your way through it, the speech-recognition program is learning to understand your voice and the way you pronounce words. If you skip the tutorial, the speech-recognition program won't be very effective.

Dictating Text

The speech-recognition program lets you issue commands to your computer and dictate text in a document. Of course, while you're dictating, you'll also be issuing some commands—for example, telling the computer to correct or change some words, to start paragraphs, and to scroll through the document. Fortunately, the speech-recognition program is usually smart enough to know when you're dictating text and when you're issuing commands. Even if the speech-recognition program gets something wrong, however, you can easily correct it.

Dictate Your Text

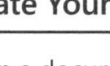 In a document that accepts text, start dictating your text. If the speech-recognition program is sleeping, say "Start listening" before you start dictating.

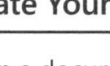 Speak as you did in the tutorial, pausing only after completing a phrase or sentence. The text will be inserted after a brief pause. Do any of the following in the table at the right:

Use the Commands

To do this	Say this
Insert a punctuation mark	The name of the mark—"Period, comma, question mark," and so on.
Insert a number	The name of the number.
Insert special characters	The name of the character—"Double quote, open parenthesis, close parenthesis, hyphen, ampersand," and so on.
Insert an unusual name or word	Spell the word one letter at a time.
Start a new paragraph	"Enter."
Undo your last entry	"Undo."
Move the insertion point around in a document	The type of move—"End, backspace, move down two lines," and so on.
Select text	"Select," and then the word or range—"Sentence" or "paragraph."
Apply formatting or other items on a toolbar	The name of the item—"Bold, italic," and so on. If you don't know the name of the item, say "Show numbers," say the number of the item, and then "OK."
Figure out how to enter or edit something if you can't remember the command	"What can I say?" and then review the Help file.

See Also

"Directing Your Computer with Voice Commands" on pages 172–173 for information about moving around windows, choosing menu commands, and improving the program's recognition of your voice.

Correct Errors

① Say "Correct" and then the word or phrase that needs to be corrected to display the Alternates Panel.

② Say the number of the correct item, and then say "OK." If the correct word or phrase doesn't appear in the Alternates Panel, say the word or phrase again, say the number of the correct item, and then say "OK."

③ If you're trying to correct a word that the program never recognizes, say "Spell it."

④ In the Spelling Panel that appears, spell the word slowly, one letter at a time. If you make a mistake, say the number of the wrong letter, and then say the correct letter. If a letter is routinely misunderstood, say it with an example, such as "H as in hotel." When the spelling is correct, say "OK."

⑤ If the Add Word To Dictionary dialog box appears, specify whether you want to add the word to the dictionary used to identify spoken words, or whether you want to insert the word just this time.

Tip ✓

Dictating text can be quite frustrating when you first start, but, as you use the program, both you and the program get better. Also, for better recognition, you can do some additional speech training.

Tip ✓

To directly add, delete, or correct words in the dictionary, say "Show speech options," and, when the shortcut menu appears, say "Open the speech dictionary."

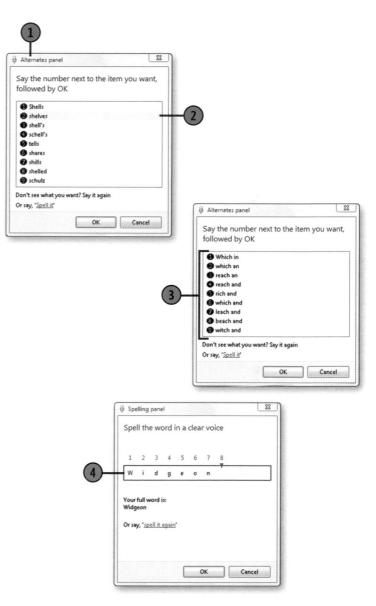

Customizing Speech Recognition

You can customize the way the speech-recognition program works so that it adjusts to your preferences, including the language you want to use, the way it spaces sentences, and its ability to recognize someone else's voice or different background sounds.

Customize Speech Recognition

1. If you want to change the way the speech-recognition program works, say "Show speech options." On the shortcut menu that appears, say "Configuration" to open the submenu, and then say "Open speech-recognition control panel."

2. In the Speech Recognition Options Control Panel, say "Advanced speech options."

3. On the Speech Recognition tab of the Speech Properties dialog box, make the modifications you want:

   - Select the language for the speech recognition.

   - Create a new profile or select a different profile.

   - Do additional training to improve speech recognition.

   - Specify the way you want speech recognition to start, learn, and space sentences.

   - Adjust the microphone.

4. Say "OK" to close the dialog box.

5. Make any other changes using the Control Panel, and then say "Close."

Talking to the Mouse

If you want to work with the mouse when you're using voice commands, you use a large grid that encompasses the entire screen to specify where you want the mouse to go. Using the grid is especially useful if you have any problems with navigating around the screen and making windows or other areas active.

Use the Grid

1 With speech recognition running and listening, say "Mouse grid" to display the large grid.

2 Say the number that identifies the region you want to work in to display a small grid for that region.

3 In the smaller grid, do any of the following:

• Say "Click" to click in the middle of the grid.

• Say a number on the grid to show a detailed grid of that region.

• Say a number and then say "Click" to click in the center of that region.

• Say "Back" to move back to the larger grid.

• Say "Cancel" to remove the mouse grid.

• Say a number and then say "Right-click" to right-click in that region.

Tip

Most voice commands, except those used with the mouse grid, aren't recognized while the mouse grid is displayed. The mouse grid will remain on the screen if you type any information, but it will go away if you click the mouse, press the Windows key, or say an appropriate voice command.

Letting Your Computer Do the Talking

Windows Vista provides a program called Narrator that actually speaks to you! Narrator can describe aloud the items that are currently displayed on your screen, and it can even read long blocks of text. Narrator has some limitations, but it can be very useful in the right circumstances. Of course, for Narrator to work, your computer must have a sound system.

Listen to Narrator

1. Start Narrator from the Start menu to display the Narrator dialog box.

2. Select this check box if you want Narrator to speak aloud each keystroke you make so that you can verify that you're pressing the keys you want.

3. Select or clear any of the check boxes to make Narrator work the way you want.

4. Choose Voice Settings to open the Voice Settings dialog box.

5. Adjust the reading speed, volume, and pitch of Narrator's voice. Click OK when you've finished.

6. Press Alt+Spacebar, and choose Minimize from the Control menu to minimize Narrator when you've adjusted all the settings to your satisfaction.

7. To close Narrator, keep pressing Alt+Tab until Narrator becomes selected, and then click the Exit button in the Narrator dialog box.

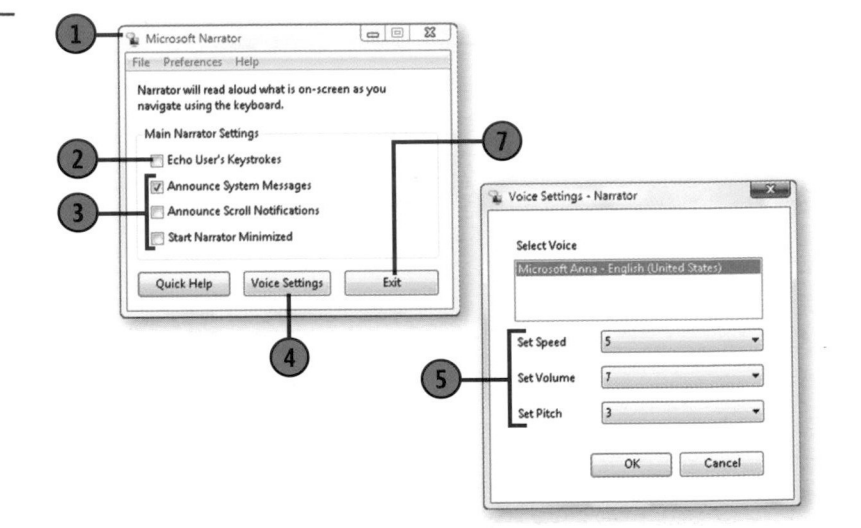

See Also

"Directing Your Computer with Voice Commands" on pages 172–173 and "Dictating Text" on pages 174–175 for information about talking to your computer.

Tip

Narrator works very well with the speech-recognition program, but it's designed primarily to work with the keyboard, so use the Tab key to move around in a dialog box, or use keyboard shortcuts to activate commands. To temporarily stop Narrator while it's reading or describing something, press the Ctrl key. To have Narrator describe the contents of a window at any time, press Ctrl+Shift+Spacebar. To hear a description of the layout, press Ctrl+Alt+Spacebar.

Creating a Sound File

You can record your own Windows Media Audio (.wma) file from a variety of sources, depending on the equipment you have on your computer. These sources can include live or recorded music, narrations, or notes. Once you've recorded it, a .wma file can be played back using Windows Media Player or Windows Media Center.

Record Sounds

① Start Sound Recorder from the Start menu.

② Click the Start Recording button, and record the sounds you want.

③ Click Stop Recording when you've finished. If you've completed the recording, use the Save As dialog box to save the sound file with the name you want in the location you want.

④ If you want to continue recording to the same sound file, click Cancel in the Save As dialog box.

⑤ Click Resume Recording, record what you want, and then click Stop Recording when you've finished. Use the Save As dialog box to save the file with the name and in the location you want.

⑥ Close Sound Recorder when you've finished.

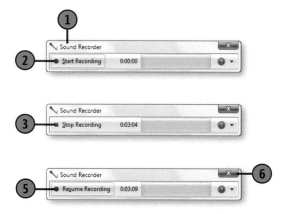

 Tip

To adjust the recording volume of your microphone, click the Start button, type **sound** in the Search box, and click Sound to display the Sound dialog box. On the Recording tab, double-click your microphone, and adjust the settings on the Levels tab.

 See Also

"Writing Quick Notes" on page 39 for information about creating voice Sticky Notes.

Associating a Sound with an Event

If you want to hear audio cues for events in Windows—the closing of a program or the arrival of new e-mail, for example—you can assign sounds to those events.

Windows Vista comes with a predesigned sound scheme that you can use, or you can create your own customized audio cues.

Use an Existing Sound Scheme

① Click the Start button, type **sound** in the Search box, and click Sound to display the Sound dialog box.

② On the Sounds tab, click the Sound Scheme list, and select a scheme. If only the Windows Default and the No Sounds schemes are shown, select the Windows Default scheme.

③ Click any event that's marked with a sound icon.

④ Click the Test button to preview the sound scheme.

⑤ If you like the sound scheme, click OK.

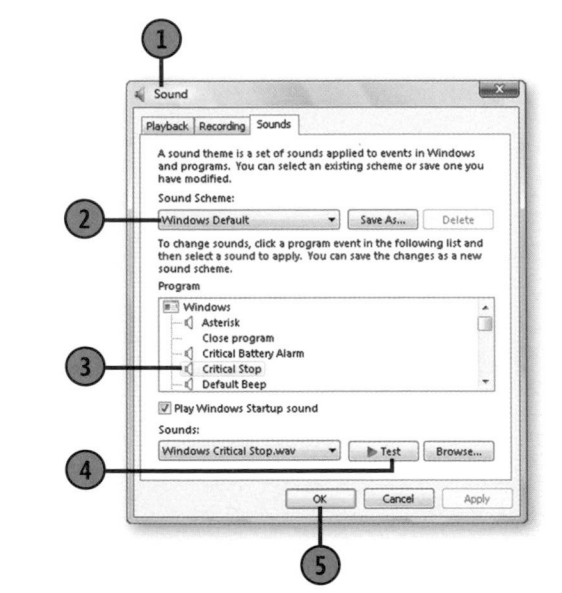

 Tip

You can also open the Sound dialog box by right-clicking the Volume icon on the taskbar and choosing Sounds from the shortcut menu that appears.

 Tip

You might or might not have numerous sound schemes available, depending on what other software you've installed, on whether the computer was upgraded from a previous version of Windows, or on whether someone else has created sound schemes on your computer. If you have only the one default Windows scheme, why not create a sound scheme of your own?

Create a Sound Scheme

1. Click the Start button, type **sound** in the Search box, and click Sound to display the Sound dialog box.

2. On the Sounds tab, click an event to which you want to assign a sound.

3. Click a sound in the Sounds list, or use the Browse button to find a sound in another folder. Click None in the Sounds list to remove a sound from an event.

4. Use the Test button to preview the sound. Continue to select events and assign the sounds you want.

5. If you want to assign a unique name to the sound scheme, click Save As, enter a name for the sound scheme you've created, and click OK.

6. Click OK.

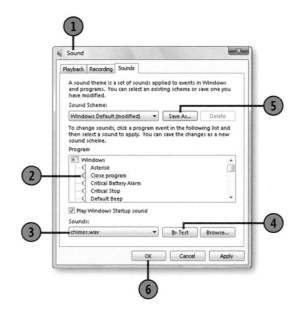

"Set the Defaults" on page 170 for information about turning the Windows startup sound on or off.

Tip

Several programs can control whether a sound is played when an event occurs. For example, if you're using Windows Mail, choose Options from the Tools menu, and, on the General tab, select or clear the check box for playing a sound. If you're using the On-Screen Keyboard, choose Settings, and specify whether you want to hear a clicking sound whenever you click a key.

Using Alternatives to Sound

If you're unable to hear the sounds from your computer—or if you simply don't want to—you can set up a visual cue such as a flash where a sound would normally be played. You can also set captions to be displayed by programs that normally signal an event with a sound. However, not all programs support the caption alternatives, so you won't always see the captions displayed.

Turn on Visual Cues

 Open the Control Panel from the Start menu, choose Ease Of Access, and choose Replace Sounds With Visual Cues.

 Select this check box to see visual cues for sounds.

3 Specify the cue you want.

4 Select this check box if you want programs to display captions for sound events.

5 Click Save.

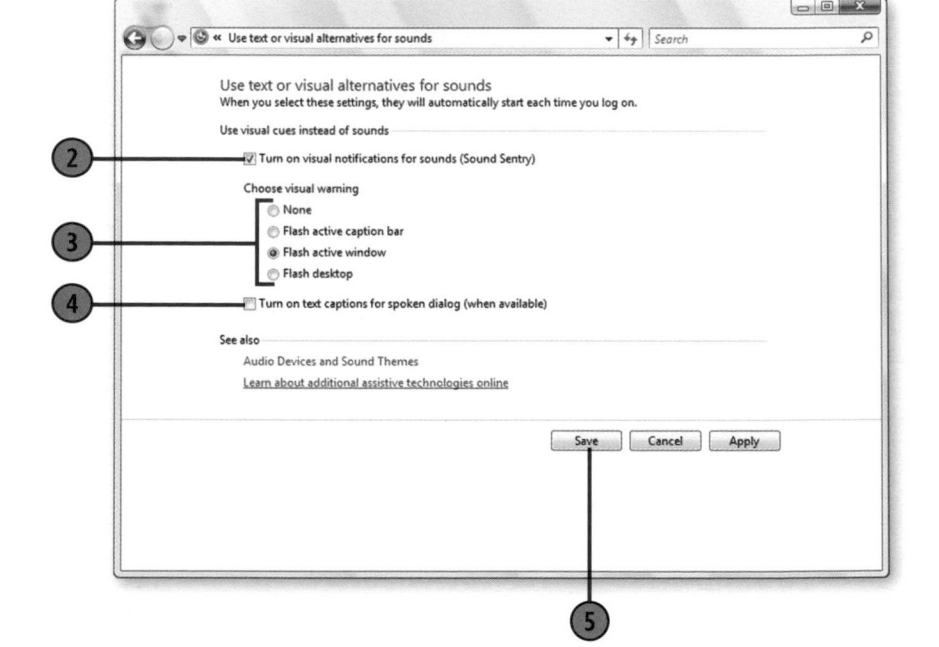

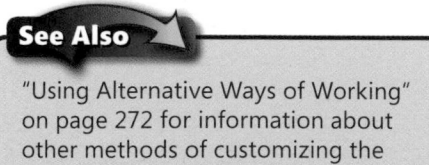
See Also

"Using Alternative Ways of Working" on page 272 for information about other methods of customizing the way Windows works.

10

Printing and Scanning

Had a frustrating experience with a surly printer? This section of the book will guide you painlessly through the printing process. If you have multiple printers installed on your computer, we'll show you how to designate one as your default printer—that is, the one you set up to automatically print all your documents—and how to target another printer when you can't or don't want to use the default printer.

We know you'll welcome a great feature in Windows Vista—a wizard that makes it really easy to print your photographs. With just a few clicks, you can choose the sizes and orientation, the number of copies you want, and the way the pictures will be laid out on the page. If you've ever printed a Web page and been unhappily surprised by the chaotic result, you'll appreciate the ability Internet Explorer gives you to print readable Web pages. We'll also discuss creating and printing a document in the new universal XPS format, which makes it possible for your document to look exactly the same as it did originally even if you open or print it on a different computer. If you have a scanner, you can access it from the Windows Photo Gallery and directly scan and digitize just about anything. It's easy and fun to do, and it gives you a great variety of images to add color and interest to your documents.

Printing from a Program

In most programs, you can print a document on any printer that's installed on your computer or shared over a network.

By using the Print dialog box, you can specify which printer to use and can customize the way your document is printed.

Print a Document

(1) With the document open in its program, choose Print from the File menu to display the Print dialog box.

(2) Specify the printer you want to use.

(3) Click Preferences if you need to change the printer settings—for example, the size of the paper being used, whether the document is to be printed in color or in black and white, and so on. (Note, however, that sometimes the program's settings will override your own settings.)

(4) Click Find Printer to find and use a printer on a network that isn't listed in the Select Printer section.

(5) Specify the pages you want to print.

(6) Specify how many copies of each page you want.

(7) Specify whether you want multiple copies to be printed with the pages in order (collated) or whether you want each page to be printed multiple times before the next page is printed. (Collated printing is usually slower than uncollated printing.)

(8) Click Print.

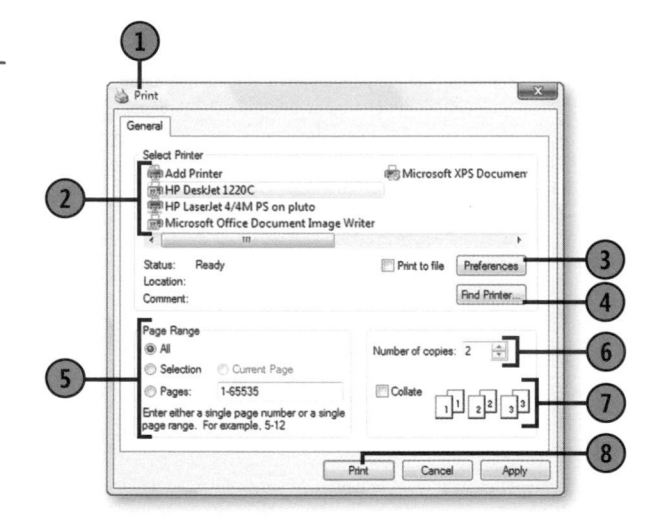

See Also

"Specifying a Default Printer" on page 186 for information about setting a printer as the default printer.

Tip ✓

The Selection option in the Page Range section of the Print dialog box tells the printer to print the text or the item that's currently selected in the document. The Current Page option tells the printer to print either the page that contains the insertion point or the page that's displayed.

Tip ✓

If the Print command on the File menu isn't followed by an ellipsis (...), the Print dialog box probably won't be displayed, and the document will be printed on the default printer using the default settings.

Printing a Document

When you want to print a document or a group of documents, you can print directly from Windows Vista without having to start the program in which the documents were created. That program, however, must be installed on your computer and will usually be started by Windows. It's a great convenience to be able to quickly send several documents to your printer and then walk away while Windows Vista does all the work.

Print a Document Using the Default Printer

(1) Open the folder that contains the items you want to print, and select the document or documents to be printed. Multiple documents must be of the same type (all Word documents or all Notepad documents, for example).

(2) Right-click a selected document, and choose Print from the shortcut menu.

> **Tip** ✓
>
> Some programs require the use of the system default printer. To print documents that were created in those programs, you have to either use the default printer or tell Windows to switch the default-printer designation to the printer you want to use.

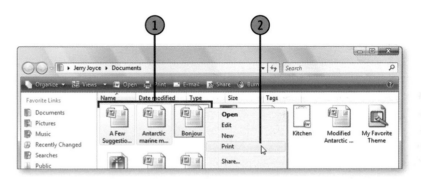

Print a Document Using a Specific Printer

(1) Click the Start button, type **printer** in the Search box, and choose the Printers folder.

(2) Locate and select the document or documents you want to print.

(3) Drag the selected document or documents onto the Printers folder and onto the printer you want to use.

(4) If a Printers dialog box appears, click Yes to confirm that you want to print multiple files.

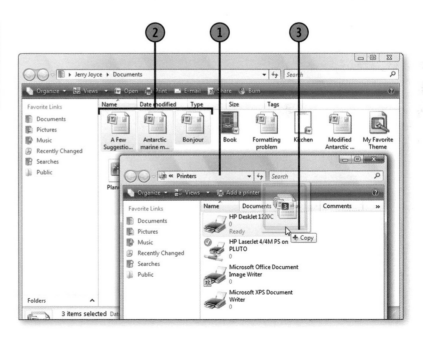

Specifying a Default Printer

Some programs are set up to print only on the system's default printer. Other programs are set up to print on the system default printer but allow you to *target*, or change to, a different printer. If several printers are available, you can designate any one of them as your default printer.

Change the Default Printer

1. Click the Start button, type **printer** in the Search box, and choose the Printers folder.

2. Click the printer you want to use as the default printer to select it.

3. Click Set As Default.

4. Close the Printers folder when you've finished.

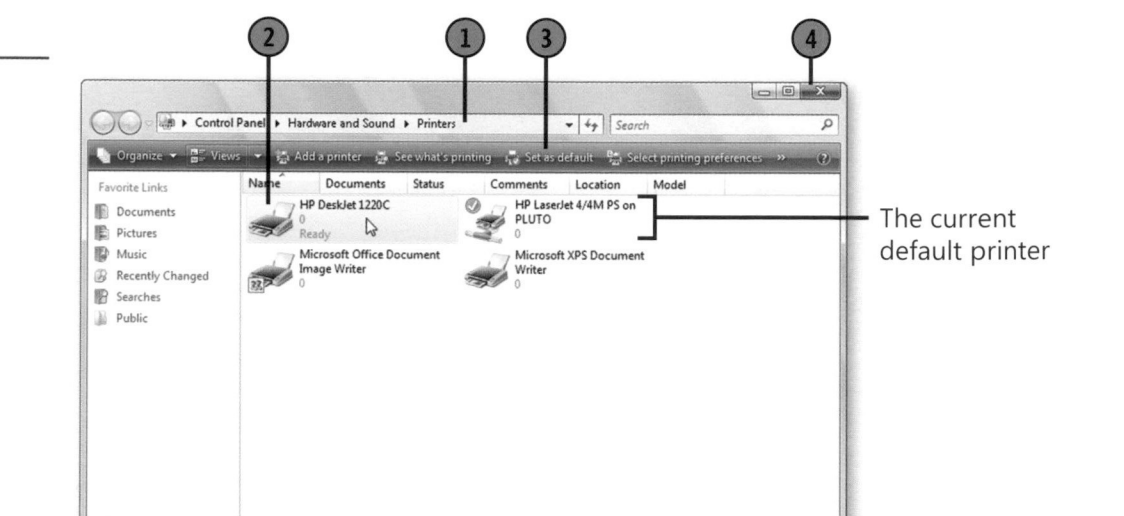

The current default printer

See Also

"Printing from a Program" on page 184 and "Printing a Document" on page 185 for information about printing on different printers.

Caution

If you normally print documents using a printer that's installed on your computer, make sure the device that's designated as your default printer is *not* the Microsoft XPS Document Writer, or any other specialized printer. If one of these other devices is set as your default printer, documents that you want to print might seem to have disappeared.

Tip

If there's a check mark next to the printer icon, the printer you've chosen is already designated as the default printer.

Controlling Your Printing

When you send your documents to be printed, each print job is *queued*, or lined up, in the order in which it's received by the print server. You can see the progress of your print job in the queue and can temporarily suspend the printing of your document or remove it from the queue if you decide that

you don't want to print it. Note that after you've paused or canceled a print job, the printer might continue to print a page or two because those pages have already been stored in the printer.

View the Queue

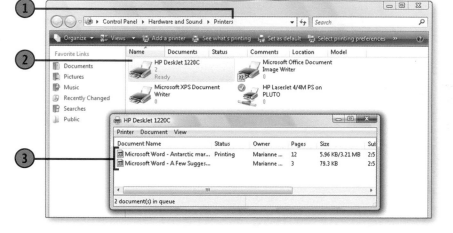

1. Click the Start button, type **printer** in the Search box, and choose the Printers folder.

2. Double-click the printer you're using to open the print queue for that printer.

3. Note the names and details of the documents in the queue.

Stop the Presses

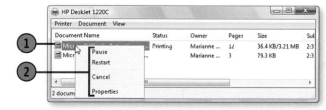

1. Right-click the name of your document.

2. Choose the action you want from the shortcut menu:

   • Pause to temporarily stop your document from printing

   • Resume to resume printing after the document printing has been paused (note that Resume appears on the menu only after you've chosen Pause)

   • Restart to restart printing the document from the beginning after the document printing has been paused

   • Cancel to delete the document from the print queue

Tip

To stop a printer from printing documents, regardless of whom they belong to, right-click the printer, point to Run As Administrator on the shortcut menu, choose Pause Printing from the submenu, and then confirm the action using an Administrator password.

Printing Your Photographs

Printing your photographs used to be quite a challenge—depending on their format and resolution, your pictures might be printed in different sizes or in different orientations on the page. Windows Vista now makes your life a lot easier by providing a wizard that lets you lay out the pictures just as you want them, so you get exactly the desired results every time.

Print the Pictures

(1) Start Windows Photo Gallery from the Start menu.

(2) Select the photograph you want to print. If you want to print multiple photos, be sure to select all of them.

(3) Click Print, and choose Print from the drop-down menu to display the Print Pictures dialog box.

(4) Select your printer and the printer settings you want. The printer settings will differ depending on which printer you chose.

(5) Select the layout you want.

(6) Click to display the printer's Properties dialog box if you want to make additional printer settings.

(7) Select this check box to enlarge or crop the photo to the specified size.

(8) Specify the number of copies you want of each photo.

(9) Look at the preview to verify that the pictures will be printed the way you want. Use the arrows to view all your pages.

(10) Click Print to print the photos.

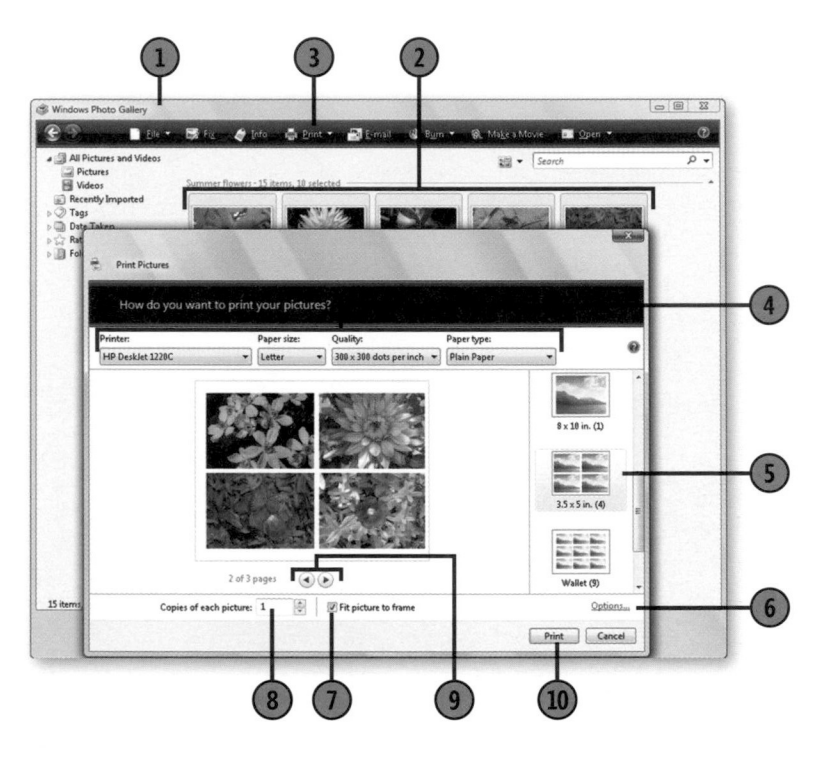

Tip

To send your pictures over the Internet to a photo-printing service, click Print in the Windows Photo Gallery, and choose Order Prints from the drop-down menu.

Printing Web Pages

If you've ever visited a Web page whose content you found so interesting or informative that you wanted to print it out for yourself or for someone else to read, the printed result might have been less than satisfactory—odd-looking pages filled with cut-off text, for example, and an indecipherable hodgepodge of disconnected graphics, tables, frames, and text. However, using Internet Explorer, you can now convert Web pages into a printable form. All you need to do is specify how you want the pages to be set up, take a quick look at the layout to make sure it includes the items you want to print, and then print the pages.

Fix the Layout

1. With the Web page you want to print displayed in Internet Explorer, click the down arrow at the right of the Print button, and choose Print Preview from the drop-down menu to display the Print Preview window so that you can preview the page.

2. Select the orientation you want for the printed page.

3. If you want to change the paper size, paper source, header and footer information, or margins, click the Page Setup button to display the Page Setup dialog box. To change the contents of the header or footer, use the codes in the table on this page. Click OK when you've finished.

4. Click to specify whether you want to show or hide the header and footer.

5. Click to adjust your view of the page or pages.

6. Select the scaling to fit the material onto the printed page. Select Shrink To Fit to automatically scale the page so that the entire width of the Web page is included, or select a scaling value for a custom fit.

7. Examine the layout based on your changes, and then click Print to print the Web page, or click Close to return to the normal view without printing the page.

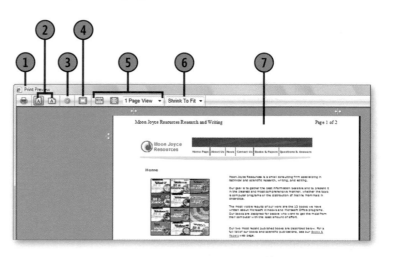

Header and Footer Codes

Code	Result
&b *your text*	Right-aligns text.
&b *your text* &b	Centers text.
&d or &D	Inserts short date or long date.
&p	Inserts page number.
&P	Inserts total number of pages.
&t or &T	Inserts time in 12- or 24-hour format.
&u	Inserts Web-page address.
&w	Inserts window title.

Creating an XPS Document

The XPS file format is a new universal format that produces a document that looks exactly the same as it looked originally, regardless of which computer you use to open or print the document. To create an XPS document, you print it to the Microsoft XPS Document Writer from whichever program you used to create the content.

Create the Document

1. Create or open the document or other item—a photo, for example—in the program you normally use, and choose to print the document. If the program doesn't let you choose a printer before printing, set the Microsoft XPS Document Writer as your default printer.

2. In the dialog box that appears, select Microsoft XPS Document Writer if it isn't already selected, make any other settings you want, and then click Print.

3. In the Save The File As dialog box that appears, specify where you want the file to be stored.

4. Enter a name for the file.

5. Click Save to create the file.

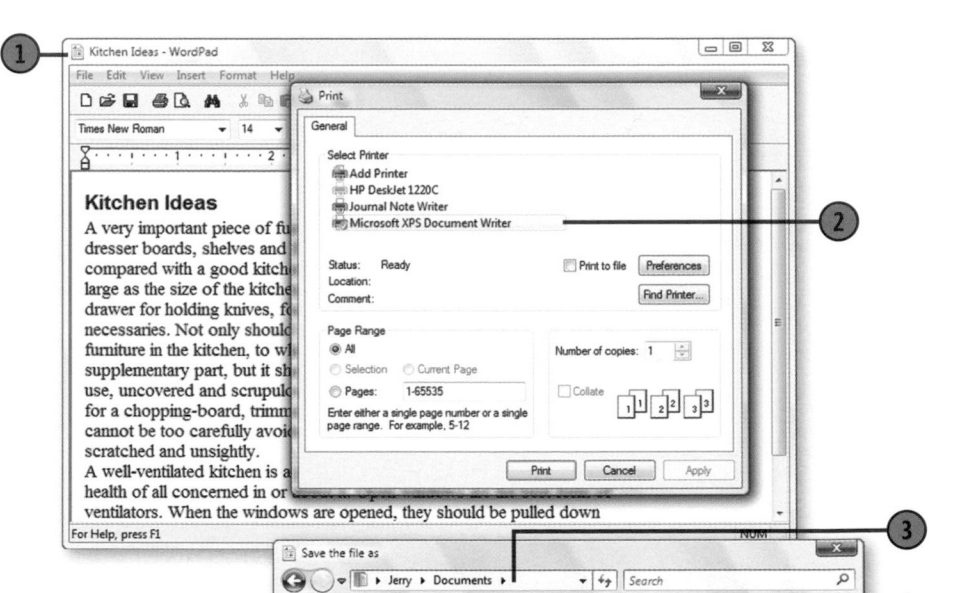

Caution

You'll need an XPS Viewer to view XPS documents. An XPS Viewer add-on to Internet Explorer is already installed on computers running Windows Vista, but the Viewer might not be installed on computers using earlier versions of Windows or on other operating systems. If the Viewer isn't installed, you can download and install it from Windows Update.

Scanning a Picture

A scanner is an excellent tool for digitizing images and making them available on your computer. Windows Vista provides access to your scanner directly from the Windows Photo Gallery, provided the scanner uses a Windows Acquisition driver (WIA) rather than a TWAIN driver. The New Scan dialog box adapts to the specific features of your scanner, so the options you see in the dialog box might be a bit different from those described here.

Scan a Picture

(1) In Windows Photo Gallery, click the down arrow next to the File button, and choose Import From Camera Or Scanner from the drop-down menu to display the Import Pictures And Videos dialog box.

(2) Double-click your scanner to display the New Scan dialog box.

(3) Make any changes you want to the scanner settings.

(4) Click Preview to do a quick scan of the picture and to preview it. Make any setting changes, such as brightness, that you want, and click Preview again.

(5) Drag the selection rectangle, if necessary, to limit the scan to your picture.

(6) Click Scan, and wait for the picture to be scanned.

(7) In the Importing Pictures And Videos dialog box that appears, type a tag for the picture, or select a tag from the drop-down list to classify the picture and provide a name for the file.

(8) Click Import to import the picture onto your computer and into Photo Gallery.

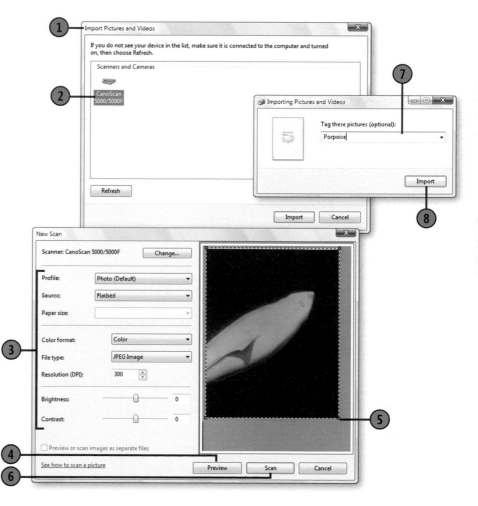

Scanning Anything

You can scan any item—a drawing, a newspaper article, a piece of patterned fabric—directly into Windows Paint, provided the scanner uses a Windows Acquisition driver (WIA) rather than a TWAIN driver, using the settings you want. Then you can save the scan of the item in the format and location you want.

Scan

① In Windows Paint, choose From Scanner Or Camera from the File menu to display the Scan dialog box.

② Select the type of scan result you want.

③ If you want to make custom settings, click Adjust The Quality Of The Scanned Picture to display the Advanced Properties dialog box.

④ Make any changes you want, and click OK.

⑤ Click Preview to do a quick scan of the picture and to preview it.

⑥ If the selected area doesn't match your item or the part of it you want, drag the handles in the preview to change the selected area.

⑦ Click Scan.

⑧ Preview the scan in Paint, and make any modifications you want.

⑨ Choose Save from the File menu, and save the scan in the file format and location you want.

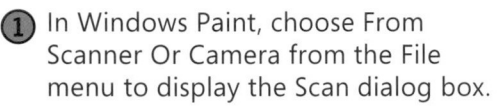

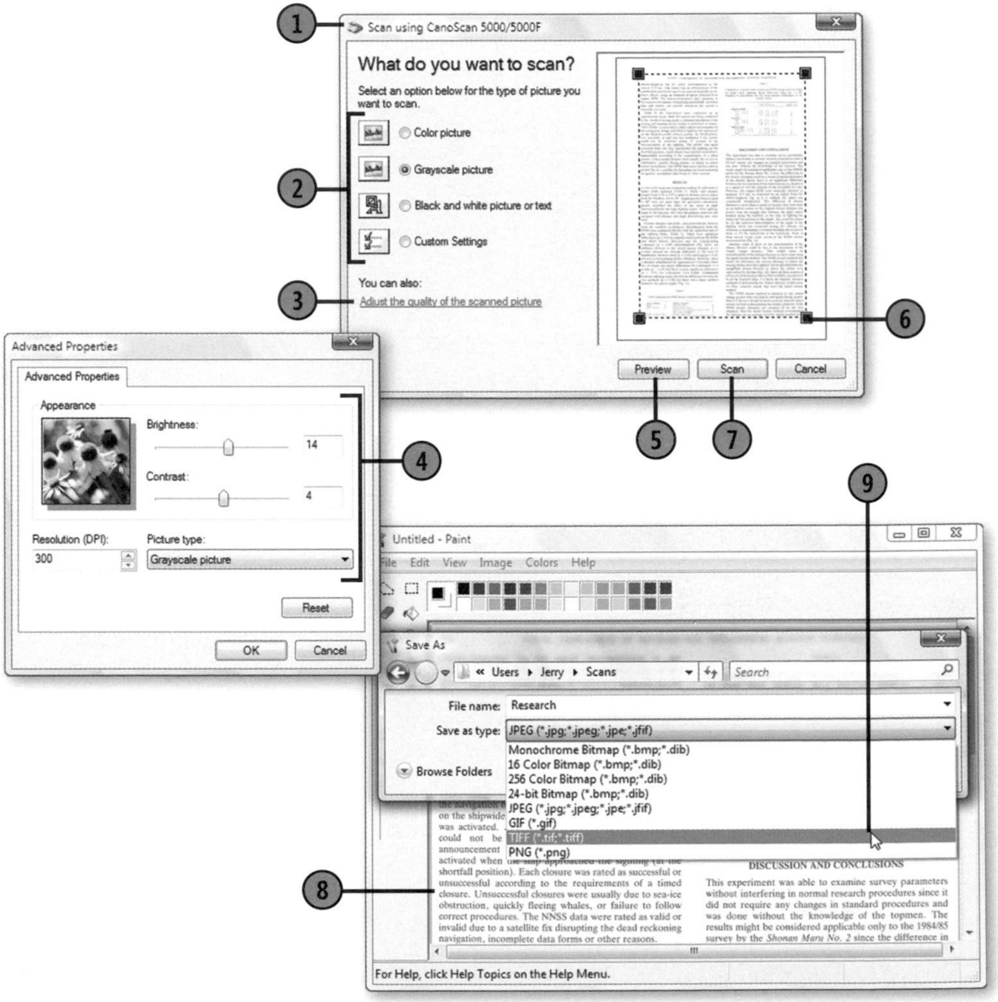

11

Managing Files and Folders

We all know that to work productively, with minimal stress and frustration, we must get organized! That's where Windows Vista comes in. Windows Vista supplies the framework—a basic file structure of drives and some ready-made folders, which you can either use as is or create your own file- and folder-management system. You can organize the files within the folders—alphabetically or by size, type, date, and so on—and move, copy, and rename files or groups of files. If you want the people who share the computer with you to have access to certain files and folders, you can put those items in folders that are designed to be shared. You can change the appearance of the windows in which you view your documents and folders, and, depending on the information you need, you can view them in any of seven different views.

You can put the items you use every day on the computer's Desktop, just as you do on a real desktop, and, to gain immediate access to a document you're preparing, you can put a shortcut to it on the Desktop. You can take your files with you by copying them onto a removable memory device, and you can compress large files, either for storage or so that you can send them via e-mail. And you can use the handy toolbars to quickly and easily navigate your way through the information on your computer.

Windows Views

Although Windows Vista has seven view settings, there are actually just four major categories, one of which is a single category with four different sizes. The four major categories are Icons view, with the choice of four different sizes of icons; and List view; Details view; and Tiles view. Additionally, you can choose an icon size setting anywhere between the four standard size settings. You'll probably want to experiment to see which view is best suited for your work and for the contents of your folders. For example, you might want to use Icons view in a folder that contains only a few files of different types, List view to see a vertical listing of files and folders, Details view when you're looking for files that were created on a specific date, Tiles view when you're managing pictures, and Extra Large Icons view when you're reviewing the pictures. The seven views are described in detail on these two pages.

Icons view: The four icon sizes are Extra Large, Large, Medium, and Small. In most cases, it's only the size of the icon—not its content—that changes in any of these four settings. However, in Small Icons view, you'll see only the icons; in the other views, Windows Vista shows you a preview of the file—if it's available—as part of the icon. Each icon size has its purpose. For example, the Extra Large Icons setting is the best way to view pictures in detail, and to get a good view of the contents of a folder and its subfolders. It is, however, an inefficient use of space to have a file represented only by an icon. On the other hand, the Small Icons setting lets you view a large number of files but provides little detail about pictures, file contents, or folder contents. The icons are arranged in horizontal rows, and, if there are too many files to be shown in the window at one time, you simply scroll vertically to see the remaining files.

Extra Large Icons view

Large Icons view

Medium Icons view

Small Icons view

List view: This view displays small icons representing files and folders in a vertical listing that can snake through multiple columns. The name of the folder or file is listed next to the icon. If there are too many files to be shown in the window, you scroll horizontally to see the additional columns and the remaining files.

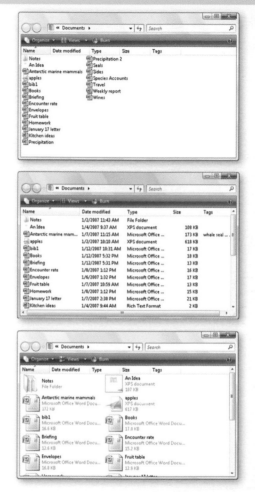

Details view: This view displays small icons in a single-column list that shows the name of the file or folder and includes details such as size, type, and date. The details shown depend on the types of files in the folder, and you can customize the details that are shown. If you can't see all the details, just scroll horizontally to see the additional details. If there are too many files to be shown in the window, you scroll vertically to see the remaining files.

Tiles view: This view displays medium-sized icons that include the name of the file or folder, the file type, and the file size. The tiles are arranged horizontally in as many columns as will fit within the window. If there are too many files to be shown in the window, you scroll vertically to see the remaining files.

After you've chosen the view you want, Windows Vista offers more options. In each view, you can arrange the way the files are sorted—for example, you can arrange the files in order by name, size, file type, or date. If you prefer, you can arrange the files in groups or include only items that fit specific parameters. You can also show different panes in the window—the Navigation pane to open other folders, the Details pane to show the *metadata* (such as title, tags, author, and size), and the Preview pane to show a preview, if available, of the selected item. These panes provide this information regardless of which view you're using.

Changing the Window View

You can change the appearance of the windows that contain your files and folders so that the information is presented in the way that's most useful for you.

Choose a View

(1) In the window whose view you want to change, click the Views button to cycle through the views in order. (Only the Large Icons view is used for the Icons view.)

(2) If you want to select a specific view, click the down arrow at the right of the Views button, and click the view you want.

(3) If you want to create a custom size for icons, click the down arrow at the right of the Views button, and drag the slider to create the icon size you want.

Try This!

Click in your folder window to select it. Hold down the Ctrl key and rotate the mouse wheel. Watch as all the views change in the same way they change when you use the slider on the Views button.

See Also

"Windows Views" on pages 194–195 for information about all the different views.

"Customizing Your Folders" on pages 268–269 for information about changing the look and type of information displayed.

Sorting Your Files and Folders

A single folder can contain a large number of files, so when you're looking for one particular file, it can be difficult to find, especially if you don't remember its name. Worse, if you need several files that are scattered all through the folder, it can be quite time-consuming to find and select the ones you want. Fortunately, you can sort the information by any of the fields, group files by numerous categories, or filter the data so that only the information you want is displayed.

Sort by Field

1 Click the field label that you want to sort by.

2 If you want to reverse the sort order, click the field a second time.

The tiny arrow above the field name indicates that the files are sorted by this field, and the arrow points in the direction of the sort.

Group, Filter, or Stack

1 Click the down arrow next to the field label.

2 If you want to group the files and folders and show all the files in the grouping, click Group.

3 If you want to show only selected files and folders, select the check boxes for the items to be displayed.

4 If you want to conduct an automatic search to group the files and folders but show only the grouping rather than the individual items, click Stack By Name. To display files and folders in a stack, double-click the stack.

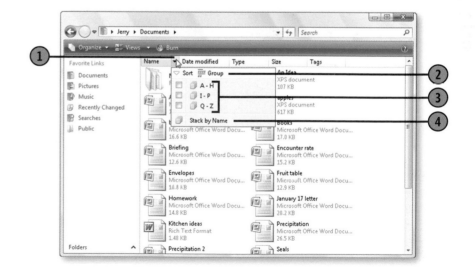

Viewing File Information

There are numerous ways to view your files and folders. In addition to changing your view of the files, the Preview and Details panes provide additional information so that you can identify whether you've located the file you want without having to open it first.

Show the Information

1. Click Organize, point to Layout on the drop-down menu, and choose Details Pane from the submenu to display the Details pane. Click Organize again, point to Layout, and click Preview Pane to display the Preview pane.

2. Click a file or folder.

3. Read the information about the file or folder. The type of information shown varies depending on the type of file or folder you're looking at.

4. View the preview of the file or the folder contents. Note that not all files display a preview.

5. Continue clicking files or folders and reviewing the material in the Details pane and/or the Preview pane until you've located the item you want.

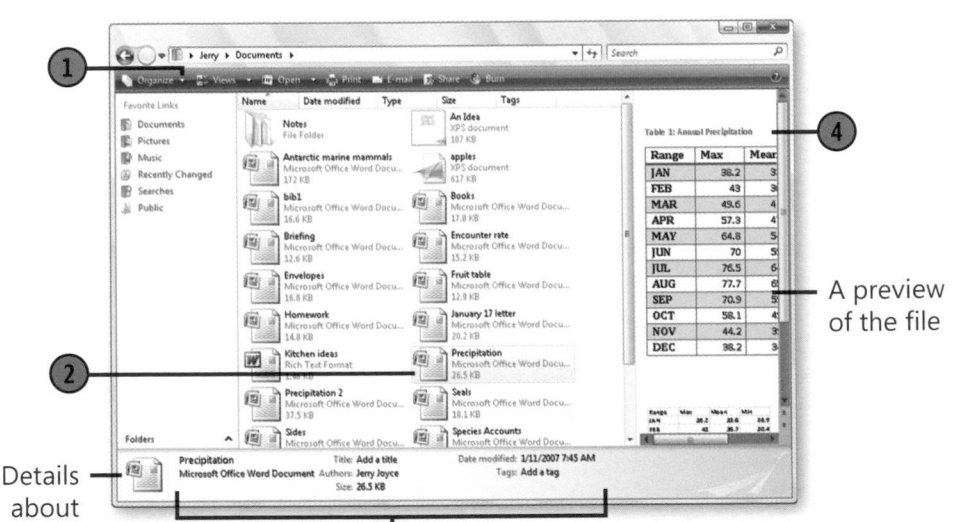

A preview of the file

Details about the file

Tip

If, when you click to show the Details or the Preview pane, you can't see it, the window is probably not large enough. Increase its size until you see the pane you want.

Tip

To change the size of the Details or the Preview pane, move the mouse over the pane's inside border until the mouse cursor changes into a Resize cursor, and then drag the border.

Classifying Your Files

Before you know it, your computer can fill up with files—pictures, music, letters, worksheets, and much more. One method you can use to help keep track of these files—and to help you find the right ones later, when you need them—is to include additional information about the file. Depending on the type of file, this information can include author name, keywords, a rating, and more. Although not all file formats support storing these extra details, called metadata, many common file formats do.

Add More Information

1 Locate the file you want to classify and click to select it.

2 Click in a field in the Details pane, and type the text you want for that field.

3 Click in another field, and enter any information you want. Continue clicking in fields and entering the text you want.

4 To add a rating for the file, click the number of stars you want for the rating.

5 Click Save.

See Also

"Sorting Your Files and Folders" on page 197 for information about sorting and grouping the files.

"Viewing File Information" on page 198 for information about displaying the Details pane if it isn't already displayed

Tip

You can't type information in some of the fields in the Details pane because these fields get their information automatically from Windows.

Navigating Folders

Although there are numerous ways to find a folder—opening it from the Start menu, running a search, or wandering around in the Computer window until you find the folder, for example—the easiest ways to move from folder to folder are to use the Favorite Links list and the Folders list in the Navigation pane.

Navigate

(1) If the Navigation pane isn't displayed, click Organize, point to Layout on the drop-down menu, and choose Navigation Pane from the submenu.

(2) Click a link to go to the location you want.

(3) If that location isn't included in the links, click the Folders up arrow if it's displayed.

(4) Scroll through the list of locations.

(5) Do any of the following:

- Click a right-pointing arrow to expand the folder list for that location.

- Click a diagonally pointing arrow to collapse the folder list for that location.

- Click a location to go to it.

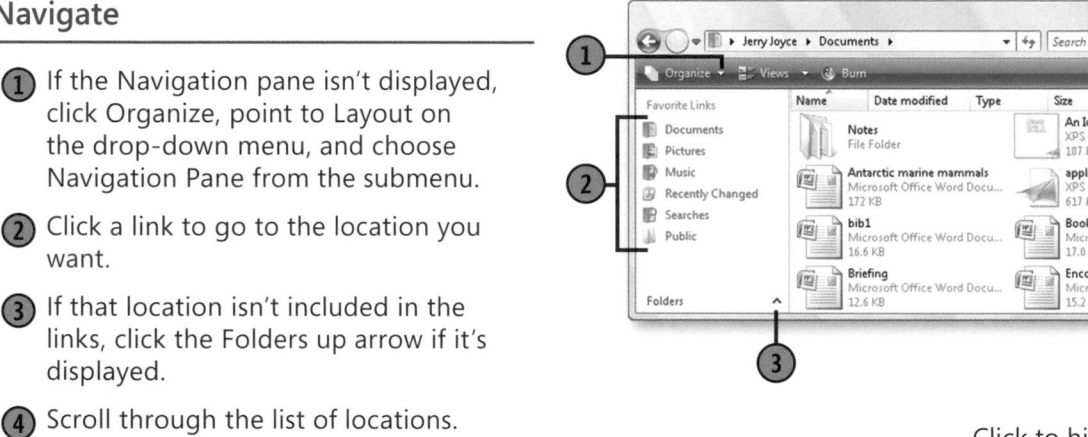

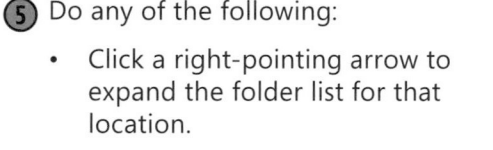

Click to hide subfolders.

Click to show subfolders.

Click to go to that location.

See Also

"Adding a Link to a Folder" on the facing page for information about adding other locations to your Favorite Links list.

See Also

"Accessing Everything" on pages 16–17 for information about navigating using the Address bar.

Adding a Link to a Folder

When there's a location that you need to go to frequently, it's a good idea to add a link to that location. After you add the link, it appears in your Favorite Links list in every folder window.

Add a Link

① If the Navigation pane isn't displayed, click Organize, point to Layout on the drop-down menu, and choose Navigation Pane from the submenu.

② Navigate to the location that contains the folder you want to link to.

③ Drag the folder onto the Favorite Links section of the Navigation pane.

④ If you want to change the order of the links, drag a link up or down into a new location.

⑤ To remove a link, right-click it, and choose Remove Link from the shortcut menu.

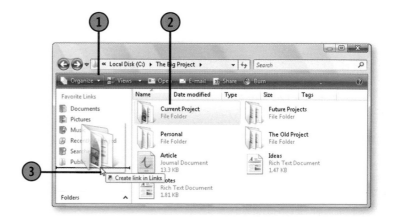

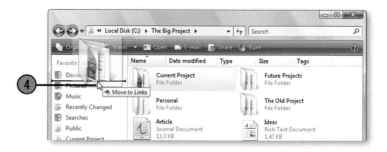

See Also

"Creating Quick Access to a File or Folder" on page 203 for information about placing a shortcut to a file or folder on the Desktop or adding a shortcut to the Start menu.

Finding Specific Types of Files

If you want to find certain files that match specific criteria, you can conduct a search, save the search, and then just open the saved search to see the updated results.

Save and Reuse a Search

(1) Set up and conduct an advanced search to find the specific types of files you want.

(2) Click Save Search.

(3) Name and save the search.

(4) The next time you want the results of the search using the same search parameters, click Searches in the Favorite Links section, and double-click the Search folder to see the updated results.

Try This!

Conduct an advanced search and save it. Click the Searches link in the Favorite Links list. In the Search folder, locate your search and drag it onto the Favorite Links list. Now you can click the link whenever you want to see the updated results of the search.

See Also

"Run an Advanced Search" on page 15 for information about conducting an advanced search.

"Navigating Folders" on page 200 for information about displaying the Navigation pane and the Favorite Links list if they aren't already displayed.

Creating Quick Access to a File or Folder

If you use a particular file or folder frequently, you can access it quickly by placing a shortcut to it on the Desktop, on the Start menu, or just about anywhere you want. A shortcut to a document opens the document in its default program; a shortcut to a program file starts the program; a shortcut to a folder opens the folder in a window.

Create a Shortcut to a File or Folder

① Open the window that contains the file or folder for which you want to create a shortcut.

② Right-click the file or folder, and choose Create Shortcut from the shortcut menu.

③ Drag the shortcut

- Onto the Desktop.

- Onto the Start button, and then onto the Start menu when it opens.

- Onto the Quick Launch toolbar.

- Onto a link in the Favorite Links list in the Navigation pane.

- To any folder listed in the Folders list in the Navigation pane, or to any open folder.

Tip

To quickly create a shortcut on the Desktop, right-click the file or folder, point to Send To on the shortcut menu, and choose Desktop (Create Shortcut).

Organizing Your Files

If you have a limited number of files, you can easily keep them all in a single folder, such as the Documents folder. However, if you have files that you want other people to have full access to, or files dealing with many different projects, you'll probably want to organize them by placing them in individual folders.

If a file doesn't have a suitably descriptive name, you can change it to one that's more useful. If there's a group of related files, you can rename each file in the group with the same group name, followed by consecutive numbering—for example, *stories, stories(1), stories(2),* and so on.

Move, Copy, or Delete a File

1. Open the window containing the file or files you want to move or copy.

2. Select the file or files to be moved or copied.

3. Hold down the right mouse button, and drag the item or items onto the destination folder in the Folders list or into the Favorite Links list in the Navigation pane.

4. From the shortcut menu that appears, choose whether you want to move or to copy the item or items.

5. To delete a file or a group of files, select the file or group of files, and press the Delete key.

See Also

"Navigating Folders" on page 200 for information about displaying the Navigation pane and using the Folders list.

"Sharing Files with Other Users" on pages 206–207 for information about keeping your files private so that other people who have access to the computer can't open them.

Rename a File or Folder or a Group of Files

1 Select the file or folder or the group of files you want to rename, and press the F2 key; or right-click the first selected file of a group, and choose Rename from the shortcut menu.

2 Type a new name, or click to position the insertion point and then edit the name. Press Enter when the name is correct.

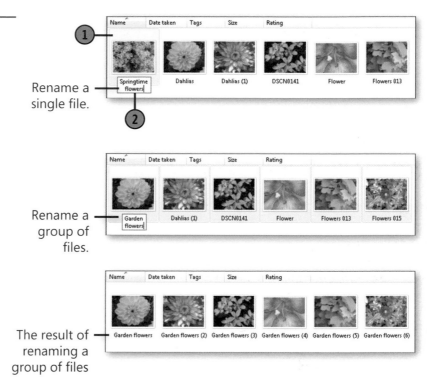

Rename a single file.

Rename a group of files.

The result of renaming a group of files

Sharing Files with Other Users

Each user of your computer has his or her individual set of folders in which to keep documents, music, and so on. Your private files and folders—Documents and Pictures, for example—are the ones that are located under your user name and that are normally accessible only by you when you're signed on to the computer or by someone with an Administrator account. However, if you want to grant the other people who use your computer full access to certain files, you can place those files in a Public folder.

Share a File or Folder with All Users

① Select the file or folder, or the group of files and/or folders, that you want to share.

② In the Folders list, expand the Desktop folder and then the Public folder to see all your Public folders.

③ Drag a file to move it, or hold down the Ctrl key while dragging to copy the file onto the appropriate type of folder.

④ Click the Public folder, and verify that the items you want to share are now available.

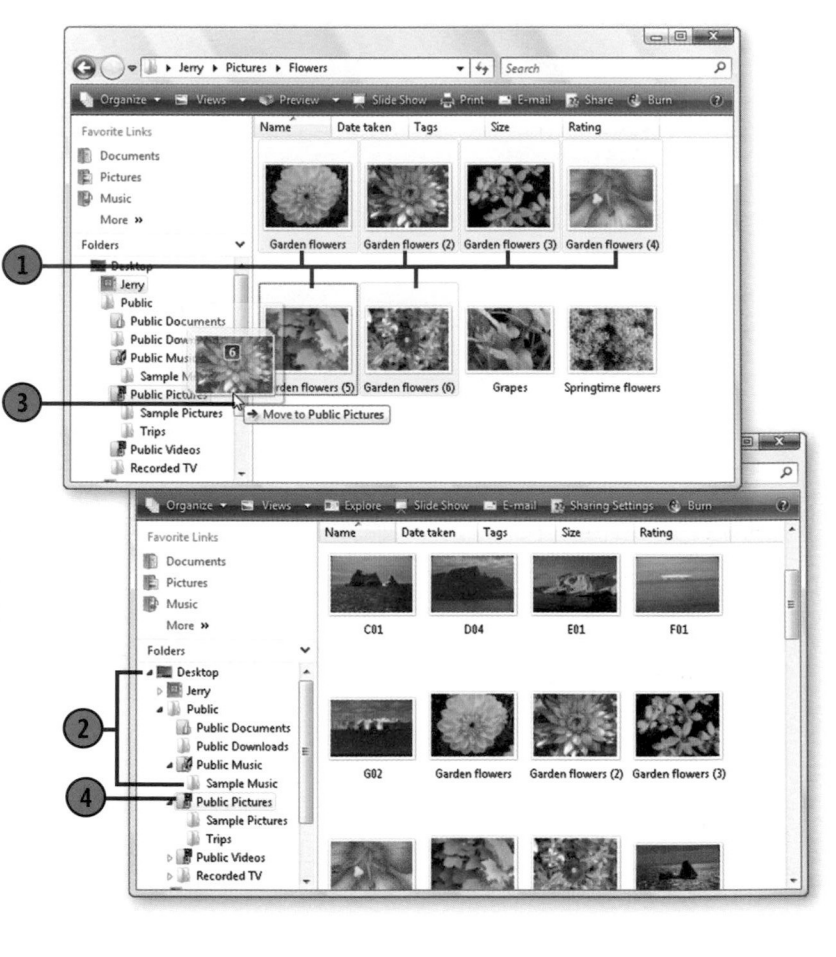

See Also

"Sharing Your Files over the Network" on page 219 for information about setting up network access to your Public folders and stipulating what changes can be made to the files.

Caution

If you see an option that gives everyone access to your shared files or folders, don't select the check box unless you want to share your files or folders with everyone on your network, including those who don't normally have access to your computer.

Share a File or Folder with Selected Users

1. Open the folder that contains the file or folder you want to share, and select the item to be shared.

2. Click Share.

3. Select a person from the drop-down list with whom you want to share the item, and then click Add. Repeat for any other people you want to include.

4. Click the down arrow for each individual to set the type of permission you're granting that person:

   • Reader to allow the person to open the file or the folder and any files in the folder, but not to save, rename, or delete that file or any files in the shared location

   • Co-Owner to allow the person to fully manage the file or folder contents, including saving, renaming, or deleting items

5. Click Share.

6. To tell someone who has permission to use the shared item how to connect to it, select the item, and then either e-mail a link to the shared item or copy the address of the shared file to provide it to that person.

7. Click Done.

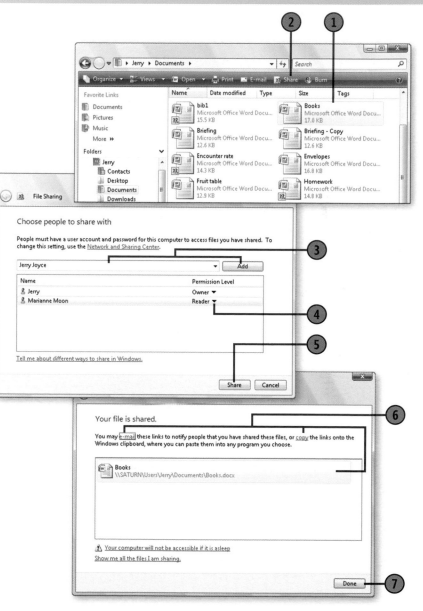

Recovering a Deleted Item

If you accidentally delete a file, a folder, or a shortcut from your computer's hard disk, you can quickly recover the item by either undoing your action immediately or restoring the deleted item from the Recycle Bin. The Recycle Bin holds all the files you've deleted from your hard disk(s) until you empty the bin or until it gets so full that the oldest files are deleted automatically. When you've deleted a folder, you have to restore the entire folder. You can't open a deleted folder in the Recycle Bin and restore selected files.

Undo a Deletion

① Point to a blank spot on the Desktop or to a blank part of any folder window, and right-click.

② Choose Undo Delete from the shortcut menu.

Caution

You can't recover any files that you've deleted from a removable disk or device, so be careful! Once they're gone, they're gone forever.

The command is available only if the deletion was your most recent action.

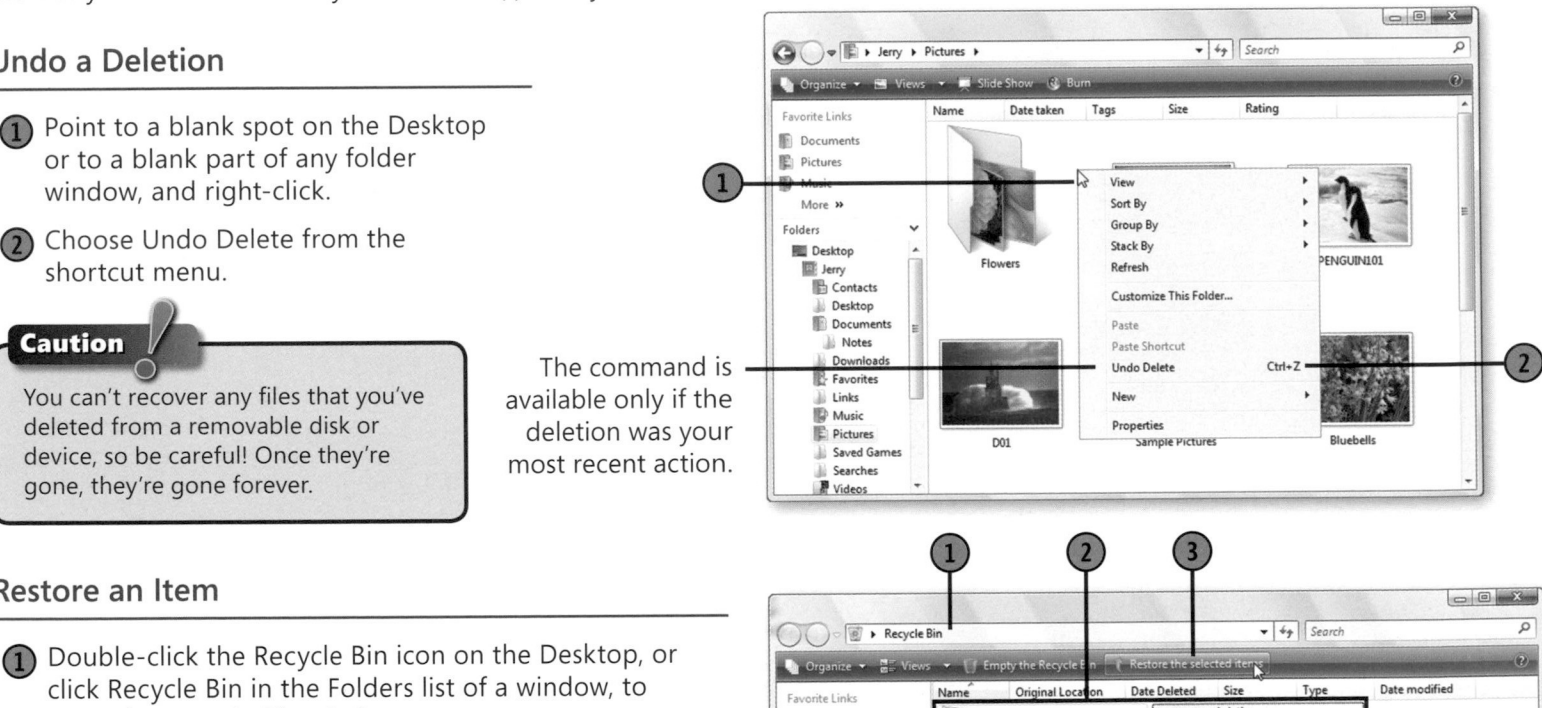

Restore an Item

① Double-click the Recycle Bin icon on the Desktop, or click Recycle Bin in the Folders list of a window, to open the Recycle Bin window.

② Select the item or items to be recovered.

③ Click Restore This Item (or Restore The Selected Items if you've selected more than one item).

Using a Removable Memory Device

The easiest way to take some of your files with you is to use a removable USB (Universal Serial Bus) memory device. There are many common names and brand names for these devices, but they all work in basically the same way: Plug the device into a USB port, copy information to or from it, and remove it when you've finished. Many people simply remove the device from the USB port when the file transfer is complete. Provided no data is being written to or from the device and there are no open files, you can do this without any loss of data. However, sooner or later you'll find that just as you start removing the device, some data is being written and you end up with some corrupted or deleted files. To avoid this disaster, make sure that you've closed all the files and stopped the device before you remove it.

Use the Device

① Plug the device into a free USB port. If Windows Vista needs to install drivers for the device, wait for the installation to be complete.

② If a window opens showing the contents of the device, use the window to manage the files on the device. If an AutoPlay dialog box appears, choose to open the folder. If the window doesn't open automatically, choose Computer from the Start menu, and double-click the drive for the device to open the window.

③ To copy files or folders from your computer to the device, select the items to copy, and right-click one of the selected items. On the shortcut menu that appears, point to Send To, and then click the device on the submenu.

④ When you've finished with the device and want to remove it, close any files or folders that are open in the device files.

⑤ Click the Safely Remove Hardware icon in the notification area of the taskbar, and click the device you want to remove. Wait for confirmation that the device can be safely removed.

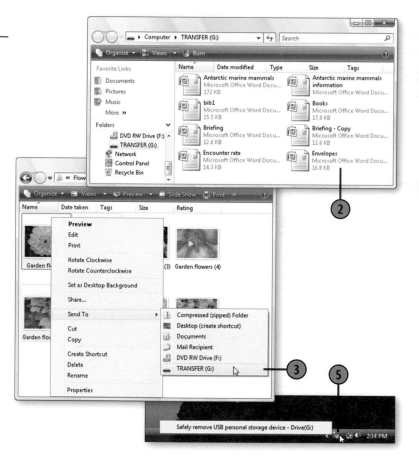

Copying Files to a CD or DVD

If you have a DVD recorder (called a *burner*) installed on your computer, you can copy your files to a CD or DVD for safe storage or distribution. When archiving, you can continue copying files to the disc until it's full. Files saved in this way are readable on Windows Vista and Windows XP computers, but they won't be readable on most other systems. When you're creating a disc for distribution, you gather all the files for the disc and record them all at once.

Archive Your Files

① Select the first files and/or folders that you want to record on the disc.

② Click Burn.

③ In the Burn A Disc dialog box, type a name for the disc.

④ Click Next, and wait for the files to be copied.

⑤ In the window showing the disc's contents, do either of the following:

- Delete any files you don't want to keep on the disc.

- Drag files from other folders and drop them in the window to add them to the disc.

⑥ When you've finished, eject the disc, and wait for Windows to close the recording session. When the session has closed, the disc is readable on compatible computers. To record more data or edit the contents on the disc, insert the disc again, and repeat steps 5 and 6.

Tip

To quickly record a file to a disc that has already been used for data, select the file or files, and click the Burn button.

Tip

By default, the disc format is the Live File System, which allows this type of multiple recording. To verify that this is the selected format, click Show Formatting Options in the Burn A Disc dialog box.

Copy Files for Distribution

(1) With a blank disc in your drive, select the files and/or folders you want to record on disc, and click Burn to display the Burn A Disc dialog box.

(2) Type a name for the disc, and click Show Formatting Options.

(3) Select the Mastered option, and click Next.

(4) In the disc-drive window, verify that all the items you want on the disc are present, and delete any items you don't want. If you want to include additional files or folders, locate and select them, and click Burn. Continue adding files until all the items you want are on the disc.

(5) Click Burn To Disc.

(6) Step through the Burn To Disc Wizard to

- Confirm or change the disc name.
- Specify the recording speed you want, and click Next.
- Specify whether you want to make another disc using the same files.

(7) Click Finish when you've finished, and remove and label your disc.

Tip

To burn all the files at once, you must have adequate free space on your hard disk to hold copies of all the files.

Compressing Files

Compressed folders are special folders that use compression software to decrease the sizes of the files they contain. Compressed folders are useful for reducing the file size of standard documents and programs, but they're invaluable when you're storing large graphics files such as bitmaps, or when you're transferring large files by e-mail.

Create a Compressed Folder

1. Select the file or files to be copied to a compressed folder.

2. Right-click one of the selected files, point to Send To on the shortcut menu, and choose Compressed (Zipped) Folder from the submenu. Rename the compressed folder if necessary.

3. Drag any other files onto the compressed folder icon to copy those files to the compressed folder.

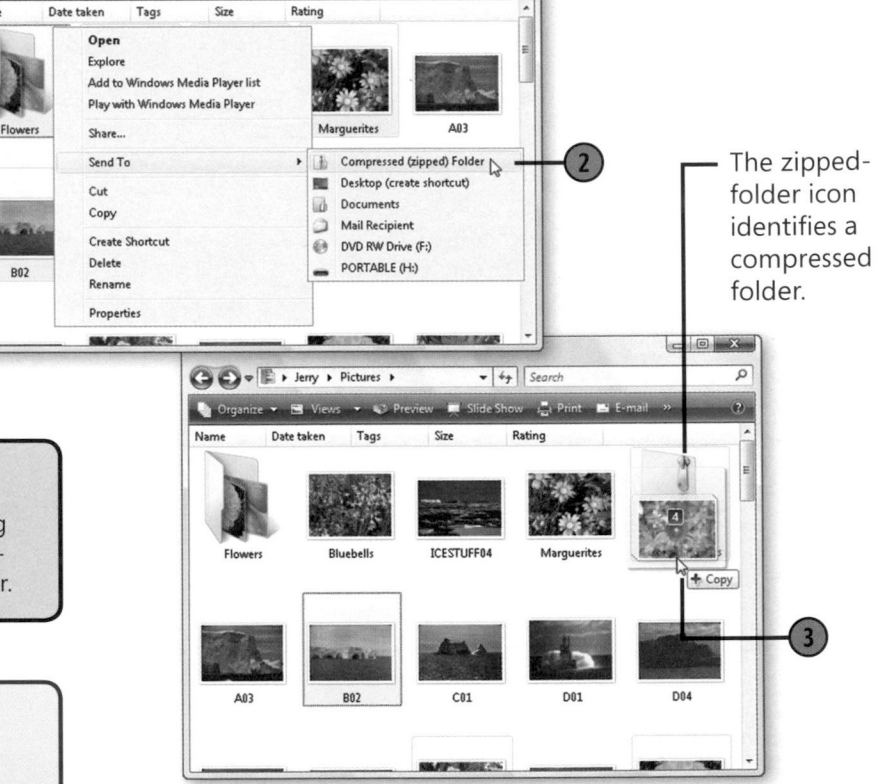

The zipped-folder icon identifies a compressed folder.

Caution

Compressed folders preserve the contents of most files, but it's possible that you could lose some data when you're using certain file formats. It's wise to test your file format in a compressed folder before you move valuable files into that folder.

Tip

Many file types, such as .jpeg pictures, are already compressed, so moving them to a compressed folder won't substantially reduce their size. However, using a compressed folder is still an excellent way to organize the files into a single file when you're transferring them.

Use a Compressed File

① Double-click the compressed folder to open it.

② Double-click an item in the folder to open it in its associated program. If the item is a program, double-click it to run it. (Note, though, that not all files and programs will function properly from the compressed folder.)

③ To decompress a single file, drag it (or copy and paste it) onto an uncompressed folder.

④ To decompress all the files in the folder and copy them to another folder, click Extract All Files.

⑤ In the Extract Compressed (Zipped) Files window, specify where you want the files to be extracted from (or copied to).

⑥ Click Extract.

Try This!

Compress a large file (or a group of files) by placing it in a compressed folder. Right-click the zipped-folder icon, point to Send To on the shortcut menu, and click Mail Recipient. Send the folder, which is now listed as a ZIP-type file, to the person who needs it. If the recipient's operating system isn't equipped with the compressed-folders feature, he or she will need to use a third-party compression program that uses ZIP-type compressed files to open the files.

Tip

A compressed folder is compatible with any file-compression programs that support the ZIP file format.

Navigating with Toolbars

There are seven toolbars associated with the Windows Vista taskbar, and they provide access to programs, folders, and documents as well as to Internet and intranet sites. You can also use the New Toolbar to create your own toolbars that link directly to the contents of folders. You probably won't see all the toolbars listed, however, because the Language Bar and Windows Media Player toolbars are shown only if you've chosen to display them, and the Tablet PC Input Panel requires the Tablet PC tools to be installed on your computer.

Display a Toolbar

1. Right-click a blank spot on the taskbar.

2. Point to Toolbars on the shortcut menu, and choose the toolbar you want to display. (A toolbar with a check mark next to its name is one that's already displayed.) Use the table at the right to identify what each toolbar does.

3. Double-click the toolbar if it isn't already expanded.

4. If the toolbar doesn't expand, right-click a blank spot on the taskbar, choose Lock The Taskbar from the shortcut menu, and repeat step 3.

The Taskbar's Toolbars

Toolbar	Function
Address	Opens the item when you specify its address. The address can be the path and the file or folder name, a computer on the network, or even the Internet address of a Web page.
Desktop	Provides quick access to the icons, files, folders, and shortcuts on the Desktop.
Language Bar	Switches input languages if Windows has been configured to use more than one language.
Links	Links you to the same locations that are shown on the Internet Explorer Links toolbar.
New Toolbar	Creates a new toolbar that shows the contents of a folder you specify.
Tablet PC Input Panel	Displays the Tablet PC's Input Panel.
Quick Launch	Launches Internet Explorer and Windows Media Player, minimizes all the windows on the Desktop, or switches to other running programs.
Windows Media Player	Provides control for operating Windows Media Player when Media Player is minimized.

12 Networking

Networking, once a requirement only in large corporations, is now almost a necessity in a multi-computer household, a home office, or a small business. With two or more computers connected, you can access files and folders on other computers that have been set up for sharing, and you can share the files and folders on your computer with other people, either in Public folders or directly from your computer. If there are items to which you want to limit other people's access—your private files, for example—you can do so. If you're working from home, you can easily connect to your office network by creating a VPN (Virtual Private Network), which ensures a secure connection to a computer on the network.

When you're away from your workplace, Windows Vista recognizes the wireless networks that are within range—some of which are open and free, and others that ask for a security key or a *passphrase* before you can connect wirelessly. If you don't have a network, you can still connect using an *ad hoc,* or improvised, network. Using Windows Meeting Space, you can hold virtual meetings, with up to ten participants, and you can send invitations to the meeting via e-mail and provide handouts in the form of shared files. There's even a network projector you can use for PowerPoint presentations or other types of demonstrations.

Connecting to a Network Computer

When your computer is connected to a small home or business network, and when other computers on the network are set up to share items, you can connect to a computer on the network and access items on that computer. The type of access you have to the contents of another computer depends, as it should, on the sharing settings on that computer to ensure that private files are kept private and public files are made available. Although networking is easiest between computers that are running Windows Vista or Windows XP, you can still connect to computers running other types of operating systems, provided those computers are properly configured.

Connect to a Computer

1. Click the Start button, and choose Network from the menu to display the Network window.

2. Double-click the computer whose files or folders you want to access.

3. If the Connect To dialog box appears, enter a user name and password for that computer, and then click OK. The user name and password must be those that have been set up on that network computer.

4. Double-click a folder to access its contents. Use the folder and the contents as you would any other folder, depending on the type of permission you've been granted.

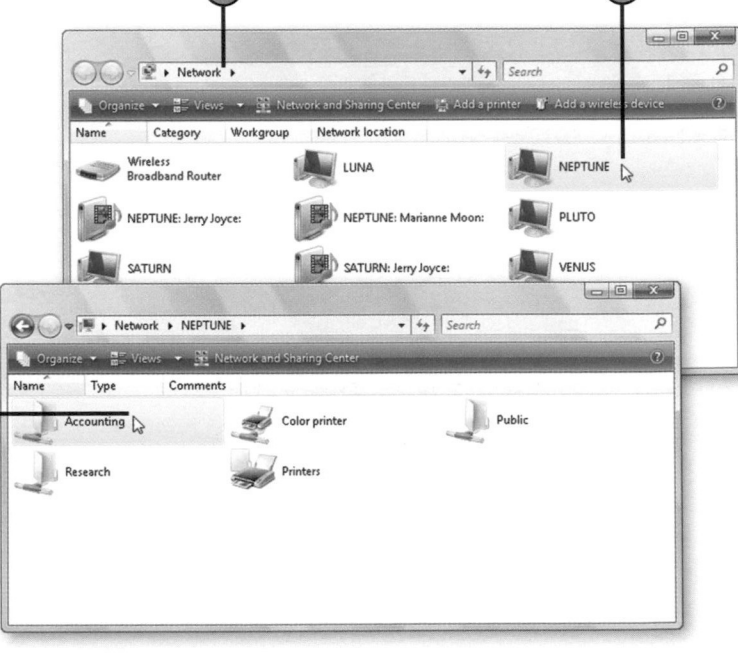

See Also

"Sharing Your Files over the Network" on page 219 for information about setting password-protected sharing.

Tip

The Connect To dialog box appears if the network computer has Password Protected Sharing turned on and you're not listed as one of the users on that computer.

Connect to a Computer That's Not Listed

(1) Click the Start button, and choose Network from the menu to display the Network window.

(2) Click the Network icon in the Address bar.

(3) Type the address of the computer in the form **\\computername**, with *computername* being the name of the computer on the network, and then press Enter.

(4) Use the shared folders as you would any other network folders.

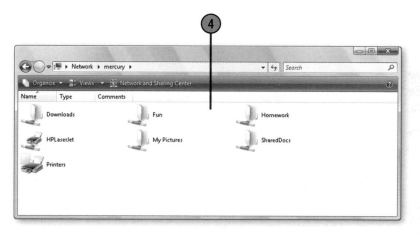

See Also

"Adding a Link to a Folder" on page 201 for information about adding a folder to the Favorite Links list in the Navigation pane of your folder windows.

"Creating a Connection to a Network Folder" on page 222 for information about creating quick access to a folder using a drive letter for compatibility with some programs.

Tip

Windows Vista shows all the computers that are on a network, but Windows XP shows only the computers that are in the same workgroup. To see all the computers on your network from a computer that's running Windows XP, set the same workgroup name for all the computers. To see or change the name of the workgroup you're using on your Windows Vista computer, click System And Maintenance in the Control Panel, and then click See The Name Of This Computer in the System Section to open the System window.

Exploring Your Network

Windows Vista will automatically explore your network, looking for the various computers, devices, and connections on your network. To allow Windows to do this, you must enable Network Discovery, even if you don't want to share anything from your computer. This type of exploration works well with computers that are running Windows Vista, but it requires computers that are running Windows XP and any other device that's connected to your network—a stand-alone network printer, for example—to have the LLTD (Link Layer Topology Discovery) protocol installed in order to be detected.

Explore

1. Click the Start button, choose Network from the Start menu to display the Network window, and click Network And Sharing Center to display the Network And Sharing Center window.

2. If Network Discovery isn't shown as On, click the down arrow to display the options, choose Turn On Network Discovery, and click Apply. When asked, verify that this is what you want to do.

3. Click View Full Map.

4. Examine the computers that are on your network.

5. Click a computer, a device, or the Internet to access each.

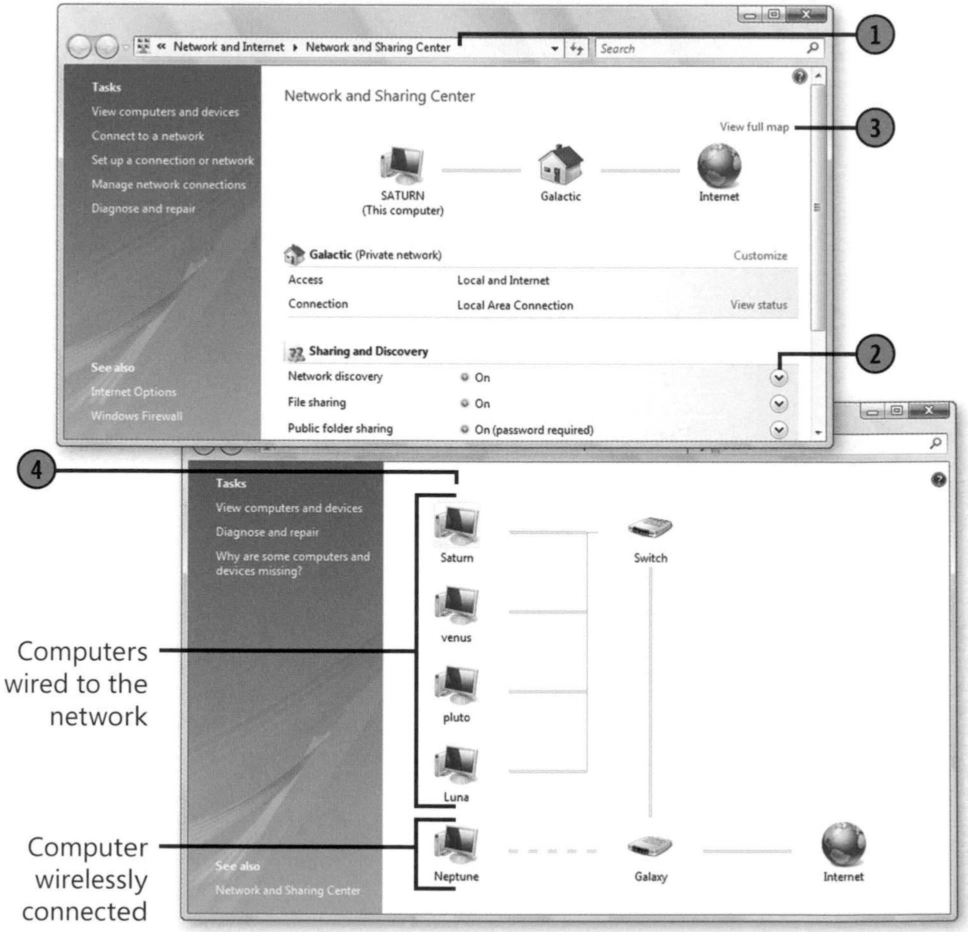

> **Tip**
>
> The LLTD protocol for Windows XP is available for download from Windows Update.

Computers wired to the network

Computer wirelessly connected

Sharing Your Files over the Network

You can share your files and folders in the Public folder with anyone who uses your computer, or you can share the Public folder with anyone who can access the network. You can also share the files or folders on your computer with only specific people or with anyone whose computer is on your network.

Set Up Sharing Permission

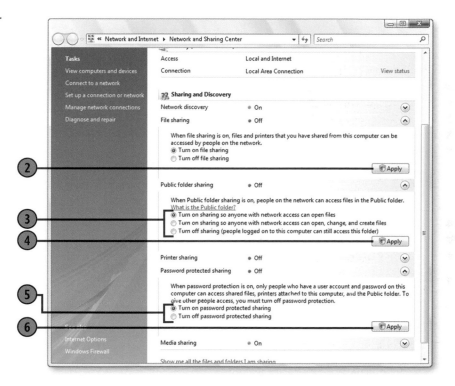

1 Click the Start button, choose Network from the menu, and click Network And Sharing Center.

2 Click the File Sharing down arrow to display the options, choose Turn On File Sharing, and click Apply.

3 Click the Public Folder Sharing down arrow, and select:

- The first option to allow people to open but not save or modify your files (read-only).

- The second option to give full access to the files, including the ability to modify or delete them.

- The third option to deny any access to the Public folders over your network.

4 Click Apply.

5 Click the Password Protected Sharing down arrow, and select:

- The first option to allow sharing to only those with user accounts on your computer.

- The second option to allow access to anyone who can access your network.

6 Click Apply.

Sharing a Folder over the Network

When your computer is on a network, the items you share are usually located in your Public folder. However, if there are folders on your computer that you want other people to be able to access, you can share those folders too.

Share a Folder

① Click the folder you want to share to select it, and then click Share.

② In the File Sharing window, select the name of a person with whom you want to share the folder. The Guest option is available only if password-protected sharing isn't turned on.

③ Click Add.

④ Click a Permission level:

- Reader to allow the user to open files from the folder but not to be able to save changes or modify files

- Contributor to allow the user to open, add, and modify or delete only those files that he or she added

- Co-Owner to allow the user to add, delete, or modify any file in the folder

⑤ Click Share.

⑥ To inform people about the location of the shared folder, click E-Mail, and send the link via e-mail.

⑦ Click Done.

Caution

If you don't have password-protected sharing turned on and you choose Everyone or Guest from the list of people to share with, anyone who has access to your network can access the shared folder.

Sharing a Printer over the Network

If there's a printer installed on your computer and you want other people on your network to use it, you can share it.

Share the Printer

① Click the Start button, choose Network from the menu, and click Network And Sharing Center.

② Click the Printer Sharing down arrow to display the options, select the Turn On Printer Sharing option, and click Apply.

③ Click the Start button, type **pri** in the Search box, and click Printers to open the Printers window. Right-click the printer, and choose Sharing from the shortcut menu to display the Properties dialog box.

④ Click Change Sharing Options, and confirm that you want to change the options.

⑤ Clear this check box if you want the preprinting work (rendering) done on this computer, or select the check box to have that work done on the computer that will be sending the print job.

⑥ Make changes on the other tabs to identify the printer and its location, to specify whether you want a separator page between print jobs, and to specify who can use and control the printer.

⑦ Click OK.

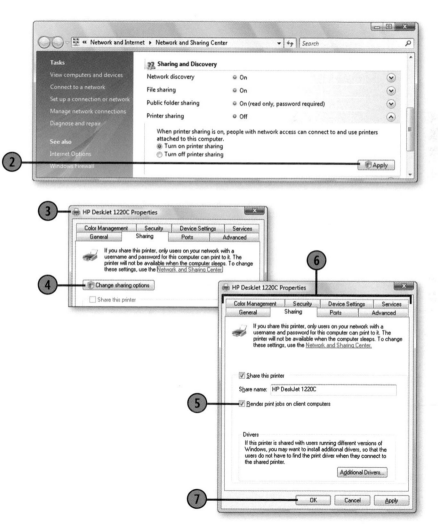

Creating a Connection to a Network Folder

If you frequently use one particular shared folder on the network, you can access that folder quickly by assigning a drive letter to it. By doing so, you'll not only gain quick access to the folder from the Computer window, but you'll also be able to access the folder in programs that don't allow you to browse the network to find a file.

Assign a Drive

1. Click the Start button, and choose Computer from the menu to display the Computer window.

2. Click Map Network Drive.

3. Select a letter for the drive. Only unused drive letters are shown.

4. Click Browse, use the Browse For Folder dialog box to locate and select the folder, and click OK.

5. Select this check box if you always want to connect to this folder. Clear the check box if you want to connect only during this session.

6. Click here if you'll be using a different user name and password to log on to the shared folder. In the Connect As dialog box that appears, enter the user name and password that have been assigned to you, and click OK.

7. Click here if you want to connect to a Web site you can use for file storage.

8. Click Finish.

Tip

If you know the name and location of the folder you want to connect to, type it in the Folder text box, using the form **\\computer\folder**.

Connecting to a Network over the Internet

To connect to a company network over the Internet, you can use a VPN (Virtual Private Network), which provides a secure connection between your computer and the network. The computer you connect to must be configured as a VPN server and must be connected to the Internet. Before you connect, verify that you have the correct name of the host computer and the correct user name and password that have been assigned to you.

Create the VPN Connection

① Click the Start button, and choose Connect To from the menu to start the Connect To A Network Wizard. If you don't see the VPN network you want, click Set Up A Connection Or Network.

② In the Connect To A Network Wizard, select the Connect To A Workplace option, and then click Next.

③ Step through the rest of the Connect To A Network Wizard:

- Click Use My Internet Connection (VPN).

- Type either the domain name or the IP address that was assigned to you.

- Enter a name for the connection.

- Enter the user name and password that were assigned to you for this connection.

- Click Connect.

④ When you're verified and connected, use the connection in any way you want.

⑤ When you've finished, choose Connect To from the Start menu, select the connection, and click Disconnect.

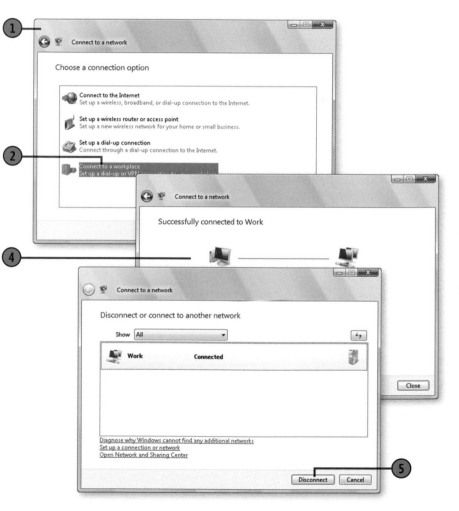

Connecting to a Public Wireless Network

The world is bristling with wireless networks, some of which are free with open access, and others that require a passphrase or a security key for access. Windows Vista recognizes the wireless networks that are within range and makes it easy for you to connect to them.

Connect to an Open-Access Network

① Click the Start button, and choose Connect To from the menu to start the Connect To A Network Wizard. If there are numerous network connections, choose Wireless from the Show list.

② Click the network you want.

③ Click Connect.

④ When you're warned that the network is unsecured, click Connect Anyway, and then complete the wizard.

⑤ Use the network. When you've finished your work, choose Connect To from the Start menu, select the network, and click Disconnect.

See Also

"Connecting Without a Network" on pages 226–227 for information about creating an ad hoc (improvised) wireless network between two computers.

Connect to a Secure Network

1. Click the Start button, and choose Connect To from the Start menu to start the Connect To A Network Wizard.

2. Click the network you want, and then click Connect.

3. Type the security key or the passphrase that was assigned to you, or insert the USB portable device that contains the network settings.

4. Click Connect.

5. Specify whether you want to save the network connection and whether you want it to start automatically whenever you start Windows.

6. Click Close, and use the network.

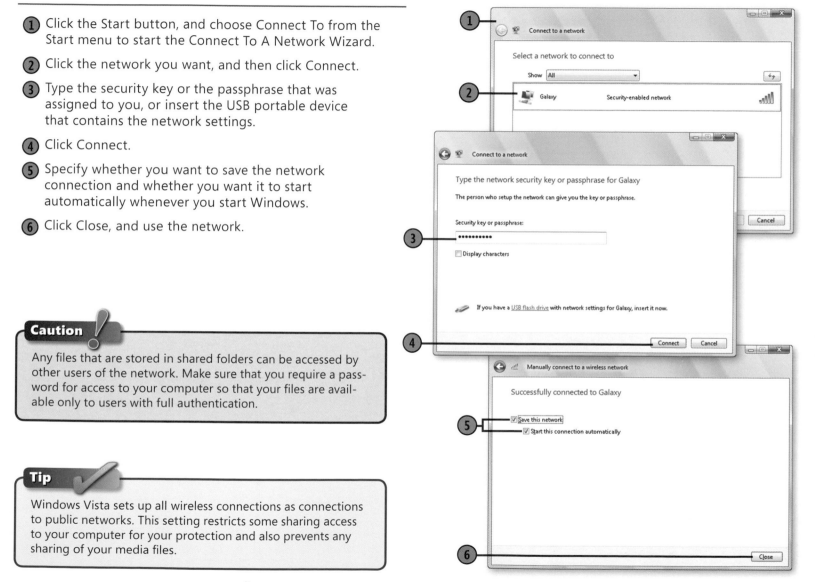

Caution

Any files that are stored in shared folders can be accessed by other users of the network. Make sure that you require a password for access to your computer so that your files are available only to users with full authentication.

Tip

Windows Vista sets up all wireless connections as connections to public networks. This setting restricts some sharing access to your computer for your protection and also prevents any sharing of your media files.

Connecting Without a Network

How do you network when you don't have a network? You can do it using two or more computers that have wireless adapters and are within range of each other. You connect them using an ad hoc network. This temporary network can work just like any wireless network and, provided you use proper security procedures, is as secure as a standard wireless connection. Once it's established, you can access files, play shared games, and do whatever you normally do over any network.

Create a Network

1. Click the Start button, and choose Connect To from the menu. In the Connect To A Network dialog box, examine the existing networks.

2. Click Set Up A Connection Or Network to start the Connect To A Network Wizard.

3. Click to setup a wireless ad hoc network.

4. Click Next, and step through the wizard to name the network and set up the security.

5. Provide others with the name of the network and the security key or passphrase you used.

Caution

Always use some level of security encryption; otherwise, anyone within 30 feet (and probably more) of any computer on your ad hoc network can access your computer.

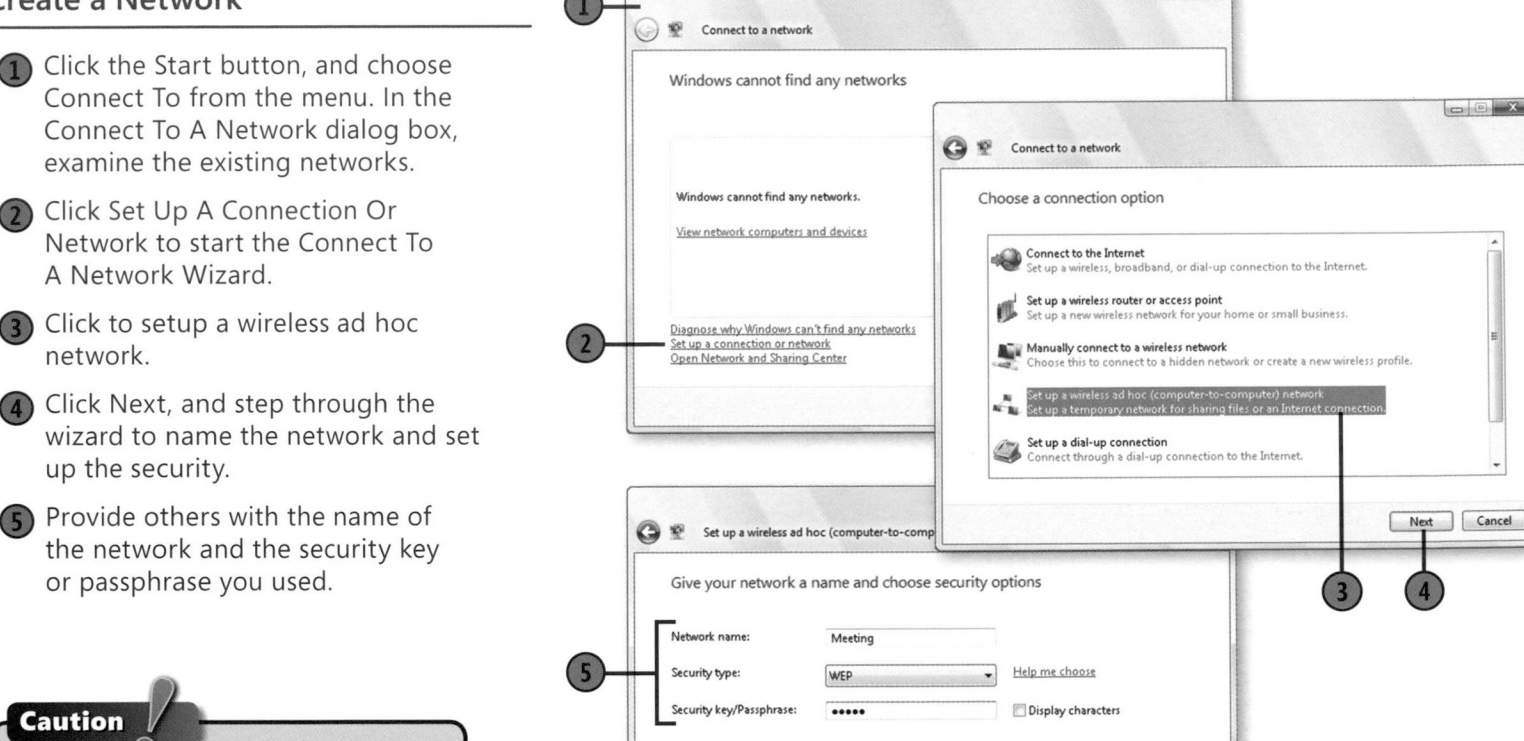

Connect to the Network

(1) With the computers you want to connect situated closely enough to receive each other's signals, choose Connect To from the Start menu to display the Connect To A Network dialog box.

(2) Click the network name that you were assigned.

(3) Click Connect.

(4) Type the security key or passphrase that you were assigned, click Connect, and complete the wizard.

(5) Choose Network from the Start menu, and connect to the other computer or computers. If you don't see other computers or are unable to connect, click Open Network And Sharing Center, and change your sharing options.

Tip

Shared media libraries are disabled if you configure the ad hoc network as a public network. To share music libraries, you must change the network type to a private network.

See Also

"Sharing Your Files over the Network" on page 219 for information about changing your network-sharing settings.

Tip

You can connect to only one network at a time unless you have multiple network adapters.

Hosting a Network Meeting

Windows Meeting Space is a program that makes it possible for you to conduct or participate in virtual meetings over your network. To arrange for a meeting in which as few as two or as many as ten people can participate, one person needs to host the meeting.

Start a Meeting

1. Click the Start button, type **meet** in the Search box, and click Windows Meeting Space. If you aren't already signed in to People Near Me, sign in when prompted.

2. Click Start A New Meeting. If you don't want everyone on the local network to see the meeting, click Options, specify that you don't want to allow the meeting to be visible on the network, and click OK.

3. Enter a meeting name and a password for the meeting, and press Enter.

4. If you want to invite people by sending them the information about the meeting, click Invite.

5. Select the people you want to invite. Only those people who are signed in to People Near Me and are on the same local (subnet) network will be shown.

6. Click Send Invitations.

7. If you want to invite people who aren't listed, click Invite again, click Invite Others, and choose to send an e-mail or create an invitation file.

8. Send the e-mail message or the invitation file, and wait for the recipients to join the meeting.

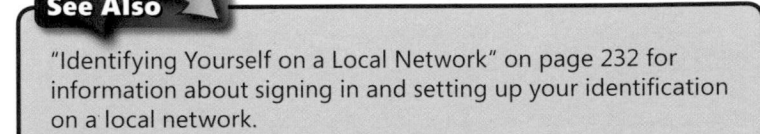

See Also

"Identifying Yourself on a Local Network" on page 232 for information about signing in and setting up your identification on a local network.

Joining a Network Meeting

With Windows Meeting Space, you have a few choices as to how you can join an existing meeting. If you're on the same local (subnet) network as those hosting the meeting, and if the host allowed the meeting to be visible on the network, you can simply browse for the meeting. You can also join a meeting by accepting an invitation or by using an invitation file that someone sent or otherwise made available to you.

Browse for a Meeting

 Choose Windows Meeting Space from the Start menu. If you aren't already signed in to People Near Me, sign in when prompted.

(2) Click Join A Meeting Near Me.

(3) Click the meeting you want, type the password that you were assigned, and press Enter to join the meeting.

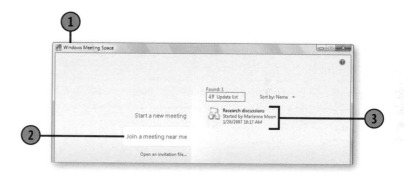

> **Caution**
>
> Be sure to verify the identity of anyone who invites you to a meeting. The safest way is to accept invitations from trusted contacts only.

Accept an Invitation

 Do either of the following:

- If the Invitation Details dialog box appears, click Accept.

- If you receive an e-mail that includes an invitation file, or if you have access to an invitation file, open the file to join the meeting immediately, or save the file for later use.

(2) Type the password that you were assigned, and press Enter to join the meeting.

Participating in a Network Meeting

A Windows Meeting Space meeting allows you to conduct or participate in a virtual meeting over a network. You can invite people to a meeting, provide handouts (in the form of files), share a program, and even show your entire Desktop. Note that Meeting Space requires all participants to have Windows Vista installed on their computers.

Share a Program

1. Start the program you want to share, and set it up the way you want others to see it.

2. With all participants signed in, click Share. Click OK if you see a dialog box about sharing.

3. Select the program, and click Share.

4. With the shared program on top of other windows, work within the program to illustrate your points.

5. If you want a participant to take control of the shared program, click Give Control, and then click the participant's name in the drop-down list. To resume control yourself, click the Give Control button again, and choose Take Back Control.

6. Use the tools to stop sharing, to pause sharing, or to see the meeting as others are seeing it.

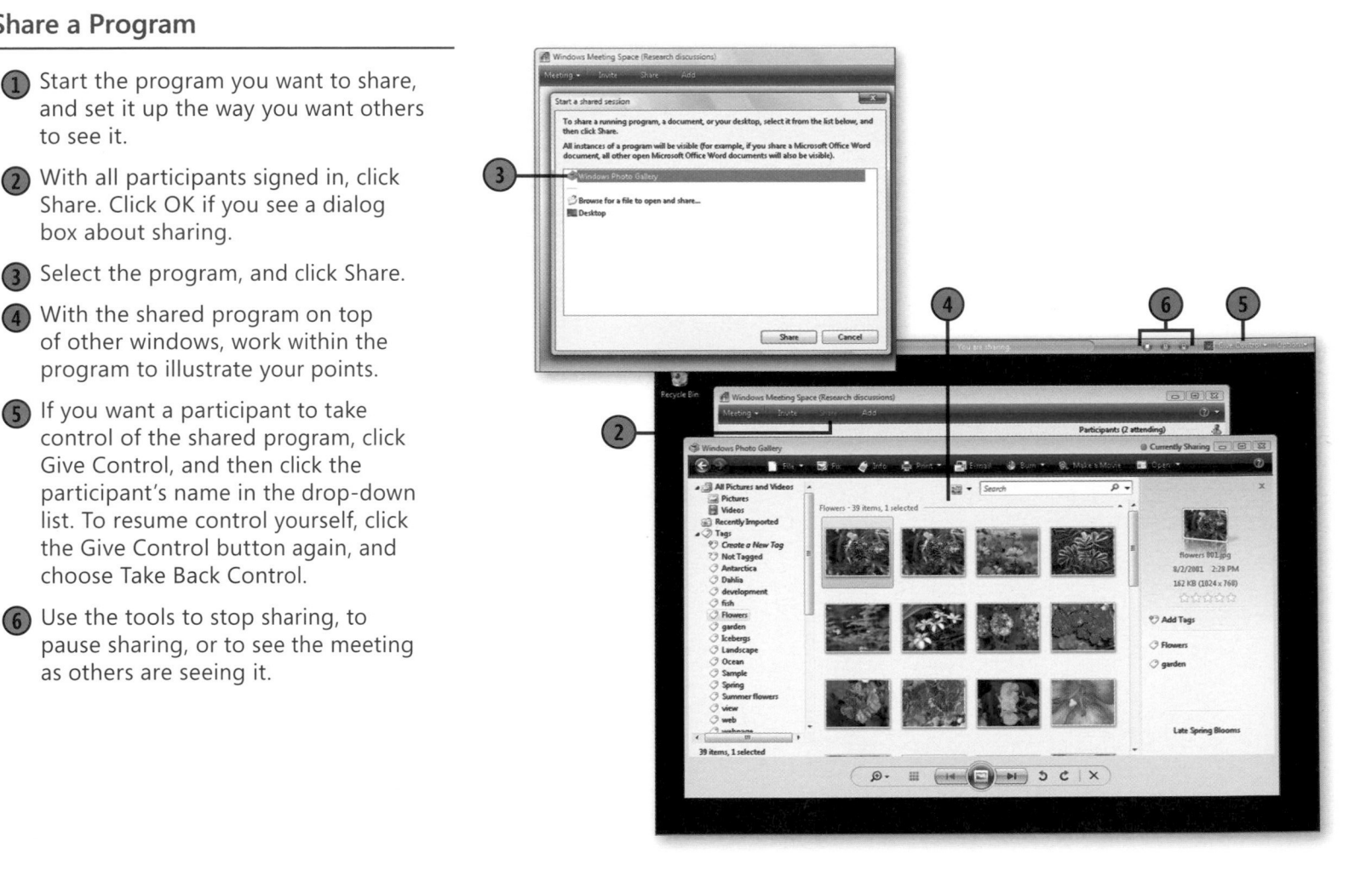

Share Handouts

① Click Add, and click OK if you see a dialog box about handouts. Use the Select Files To Add window to select the files you want to use as handouts, and click Open. The files will then be copied to each participant.

② Double-click a handout, and confirm that you want to open it. If you need to edit the handout, edit it in its program, and then save and close it. The changed version will be copied to all the meeting participants. Note that only one person at a time can edit and save a document.

③ When the meeting is over, click Meeting, and choose

- Save Handouts if you want to save the handout files to your computer.

- Leave Meeting if you need to leave but want Meeting Space to continue to run.

- Exit to leave the meeting and close Meeting Space.

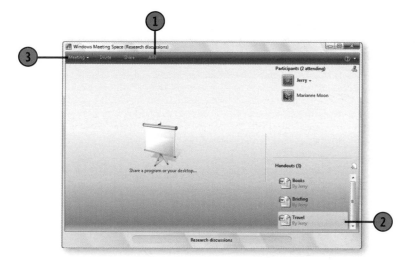

> **Tip**
>
> If, when you're hosting a meeting, you need to leave to attend to something else, the meeting will continue until all the participants leave. That way, you can leave a meeting for a while and rejoin it later.

> **Tip**
>
> To view a handout, you need to have a program that can open the handout file. For example, you'll need Microsoft Excel if the handout is an Excel workbook.

Identifying Yourself on a Local Network

The People Near Me listing service lets you control the way you're identified on a local network and from whom you'll accept invitations for meetings.

Make Your Settings

1. Click the Start button, type **people** in the Search box, and click People Near Me to display the People Near Me dialog box. (If you're already signed in to People Near Me, you can quickly open the People Near Me dialog box by double-clicking the People Near Me icon in the notification area of the taskbar.)

2. On the Settings tab, type the name you want to use for identification.

3. Select this check box if you want your user account picture to be included with your contact information.

4. Specify whom you'll accept meeting invitations from.

5. Select this check box if you want to be notified when you receive an invitation.

6. Select this check box if you want to be signed in automatically every time Windows starts, or clear the check box if you want the information available only when you sign in manually.

7. On the Sign In tab, sign in to or out of People Near Me.

8. Click OK.

> **See Also**
>
> "Creating Trusted Contacts" on page 298 for information about creating a Trusted Contacts list.

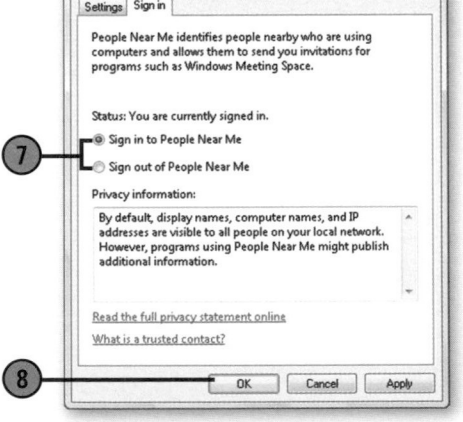

Controlling a Computer over the Network

If you want to give control—or as much control as you're authorized to have—to someone else on the network, you can use Windows Meeting Space to turn over your entire Desktop to a meeting participant.

Turn Over Control

1. Start Windows Meeting Space, start a meeting, and invite the person to whom you want to give control of your Desktop.

2. After he or she has joined the meeting, click Share. Click OK if you see a dialog box about sharing.

3. Select Desktop, and click Share.

4. Click Give Control, and select the name of the person who'll be controlling your computer.

5. Let him or her use any items on the Desktop or open any program from the Start menu.

6. To regain control, click Control again, and choose Take Control or press the Windows key+Esc.

Caution

Sharing your Desktop can be dangerous. Make sure you know who's sharing your Desktop, and watch what's being done. You'll also need to provide administrative permission from your computer anytime it's needed.

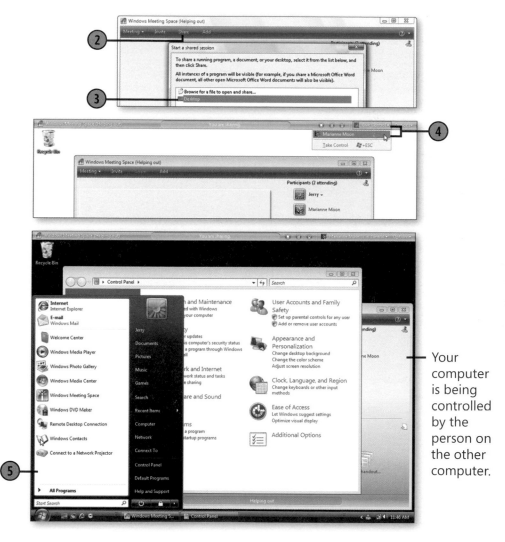

Your computer is being controlled by the person on the other computer.

Holding a Wireless Meeting

Even if you aren't connected to a network, you can still hold an electronic meeting by using Windows Meeting Space and creating a wireless ad hoc network.

Create the Meeting

1. Using a computer that isn't connected to a network, start Windows Meeting Space, and start a new meeting.

2. Enter a name and password for the meeting.

3. Click Options.

4. Select this check box to create an ad hoc network, verify that the country or region is correct, and click OK.

5. Click the Create A Meeting button.

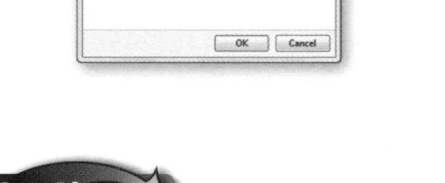

See Also

"Hosting a Network Meeting" on page 228 for information about hosting a Windows Meeting Space meeting.

Tip

You can create an ad hoc wireless network connection using a computer that's already connected to a different network, provided the computer has a separate wireless adapter that will be dedicated to the ad hoc network.

See Also

"Participating in a Network Meeting" on pages 230–231 for information about hosting or participating in a meeting using Windows Meeting Space.

Connect to the Meeting

(1) On the other computer or computers, have the other person or people start Windows Meeting Space.

(2) With Join A Meeting Near Me selected, click the name of the meeting.

(3) Enter the assigned password, and press Enter.

(4) Wait for the network connection to be established, and then conduct the meeting as you would any other Windows Meeting Space meeting.

(5) When the meeting is over, stop sharing any program that's being shared, save any handouts you want to keep, and choose Leave Meeting or Exit from the Meeting drop-down menu to leave the meeting and disconnect the ad hoc network.

Caution

When you create an ad hoc network for your meeting, the network also provides normal network access among computers. This means that if you've shared your Public folder, or any other folders, and you haven't protected them by requiring a user name and password (password-protected sharing), anyone in the meeting can access those folders.

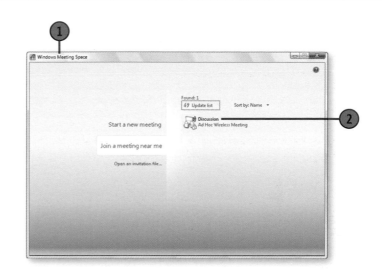

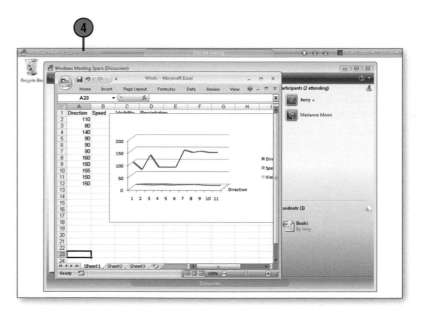

Using a Network Projector

A network projector is one that can display large images of your screen for items such as PowerPoint presentations or demonstrations. There are two main types of projector: a stand-alone projector that you connect to your computer by using cables or a wireless connection, and a network projector. The connection to a stand-alone projector is usually pretty straightforward, but Windows Vista has greatly simplified the sometimes complex connection to a network projector.

Connect

(1) With your computer connected to the network that's hosting the projector, choose Connect To A Network Projector from the Start menu to start the Connect To A Network Projector Wizard.

(2) Select the Search For A Projector (Recommended) option if you know that there aren't many projectors on the network or if you don't know the projector's address. Click the projector you want, click Next, and then provide the password for the projector.

(3) If the search didn't find the projector and you know its address, click to enter the address.

(4) Enter the assigned address.

(5) Enter the assigned password.

(6) Click Next, complete the wizard, and start using the projector.

See Also

"Managing Settings for a Presentation" on pages 310–311 for information about making settings on a portable computer while giving a presentation.

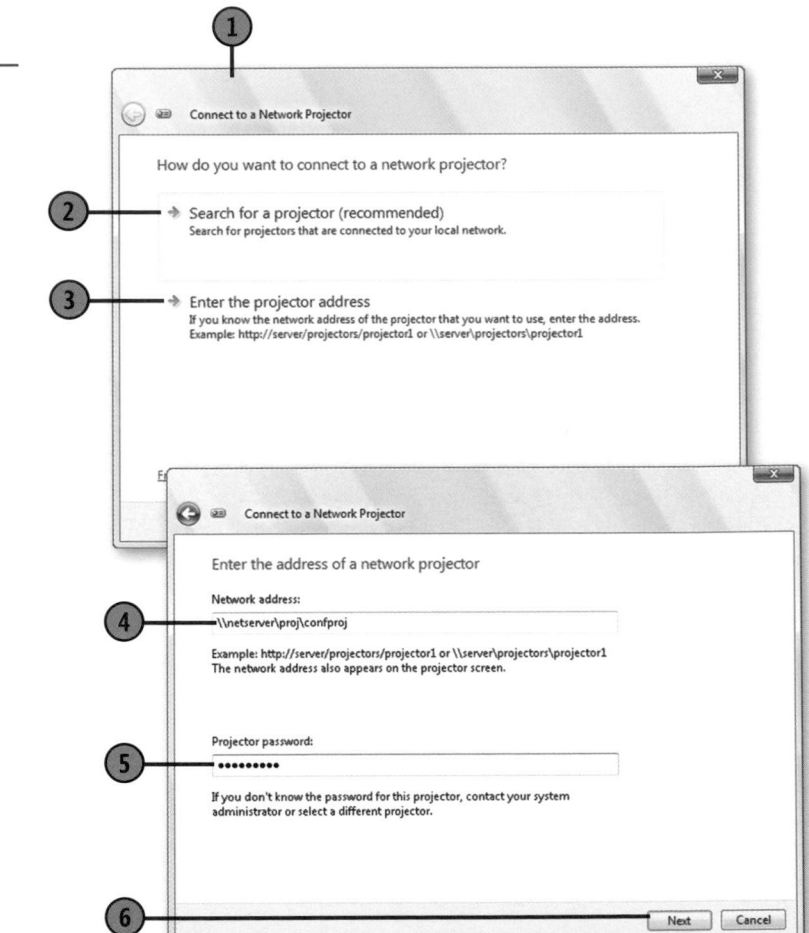

13 Setting Up

One thing that usually takes all the fun out of buying a new computer is having to set up all over again the files and settings that took such a long time to get exactly right on your old computer. Well, we have good news for you! You can transfer your files and settings easily and quickly with the help of a wizard that walks you through the process. If you choose to transfer the information over your network or by using a cable, you provide a few pieces of information and type a password, and the transfer happens automatically. If you use discs to transfer the information, just follow the instructions on the screen until the transfer is complete.

You'll also find information here about setting up dial-up Internet access if a broadband connection isn't available so that you can explore the Web's vastness; setting up Windows Mail for sending and receiving e-mail messages and subscribing to newsgroups; and setting up a printer that's attached to your computer. In addition, we'll talk about turning on or off Windows Vista components or parts thereof, and adding hardware devices to your computer. If these all sound like daunting tasks, rest assured that they're not. With the instructions on the pages that follow, and with help from the wonderful wizards of Microsoft, you'll sail right through them.

Transferring Files and Settings

When you need to transfer your accounts—personal files, computer settings, and the contents of shared folders—from your old Windows XP computer to a new super-duper computer loaded with Windows Vista, Windows provides a wizard that helps you transfer the files automatically using a network or a transfer cable, or manually using removable media. Each method has its own procedures, and the wizard guides you through the specific steps. When connected by a network or a cable, the wizard transfers the information directly from one computer to the other when you enter the key code that's generated by the wizard. If you're using removable media—a CD or a USB device, for example—you record the information on one computer, remove the media, insert the media into the other computer, and then have the wizard copy the information to that second computer. You can also use this method to transfer files and settings from a computer running Windows Vista and, to a limited extent, to a computer running Windows 2000.

Set Up the Computers

① On the new computer, log on as an Administrator, click the Start button, type **easy** in the Search box, and click Windows Easy Transfer to start the Windows Easy Transfer Wizard. Step through the wizard, completing the following information and actions:

- Specify that this is a new transfer.

- Specify that this is the new computer.

- Specify which device you're going to use for the transfer: an Easy Transfer cable, a network, a CD, a DVD, or a USB storage device.

- Select the way you're going to install Easy Transfer on your old computer.

- Create the Easy Transfer setup disc, or copy the material to a USB device or a network folder, if necessary.

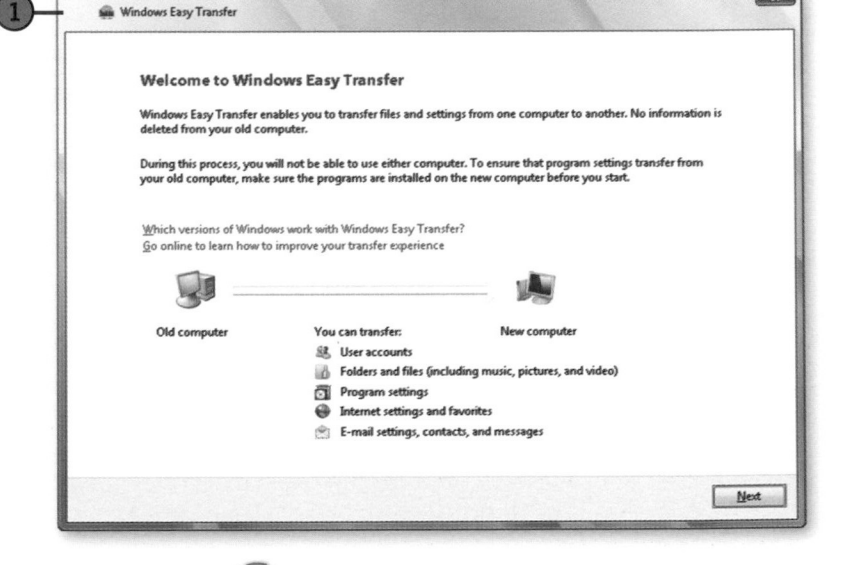

Tip

To transfer your programs from your old computer to your new computer using the Easy Transfer cable or your network, use the Windows Easy Transfer Companion program available for download from Microsoft.

Transfer the Information

① Start the Easy Transfer Wizard on the new computer if the wizard isn't already running.

② On the old computer, close all your running programs, connect any cable or device you'll be using in the transfer, and insert the disc or the USB device; or connect to the network folder that contains the Easy Transfer installation files. When it starts, step through the Easy Transfer Wizard, specifying

- That this is the old computer, if you're asked.

- The way you want to transfer the information.

- Whether you want to copy your own files and settings or the files and settings of all the computer's users. Otherwise, select each item you want to transfer.

- Whether you want to include files other than those selected by the wizard.

③ If you're transferring the information over a network or a cable, choose to get a key, write it down, and then enter it on the other computer when requested. The transfer will take place automatically.

④ If you're using removable media or copying the material to a shared network folder, enter a password to protect the material, and then copy it. Take the completed copy to the new computer, or access the shared network folder, double-click the transfer file on the removable media or in the shared folder to open it, and step through the Easy Transfer Wizard to copy the information.

⑤ Examine the results of the transfer to verify that the files you want have been transferred from the old computer to the new one.

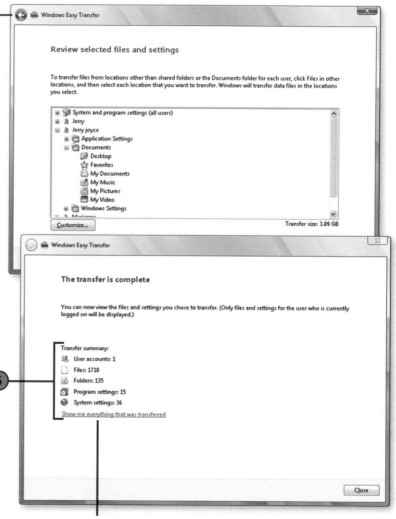

Click to modify the items to be transferred.

Setting Your Default Programs

When you set up Windows Vista, certain programs are designated as the default programs for specific tasks: Windows Mail for your e-mail, for example; Internet Explorer for Web browsing; Windows Media Player for playing videos and digital music; and Windows Media Center for recording TV programs.

However, if there are other programs you'd prefer to use instead, you can set them as your default programs. You can also modify which file types are associated with which programs.

Set the System Defaults

1. Click the Start button, choose Default Programs from the Start menu, and, in the Default Programs window, click Set Program Access And Computer Defaults.

2. In the Set Program Access And Computer Defaults dialog box, click the down arrows for any configuration you might want to use.

3. Review the configuration.

4. Select the type of configuration you want to use. If you chose the Custom configuration, make any changes you want to it.

5. If you don't want the Microsoft program to be available on your computer, clear this check box.

6. Click OK.

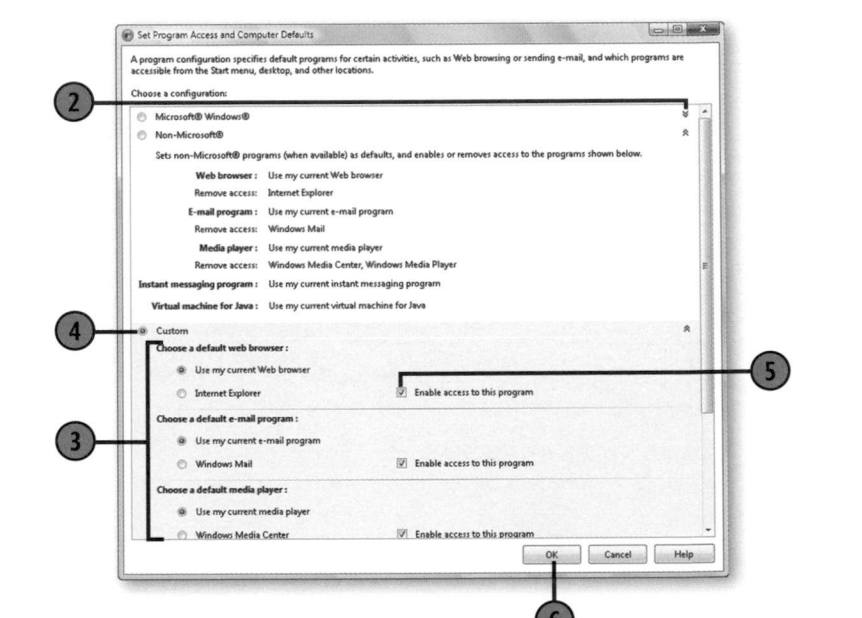

Customize the Settings

1. In the Default Programs window, click Set Your Default Programs to display the Set Default Programs window.

2. Click a program.

3. Click Choose Defaults For This Program.

4. In the Set Program Associations window that appears, specify which file types (extensions) and protocols you want to be used by this program. Items currently checked are already defaults for this program.

5. Click Save.

6. Continue going through the list of programs until you've customized all of them.

7. Click OK when you've finished.

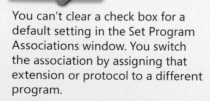

Tip

You can't clear a check box for a default setting in the Set Program Associations window. You switch the association by assigning that extension or protocol to a different program.

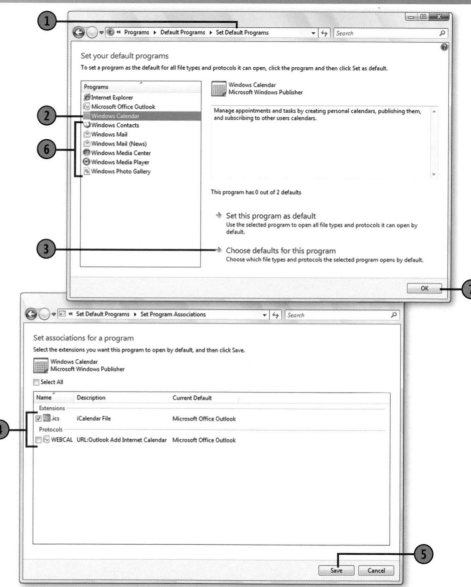

Turning Windows Components On or Off

When Windows Vista is installed on your computer, some—but not all—of its components are available. If any components you need aren't active, you can turn them on, and, by the same token, if there are components you never use, you can turn them off.

Turn a Component On or Off

① Save any documents you're working on, and close all your running programs.

② Click the Start button, choose Control Panel from the Start menu, choose Programs from the Control Panel, and click Turn Windows Features On Or Off in the Programs window that appears.

③ If a plus sign (+) appears next to a component, click it to see the items listed under that component group.

④ To turn a component on, select its check box. To turn a component off, clear the check box.

⑤ Click OK.

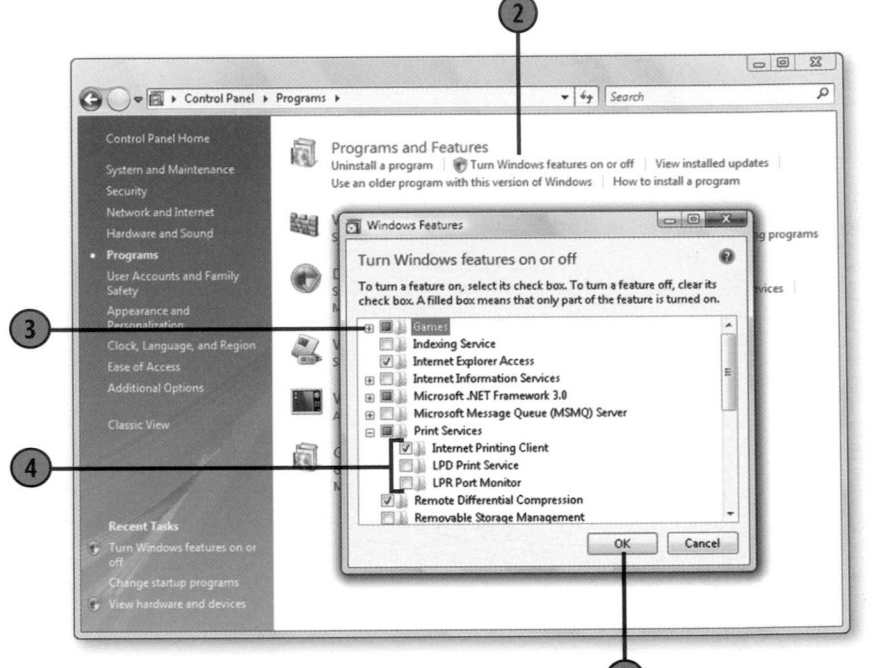

See Also

"Installing Critical Fixes" on page 300 and "Downloading Free Software" on page 314 for information about updating existing Windows components or adding components that have recently been released.

Tip

To install new fonts on your system, click the Start button, type **font** in the Search box, and click the Fonts folder. In the Fonts window, press the Alt key to display the menu bar, and then choose Install New Font from the File menu.

Associating a File Type with a Program

Most of us seem to end up with different programs installed that handle the same file types, although not always in the same way—for example, one program to view and organize your photos and another to edit them. You can tell Windows Vista which program you want to open which file type.

Set a Program to Always Open a File

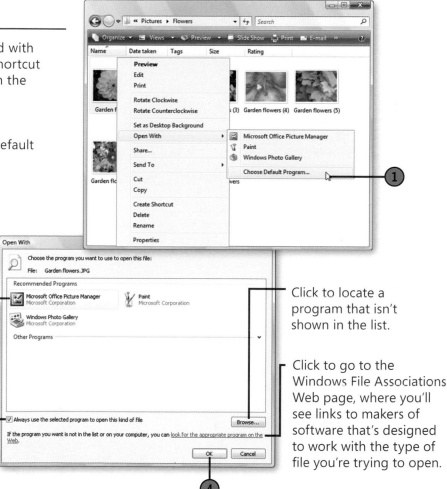

① Right-click the file that you want to be associated with a specific program, point to Open With on the shortcut menu, and choose Choose Default Program from the submenu to display the Open With dialog box.

② Click the program you want to use.

③ Select this check box to make the program the default program for all files of this type.

④ Click OK.

Click to locate a program that isn't shown in the list.

Click to go to the Windows File Associations Web page, where you'll see links to makers of software that's designed to work with the type of file you're trying to open.

Tip

If you choose a program listed on the shortcut menu, the file will open in that program this one time, but the program won't become the default for future use.

Tip

To set the association for any of the file types or protocols on your computer, choose Default Programs from the Start menu, and choose Associate File Types Or Protocols With A Program.

Setting Up Dial-Up Internet Access

Many ISPs (Internet Service Providers) supply installation CDs or other setup discs, and all you have to do is insert the CD or the discs into the appropriate drive and follow the instructions on the screen. However, if you don't have the installation materials, you can easily set up your connection manually.

Set Up a Connection

① Click the Start button, choose Connect To from the Start menu, and click Set Up A Connection Or Network to start the Connect To A Network Wizard.

② Choose Set Up A Dial-Up Connection, and click Next.

③ Enter the connection information you received from the ISP.

④ Click Dialing Rules, and, in the Location Information dialog box that appears, enter your location information and any access codes you need. Click OK when you've finished.

⑤ Select this check box if you want your password to be filled in automatically whenever you use this connection.

⑥ Name the connection.

⑦ Select this check box if you're willing to share the connection with anyone who has a user account on this computer.

⑧ Click Connect to try out the connection.

Control the Connection

① Click the Start button, choose Control Panel from the Start menu, click Network And Internet, and then click Internet Options to display the Internet Properties dialog box.

② On the Connections tab, if you have more than one connection, select the one you want to use.

③ Click Set Default.

④ Specify when you want the connection to be used.

⑤ Click Settings, and, in the Dial-Up Settings section of the Settings dialog box that appears, click Advanced to display the Advanced Dial-Up dialog box.

⑥ Specify how many times you want the number to be redialed if the connection can't be made, and how long to wait between redialings.

⑦ Select the check boxes you want to use to control automatic disconnect.

⑧ Click OK in the Advanced Dial-Up dialog box and in the Settings dialog box.

⑨ Click OK in the Internet Properties dialog box.

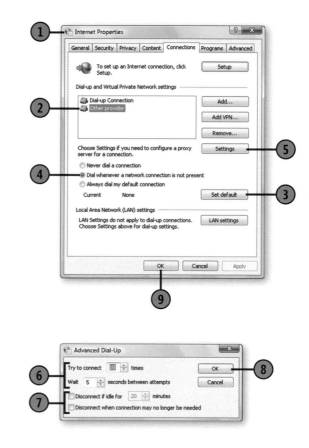

Setting Up Windows Mail

When you first set up Windows Vista, you probably set up your e-mail account at the same time. However, if you didn't set up the account, or if you want to add newsgroups or another e-mail account, you can easily make changes to the Windows Mail setup.

Set Up Your E-Mail Account

1 Click the Start button, and choose Windows Mail from the Start menu. If this is the first time you've started Windows Mail, a wizard will start to help you set up your e-mail account.

2 Step through the wizard, specifying

- Your name as you want it displayed in your e-mail.

- Your e-mail address.

- The type of incoming mail server (POP3 or IMAP, for example) that you obtained from your service provider.

- The addresses of the incoming and outgoing e-mail servers, if they haven't already been supplied.

- Your e-mail account name (usually the same as your e-mail address) and your password.

- Whether your e-mail provider requires you to log on using Secure Password Authentication.

- Whether you want to download all your mail from your mail server.

Your Name

When you send e-mail, your name will appear in the From field of the outgoing message. Type your name as you would like it to appear.

Display name: Jerry

For example: John Smith

Internet E-mail Address

Your e-mail address is the address other people use to send e-mail messages to you.

E-mail address: Jerry@baldwinmuseumofscience

For example: someone@microsoft.com

Where can I find my e-mail account information?

Next   Cancel

Tip ✓

In case you're wondering, POP3 is Post Office Protocol 3, IMAP is Internet Message Access Protocol, HTTP is Hypertext Transfer Protocol, and NNTP is Network News Transfer Protocol. Now you know!

See Also

"Transferring Files and Settings" on pages 238–239 for information about transferring your Windows Mail settings and messages from another computer.

Add an Account

(1) In Windows Mail, choose Accounts from the Tools menu to display the Internet Accounts dialog box.

(2) Click Add.

(3) Choose the type of account you want.

(4) Step through the wizard as you did when you set up your first account. If you're adding a news account, specify the newsgroup account server instead of your e-mail server.

(5) Close the Internet Accounts dialog box when you've finished.

Tip ✓

Gather up all your account information from your ISP before you set up your e-mail account. Mail protocols and server names can be complex and confusing.

Tip ✓

You can't access Web-based mail, such as Hotmail or Windows Live Mail accounts, using Windows Mail, but you can download and use Windows Live Mail Desktop from Microsoft to access these and other accounts.

Setting Up a Printer

Windows Vista might or might not detect your printer, depending on how and to what the printer is attached. Windows should detect and install any printer that's attached to your computer's USB (Universal Serial Bus) or infrared port (provided the printer has been turned on). If the printer is attached to a parallel or serial port, however, Windows might not have detected the printer when it was installed, so you'll need tell Windows about it yourself. If the printer is a network printer, it's usually detected automatically, but, if not, you can manually add it to your printers list.

Set Up a Local Printer

1. If the printer came with an installation disc that's designed to work with Windows Vista, follow the directions that came with the printer to run the installation program. The printer should then be installed correctly.

2. If you don't have an installation disc, with the printer connected and turned on, click the Start button, type **printer** in the Search box, and choose Printers from the menu to display the Printers window.

3. Click Add A Printer to start the Add Printer Wizard.

4. Click Add A Local Printer.

5. Step through the wizard, specifying

   • The port the printer is attached to.

   • The manufacturer and model of the printer.

   • A display name for the printer—that is, the name by which you'll identify it.

   • Whether the printer will be your default printer.

   • Whether you want to print a test page.

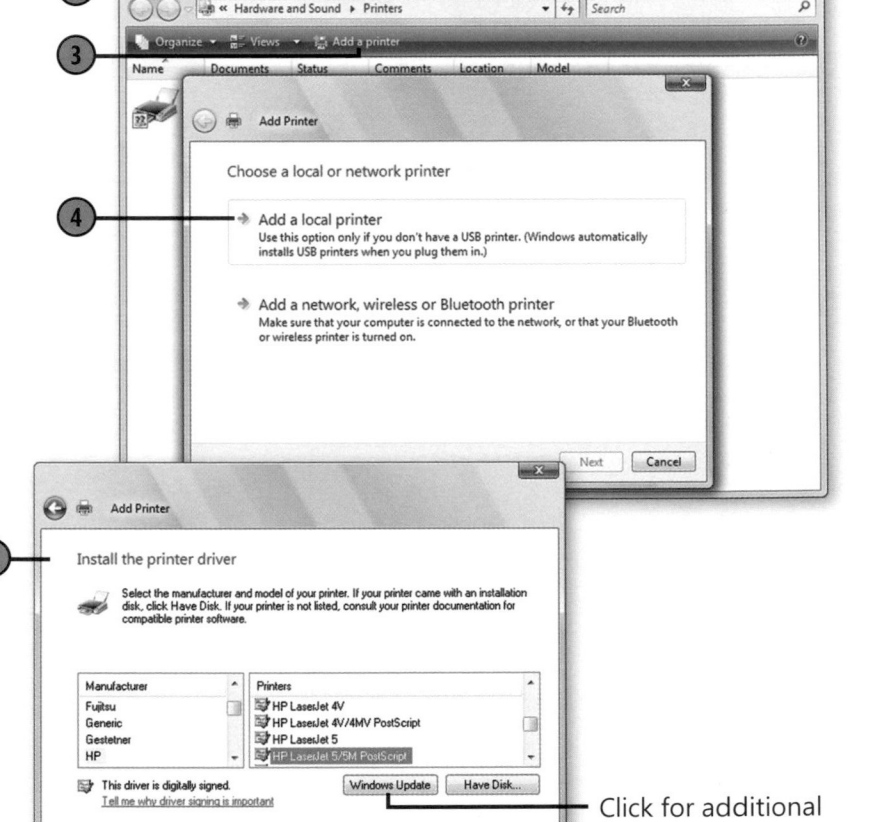

Click for additional printers if your printer isn't listed.

Connect to a Network Printer

1. Open the Printers window, and click Add A Printer to start the Add Printer Wizard.

2. Click Add A Network, Wireless Or Bluetooth Printer.

3. When the search for printers on the network is complete, click the printer you want to use, click Next, and skip to step 6.

4. If the printer you want isn't found, click here to connect manually.

5. Choose to browse your network to locate the printer; enter its location and name; or connect using the TCP/IP address. Click Next.

6. Complete the wizard by assigning a name for the printer and printing a test page.

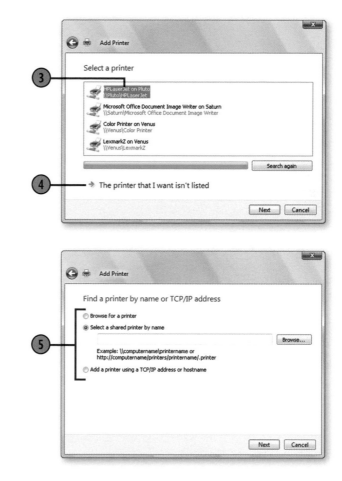

Tip

Make sure the computer that hosts the shared printer is turned on, or you won't see the shared printer in the list of available printers.

See Also

"Sharing a Printer over the Network" on page 221 for information about sharing your printer over a network.

Setting Up Hardware

Most hardware comes with helpful (usually!) installation instructions and an installation disc. However, sometimes all you have is the device. Now what? In most cases, all you need to do is plug the device into your computer and wait for Windows Vista to recognize it and install the necessary drivers for the device to work. Once in a while, though, you might need to do a little more work to get the device running.

Set Up the Hardware Automatically

1. Plug the device into your computer, turn the device on if necessary, and wait for Windows Vista to recognize it and install the necessary driver software.

2. If Windows Vista can't set up the device, connect to the Internet if you aren't already connected, and click this option to search for the driver on Windows Update.

3. If you have a disc that contains the driver software, insert it into the computer, and wait for Windows Vista to find and install the software.

4. If you still can't install the device, click

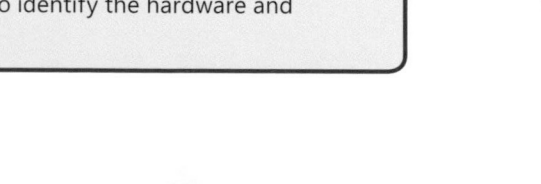

Tip

If you need to attach older hardware that isn't recognized as being connected and that you can't install using the installation disc, choose Control Panel from the Start menu, choose Classic View, and double-click Add Hardware. Step through the Add Hardware Wizard to identify the hardware and (we hope!) install it.

Set Up the Hardware Manually

① With the device not attached to your computer, contact the manufacturer of the device, or search its Web site for the necessary drivers and software for the device. If the software provides an installation program, use it to install the software.

② If there was no installation program, plug the device into the computer, step through the Found New Hardware Wizard, and choose to see other options.

③ Click this option to locate the software on your computer.

④ Click Browse, select the folder that contains the software, and click OK.

⑤ Click Next, and wait for the software to be installed.

Click if you don't have the software and you want more information.

Caution

Make sure that you obtain the driver software from a known and reputable source. Illicit driver software is sometimes used to plant viruses or spyware. Also, make sure that the driver software is designed to work with Windows Vista.

Setting Up a SideShow Device

Windows SideShow is a new technology that lets you see information from your computer on a SideShow-enabled external device even when the computer is sleeping. This is achieved by using certain gadgets that work with your computer's power-management system. Gadgets are specialized small programs, each of which is designed to provide a single type of information—new e-mail messages, for example, or appointments, news headlines, or pictures.

Set Up SideShow

1. Set up the device according to the manufacturer's instructions. Install any gadgets you want to use that came with the device.

2. Click the Start button, type **sides** in the Search box, and click Windows SideShow to open the SideShow window.

3. Select the gadgets that you want to run on the device.

4. Click to set a schedule for when you want your computer to automatically wake up and update the device.

5. Click to modify the settings for the device.

6. In the Change Device Settings window, make any changes you want to the settings. Each SideShow device has its own settings.

7. Click OK.

8. Close the Windows SideShow window when you've finished, and use the controls on your SideShow device to control the display.

Click to connect to the Internet to find more gadgets.

14 Customizing

You can customize just about everything on your computer to make it look and work exactly the way you want. It's fun to experiment with the various themes, and to try out the Windows Aero glass feature for a cool transparent look in parts of Windows components. You can not only create a screen saver with pictures from your Photo Gallery—you can even use a video clip as part of your screen saver. You can change the size and color of almost everything; set items to open with one click instead of two; and rearrange or hide the taskbar, toolbars, Start menu, and Desktop items. You can even customize your little friend the mouse.

You can use a single window in which to open all your folders, or use a separate window for each folder; and you can choose the details—date, author, and so on—that you want to be shown in your folder windows. If you sometimes work in a different language, you can switch the layout of your keyboard to conform to that language, and you can add clocks that let you check the time in other cities or countries. If you have any problems with your vision, hearing, or manual dexterity—or if you just want to try a different way of working—the Ease Of Access Center presents an array of alternative tools that you'll want to try.

Changing the Overall Look

The visual and auditory interface elements of Windows Vista—colors, Desktop background, icons, sounds, screen savers, mouse pointers, and so on—are all part of a *theme*. Windows Vista comes with a few themes, other themes are available as add-ons, and you can also create your own themes. If the new look of Windows Vista doesn't appeal to you, you can revert to the look of earlier versions of Windows.

Change the Theme

1. Click the Start button, type **pers** in the Search box of the Start menu, click Personalization to open the Personalization window, and choose Theme to display the Theme Settings dialog box.

2. If you already have some customized settings that you want to save, with Modified Theme selected, click Save As. In the Save As dialog box that appears, name the current theme, select a different location in which to save it if you want, and click Save.

3. Select a different theme.

4. Preview the theme.

5. If you like the appearance of the theme, click OK.

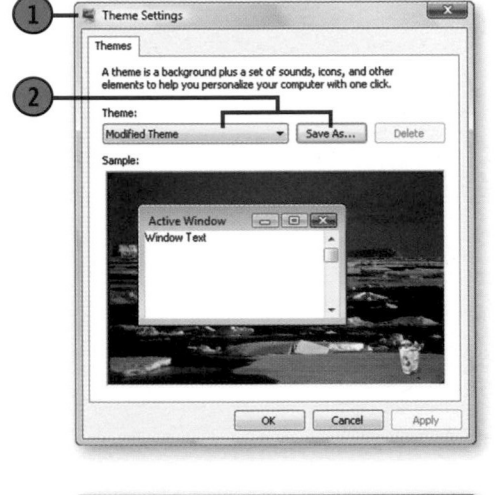

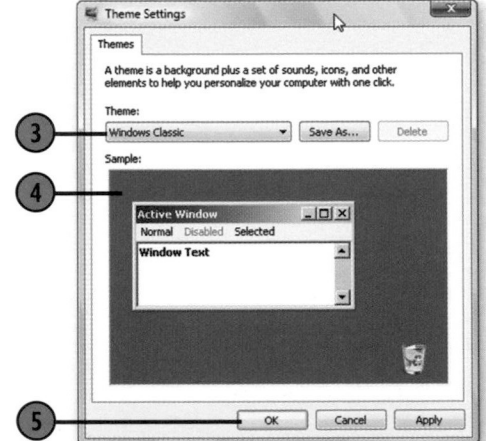

Adjusting the Windows Aero Glass Effect

One of Windows Vista's most dramatic appearance effects is the color and the transparency of windows and other objects. You can adjust this effect to create the look you like. Note that you must be using the Windows Aero color scheme to apply these effects, and that the Aero glass effect is available only on computers that have display adapters powerful enough to show it. It's also not available in the Windows Vista Home Basic version.

Adjust the Color Scheme and Glass Effect

① Click the Start button, choose Control Panel from the Start menu, and, in the Appearance And Personalization section, click Customize Colors to display the Window Color And Appearance window.

② Choose the color scheme you want.

③ Select this check box if you want window components to contain transparent portions.

④ Adjust the intensity of the color.

⑤ If you want to create a custom color, click Show Color Mixer.

⑥ Use the sliders to adjust the hue, saturation, and brightness to create the color you want.

⑦ Click OK.

See Also

"Changing the Color Scheme" on page 256 for information about selecting the Aero color scheme if your computer supports displaying it and if it isn't already selected.

"Checking the Status of Windows" on page 306 for information about whether your computer can display the Aero glass effect.

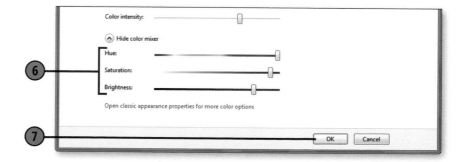

Changing the Color Scheme

If Windows Vista's master color scheme doesn't appeal to you, you can easily change it to look exactly the way it looked in earlier versions of Windows. You can also adjust the color scheme to increase the contrast so that items are easier to see. (Note that the Window Color And Appearance window appears if you have the Windows Aero color scheme enabled. Not all computer systems support or offer the Windows Aero color scheme.)

Change the Color Scheme

1. Click the Start button, choose Control Panel from the Start menu, and, in the Appearance And Personalization section, click Customize Colors.

2. If the Window Color And Appearance window appears, click this option to open the Appearance Settings dialog box.

3. Select the color scheme you want.

4. Click Effects if you want to

   • Choose the method for smoothing screen fonts.

   • See shadows under menus.

   • See the window contents while you're dragging a window.

5. Click Advanced if you want to change the color, size, or font of individual items in the scheme you're using.

6. Click OK.

> **Tip**
>
> The ClearType option in the Effects dialog box smoothes the edges of screen fonts and can dramatically improve the readability of text, especially on a flat screen.

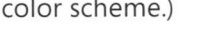

Setting Your Desktop Background

One of the ways you can personalize your computer is to choose an image you like for the background of your Desktop.

The image can be a single color, a pattern, or your favorite picture or photograph.

Set the Background

① Click the Start button, choose Control Panel from the Start menu, and, in the Appearance And Personalization section, click Change Desktop Background to display the Desktop Background window.

② Select the wallpaper picture or color you want, and specify its location:

- Windows Wallpapers to use one of the background patterns or pictures that came with Windows Vista

- Pictures, Sample Pictures, or Public Pictures to use a picture from one of those locations

- Solid Colors to use a single color

③ Click Browse if you want to locate and use a picture from another location.

④ Select the item you want as your Desktop background.

⑤ Specify whether you want the picture stretched to fit the screen, shown at its standard size and repeated to fill the screen (tiled), or shown at its normal size and centered within a colored background that fills the rest of the screen.

⑥ If you chose to center the picture, click this option to set the background color.

⑦ Click OK.

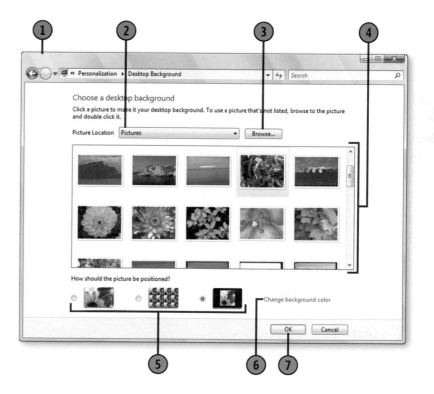

Using a Screen Saver

A screen saver can provide a nice little respite from your work, as well as some privacy. If you work with other people, you might not want them to be able to read your screen, albeit unintentionally, any time your computer is unattended. To prevent anyone from using your computer—but still allow network access to it—when you're away from your desk, you can use the password option. You'll need sign in to Windows Vista using your password when you're ready to get back to work.

Choose a Screen Saver

① Click the Start button, type **pers** in the Search box, click Personalization, and then click Screen Saver in the Personalization window to display the Screen Saver Settings dialog box.

② Click a screen saver in the Screen Saver list.

③ Click Settings.

④ Specify the options you want for the screen saver. (Some have no options; those that do have their own unique settings.) Click OK when you've finished.

⑤ Click Preview to see the screen saver in full-screen view. Move your mouse to end the preview.

⑥ Specify the length of time you want your computer to be inactive before the screen saver starts.

⑦ Select this check box to require you to log on so that you can get back to work.

⑧ Click OK.

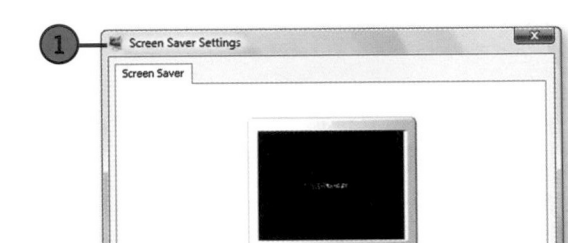

Create a Custom Screen Saver

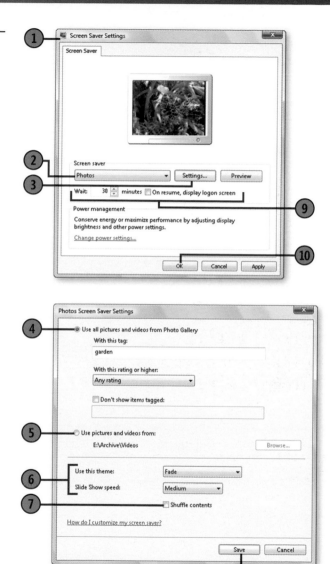

(1) Click the Start button, type **pers** in the Search box, click Personalization, and then click Screen Saver in the Personalization window to display the Screen Saver Settings dialog box.

(2) Select Photos in the Screen Saver list.

(3) Click Settings.

(4) Select this option to use items from your Photo Gallery. You can limit which items you want to be shown by specifying tags or ratings.

(5) Select this option if you want to use items from a specific folder, and click Browse to specify the folder.

(6) Select a theme for the display, and select the speed at which you want the pictures to change.

(7) Select this check box to have the pictures appear in random order.

(8) Click Save.

(9) Make any additional settings for the screen saver.

(10) Click OK.

Tip

If you use the Photos option for your screen saver, you can include videos as part of the screen saver.

See Also

"Controlling the Volume" on page 170 for information about setting the sound volume for your screen saver.

Customizing Your Mouse

You're probably on pretty friendly terms with your mouse, but haven't you sometimes wished that you could build a better one? If your mouse's occasional disobedience is a source of frustration, you can lay down the law and tell that critter how to behave, and then you'll live together happily ever after.

Set the Buttons

1. Click the Start button, type **mou** in the Search box of the Start menu, and click Mouse to display the Mouse Properties dialog box.

2. On the Buttons tab, select this check box to switch the function of the buttons for left-handed or right-handed operation.

3. Move the slider to set the speed at which you need to double-click for Windows to recognize your double-click. Double-click the folder icon as a test to see whether the setting is correct for your clicking speed.

4. Select this check box if you want to be able to select content or drag the mouse without having to hold down the mouse button. With the check box selected, the ClickLock feature is activated when you hold down the mouse button for a short time and is then deactivated when you click the mouse button. Use the Settings button to set the length of time the mouse button needs to be held down to activate ClickLock.

5. Click Apply.

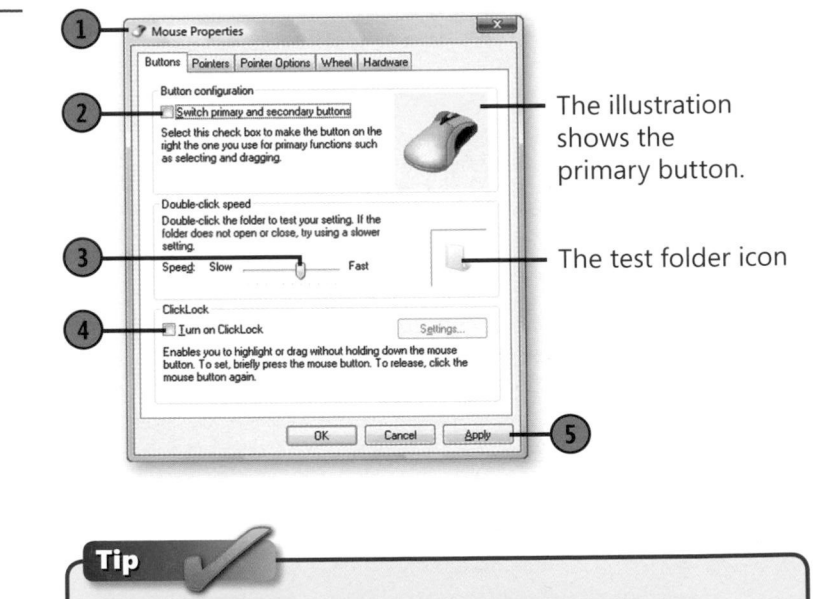

The illustration shows the primary button.

The test folder icon

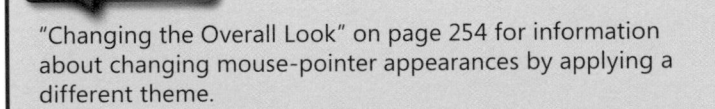

Tip

You can also open the Mouse Properties dialog box by choosing Mouse in the Hardware And Sound section of the Control Panel.

See Also

"Changing the Overall Look" on page 254 for information about changing mouse-pointer appearances by applying a different theme.

Set the Mouse Pointer

1 Click the Pointer Options tab of the Mouse Properties dialog box.

2 Use the slider to set the speed at which you want the mouse pointer to move. Move your mouse to see how the setting affects its speed.

3 Select this check box if you want to increase the precision of the pointer when you move short distances.

4 Select this check box if you want the mouse to automatically move to the default button in a dialog box to facilitate quick selection of the button.

5 Select this check box, and use the slider to set the length of the trails if you want to increase the mouse pointer's visibility by temporarily showing its path.

6 Select this check box if you find the mouse pointer's visibility annoying or distracting when you're typing and not using the mouse. The pointer will reappear when you move the mouse.

7 Select this check box if you need help locating the mouse pointer on your screen. When you press the Ctrl key, an animated bull's-eye will appear, indicating the pointer's location.

8 On the Pointers tab, choose a theme to change the overall appearance of the mouse.

9 Use the options on the Wheel tab to specify the way you want the mouse to move when you scroll the wheel.

10 Click OK when you've finished.

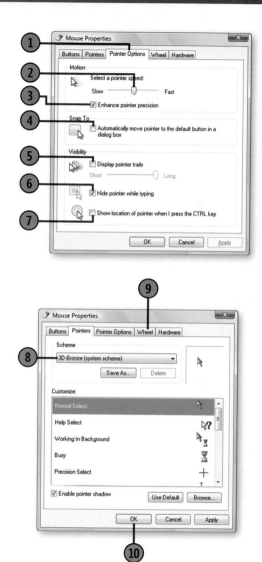

Customizing the Taskbar

The taskbar is a really handy navigation device, and you can make it even more useful by customizing it to your work habits. You can specify which items you want to be displayed on the taskbar and how you want them displayed, and you can even hide the taskbar when you aren't using it and then make it reappear when you need it.

Customize the Taskbar

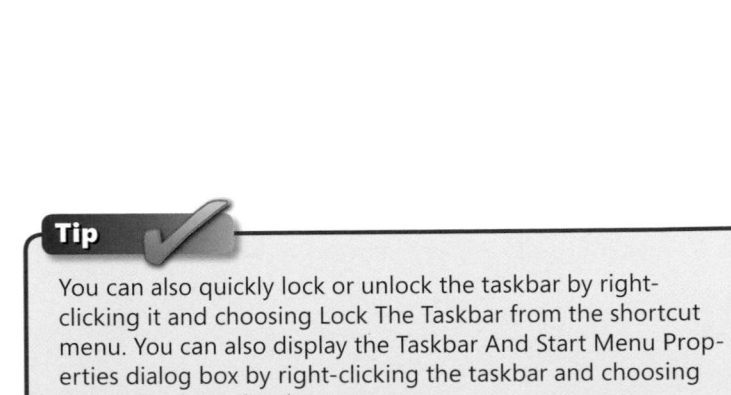

1. Click the Start button, type **taskb** in the Search box of the Start menu, and click Taskbar And Start Menu to display the Taskbar And Start Menu Properties dialog box.

2. Select this check box to prevent the taskbar from being moved to a new location or to prevent toolbars from being resized.

3. Select this check box to hide the taskbar when you're not using it. The taskbar will reappear when you move the mouse to whichever edge of the screen contains the taskbar.

4. Select this check box to prevent other windows from obscuring the taskbar.

5. Select this check box to have similar items grouped on one button when the taskbar is crowded.

6. Select this check box to display the Quick Launch toolbar.

7. Select this check box to show a thumbnail image of the window when you point to the button on the taskbar.

8. Click Apply if you've made any changes.

Tip

You can also quickly lock or unlock the taskbar by right-clicking it and choosing Lock The Taskbar from the shortcut menu. You can also display the Taskbar And Start Menu Properties dialog box by right-clicking the taskbar and choosing Properties from the shortcut menu.

Customize the Notification Area of the Taskbar

 On the Notification Area tab of the Taskbar And Start Menu Properties dialog box, select this check box to hide the icons for items that aren't running or aren't currently active.

② Click Customize to specify when you want icons to be displayed on the taskbar.

③ In the Customize Notification Icons dialog box, click an item, and, in the drop-down list that appears, specify whether you want the icon to be hidden when inactive, to always be hidden, or to always be displayed.

④ Click OK.

⑤ Select this check box to have the clock displayed on the taskbar.

⑥ Select this check box to have the Volume icon displayed on the taskbar.

⑦ Select this check box to have the network status displayed on the taskbar.

⑧ Select this check box to have the power status displayed (for portable computers only).

⑨ Click OK.

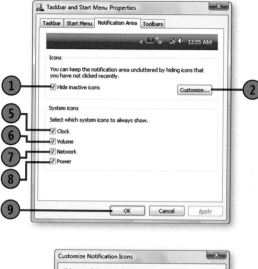

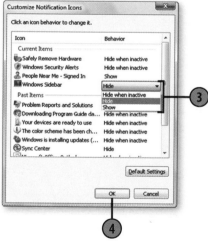

Tip

Whenever you need to access a hidden icon, just click the Show Hidden Icons button on the left side of the notification area of the taskbar.

Moving the Taskbar

The taskbar normally resides at the bottom of your computer's Desktop. However, you can move the taskbar to any side of the Desktop and then resize it to work best at that location.

If you're using multiple monitors, especially if you're giving a presentation, you can also move the taskbar onto one of the monitors so that it won't be visible during your presentation.

Move and Resize the Taskbar

(1) Point to a blank spot on the taskbar, and drag the taskbar to the side of the Desktop where you want it. If the taskbar doesn't move, right-click it, and if the Lock The Taskbar command has a check mark next to it, click the command to unlock the taskbar. When the taskbar is unlocked, you can drag it to the new location.

(2) Place the mouse pointer on the outer edge of the taskbar until the pointer turns into a two-headed arrow.

(3) Drag the border to change the width of the taskbar.

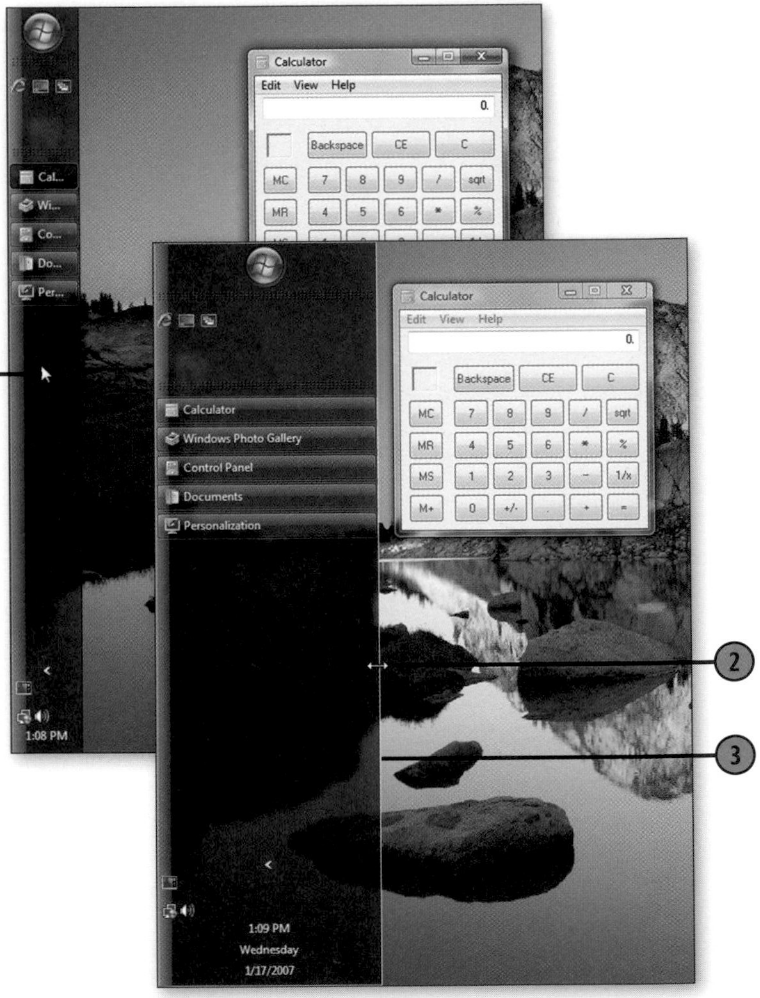

See Also

"Move the Sidebar" on page 47 for information about moving the Sidebar.

Tip

The Start button and the Start menu move with the taskbar, so if you move the taskbar to either side of your Desktop, you won't be able to see most of the items on the taskbar when you open the Start menu. Therefore, unless you have any reason not to do so, it's best to place the taskbar at the top or bottom of the Desktop window.

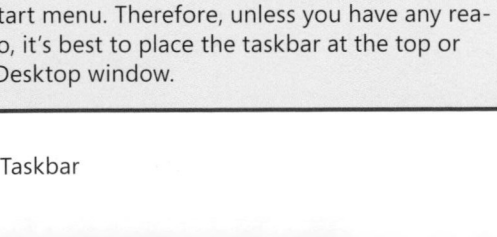

Customizing the Desktop Icons

You can display all the standard Desktop icons, hide them, or show only the ones you want. You can also change the image for each icon and adjust its size, and then arrange the icons however you want to see them on your Desktop.

Select and Modify the Icons

1 Click the Start button, type **pers** in the Search box of the Start menu, and click Personalization to display the Personalization window.

2 Click Change Desktop Icons to display the Desktop Icon Settings dialog box.

3 Select the icons you want to be shown on the Desktop.

4 To change the appearance of an icon, select it, click Change Icon, and, in the Change Icon dialog box that appears, click the image you want to replace that of the selected icon. Click OK.

5 Click OK.

6 Right-click a blank spot on the Desktop, point to View, and specify

- The size you want for the icons.

- The alignment you want.

- Whether you want the icons to be shown on the Desktop or hidden.

> **Tip**
>
> You can also open the Personalization dialog box by right-clicking anywhere on the Desktop and choosing Personalize from the shortcut menu.

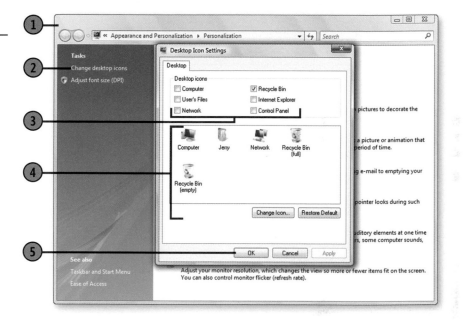

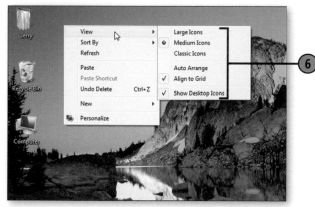

Customizing the Start Menu

The Start menu is your main resource for organizing your programs and files and getting your work done in Windows Vista. You can customize the Start menu in several ways: You can change its new Windows Vista look so that it looks like the Start menu in an earlier version of Windows, you can modify the way items are displayed on the Start menu, and you can add items to or delete items from the main part of the Start menu and from the All Programs folder or its subfolders.

Choose and Customize the Style

① Click the Start button, type **start** in the Search box of the Start menu, and click Taskbar And Start Menu to display the Taskbar And Start Menu Properties dialog box.

② On the Start Menu tab, click an option to specify the style you want for the Start menu.

③ Click Customize to display the Customize Start Menu dialog box. (The contents of the dialog box that appears might differ from the one shown here, depending on the style you selected for the Start menu.)

④ Specify the items to be displayed and how you want them displayed.

⑤ Specify how many recently used programs you want to be listed.

⑥ Select these check boxes if you want links to your Internet browser and e-mail program to appear on the Start menu, and, if so, specify the programs.

⑦ Click if you want to remove all custom settings.

⑧ Click OK.

⑨ Click OK to close the Taskbar And Start Menu Properties dialog box.

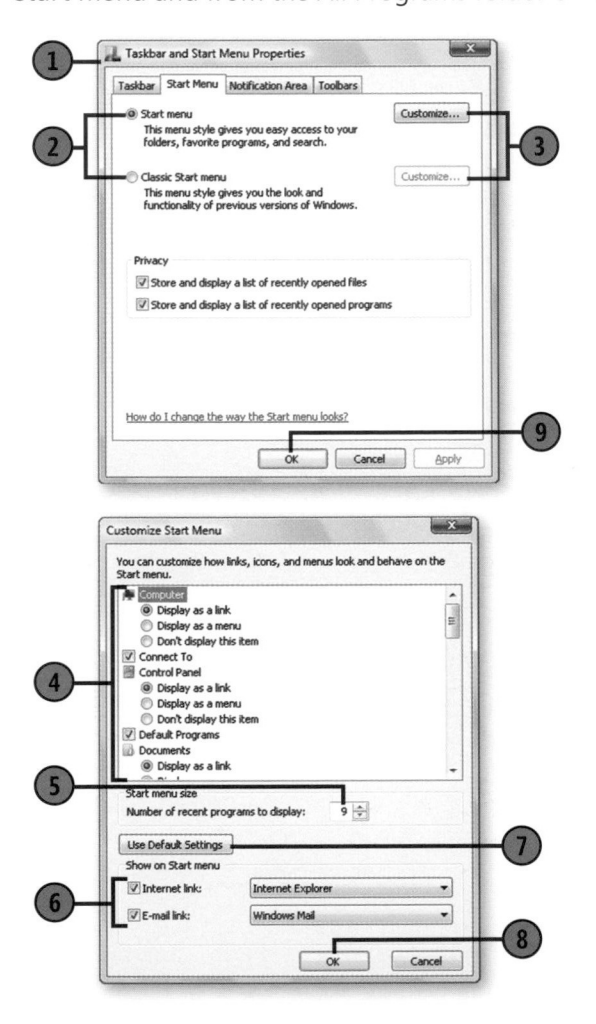

Add or Remove a Start Menu Program

① Click the Start button, and choose All Programs from the Start menu.

② Open any folder you need to locate the program you want to add to the main part of the Start menu, and right-click the program.

③ Choose Pin To Start Menu from the shortcut menu.

④ Right-click a program that has been "pinned" to the Start menu, and choose Unpin From Start Menu from the shortcut menu to remove the program.

Add a Link to an Item

① Locate the item, and drag it onto the Start button.

② Click the Start button, and verify that the item is now on the Start menu.

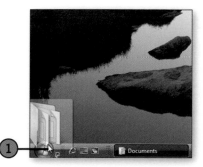

Customizing Your Folders

Working in Windows Vista means that you work with folders. To adapt the folders to your working style, you can customize them so that they look and work in exactly the way you want. Some of the changes you make will apply to all your folders, and other changes will apply to the single folder that's open. In some cases, you can first apply the changes to a single folder, and then, if you want, you can apply the changes to all your folders.

Change the Way All the Folders Work

1. In a folder that you want to modify, click Organize, and choose Folder And Search Options from the drop-down menu to display the Folder Options dialog box.

2. Specify whether you want to use the Windows Vista style or an earlier Windows style.

3. Specify whether you want all your folders to open in the same window (that is, to replace the window's current content), or to use a separate window for each folder that you open.

4. Click the first option if you want to click only once to open an item in a folder. Click the second option if you want to double-click to open an item. If you chose the first option, specify how you want the icon text to be underlined.

5. Click the View tab.

6. Select the check boxes for the options you want and clear the check boxes for the options you don't want.

7. Click if you want to apply the current view setting to all folders of this type.

8. Click OK.

Change the Content That's Shown

① Right-click the descriptive label, or detail, of one of the columns in the folder window (Name, for example), and, on the shortcut menu that appears, click an unchecked item to display that label if it isn't shown, or click a checked item to hide that label. If you don't see the item you want, click More.

② In the Choose Details dialog box, select the check boxes for the labels, or details, that you want to be shown in the folder window, and clear the check boxes for the details that don't need to be shown.

③ Use the appropriate buttons to change the order of the labels or to show or hide them.

④ Specify the width in pixels of the column for the selected label.

⑤ Click OK when you've finished.

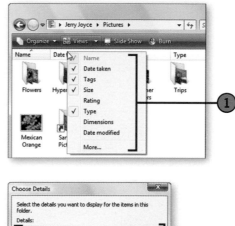

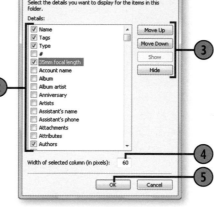

Try This!

To apply the same view to all folders of the same type, select a view from the Views button, choose Folder Options from the Tools menu, and, on the View tab, click the Apply To Folders button. Click OK.

Tip

Windows Vista looks at the content of a folder and applies a template for that type of content. For example, it uses one template for a folder of pictures and another template for a folder of music. If you want to change the template, press the Alt key to show the menu bar, and choose Customize This Folder from the View menu.

Changing Your Account Picture

When you set up your account, you have a selection of pictures to choose from to use next to your name. The picture you choose is important because not only does it appear when you log on to Windows Vista and at the top of the Start menu, but you can also use it when you sign in to People Near Me, in your Contacts file and business cards, in Windows Meeting Space, and in other programs. If you don't like the current picture, or if it has no relevance to your personality—and if you have a picture that's just right—you can change the picture.

Change Your Picture

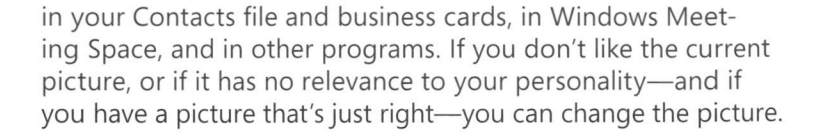

1. Click the Start button to open the Start menu, click your account picture at the top of the menu, and, in the User Accounts window that appears, choose Change Your Picture.

2. Click a picture you want to use.

3. If you don't like any of the pictures, click Browse For More Pictures, locate and select any picture you want, and click Open.

4. Click Change Picture.

5. In the User Accounts window and/or on the Start menu, verify that you can now see the picture you want.

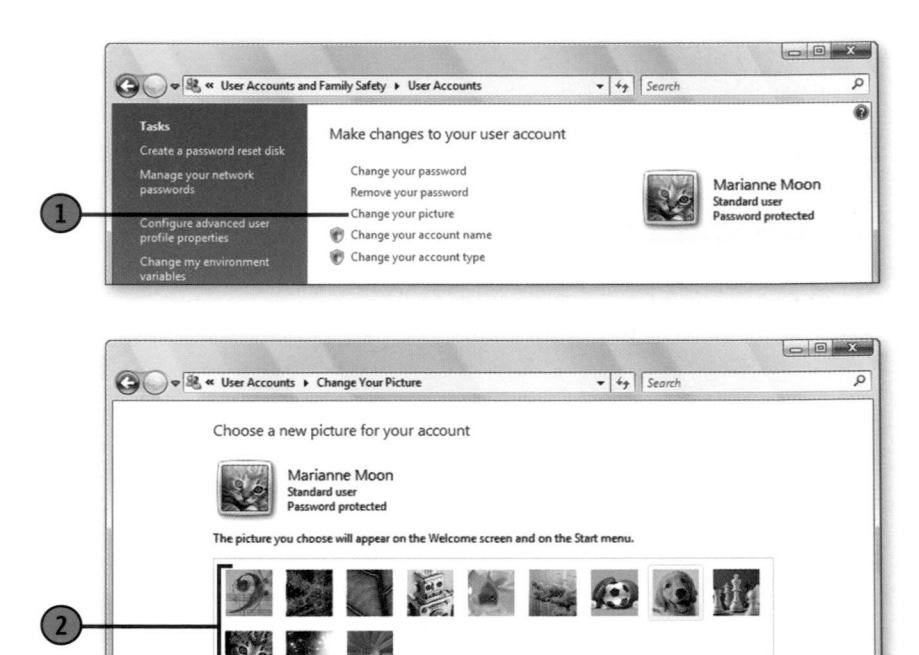

> **Tip**
>
> The space where the user account picture goes is designed for a square picture, so if your picture isn't square, you might want to crop it in Paint or in another photo-editing program to eliminate any blank space.

Changing the Way a CD Starts

When you insert a CD, a DVD, a USB media device, or any other removable media device, Windows Vista detects the type of content—music, pictures, or a movie, for example.

You can set Windows to perform a specific action for each media type and/or device.

Set the AutoPlay

(1) Click the Start button, choose Control Panel from the Start menu, and, in the Hardware And Sound section, click Play CDs Or Other Media Automatically to display the Auto-Play window.

(2) If you want some action to take place when you insert or attach a media type or media device, select this check box. If you want the action only for the media types and devices for which you set the default action, clear the check box.

(3) For a media type or device for which you want to set the default action, choose the action you want to take:

• An action using a program or a Windows feature

• Open Folder to view files using Windows Explorer

• Take No Action for Windows to do nothing

• Ask Me Every Time to display the AutoPlay dialog box showing available actions

(4) Repeat step 3 for other media types or media devices.

(5) Click Save.

Using Alternative Ways of Working

If you have any difficulties when you're working with your computer, the Ease Of Access Center provides easy steps you can use to set up your computer with alternative tools and settings that will make the work easiest for you.

Set the Options

(1) Click the Start button, type **access** in the Search box, and click Ease Of Access Center to display the Ease Of Access Center window.

(2) Select these check boxes if you want the contents of this section read aloud and want to have each of the tools highlighted in order.

(3) If you want to use any of the listed tools to improve the view, to have the window's contents read to you, or to use the On-Screen Keyboard for alternative input, click the tool or press the Spacebar to select the highlighted tool.

(4) Select the scenario that best fits the way you want to adjust the system.

(5) Select the item or items you want to use.

(6) If necessary, for each item, select an option or click an item to make additional settings. Click Save when you've finished.

(7) Select any other scenario that fits your needs, and repeat steps 4 through 6.

> **Tip** ✓
>
> To quickly open the Ease Of Access Center, press the Windows key+U. Alternatively, you can click Ease Of Access and then click Ease Of Access Center in the Control Panel.

Working Alternatives

Windows Vista provides several tools and settings that let you change the way you enter information into, or receive information from, the computer. These tools and settings—although designed primarily for people who experience difficulty when typing, using the mouse, seeing details on the screen, concentrating, or hearing sounds—can be used by anyone who'd like to try different ways of working on the computer. For example, you can use the keyboard to execute mouse actions, or use the mouse or another pointing device for keyboard input.

You can access these tools and settings from the Ease of Access Center, or you can walk through a five-step wizard that tries to identify the best settings for your needs by choosing the Let Windows Suggest settings in the Ease Of Access section of the Control Panel. You can also access six tools and settings (Narrator, Magnifier, High Contrast, On-Screen Keyboard, Sticky Keys, and Filter Keys) from the Logon screen when you sign in by pressing the Windows key+U to display the Ease Of Access Center window.

Alternative Tools

Windows Vista provides four major tools to help you do your work.

Narrator: Reads aloud the text on your screen.

Magnifier: Enlarges the active section of your screen.

On-Screen Keyboard: Displays a keyboard on your screen; you then use the mouse or another pointing device to type your text.

Speech Recognition: Recognizes your voice commands and standard dictation commands.

Alternative Settings

Windows Vista provides numerous settings that help you work, some of which change the way Windows works and others that adjust the look of your screen. The most common settings are listed below.

StickyKeys: Sets key combinations with the Alt, Ctrl, and Shift keys to be pressable one key at a time.

FilterKeys: Ignores repeated characters or too-rapid key presses.

ToggleKeys: Makes different sounds when you turn the Caps Lock, Num Lock, or Scroll Lock key on or off.

SoundSentry: Flashes a specified screen component when the system beeps.

High Contrast: Sets the color scheme for Windows Vista to High Contrast to improve the visibility of components.

MouseKeys: Sets the numeric keypad to control mouse movements.

You can also adjust the general Windows Vista environment by changing the size and color of the mouse, execute mouse actions by pointing (hovering) instead of clicking, underlining access and shortcut keys, and setting the duration for which notification dialog boxes that appear from the notification area of the taskbar are shown. Other settings depend on whether a program or a file supports those features—turning off unnecessary animations, for example, or removing backgrounds, showing text captions for spoken dialog, or providing audio descriptions of actions in videos.

Working in a Different Part of the World

If you're working in, or producing documents for use in, a region or country other than the one for which your computer was configured, you can change the default region and have Windows Vista adjust the numbering format, the type of currency, and the time-and-date schemes used by your programs. If you're working in a different language, you can switch the layout of your keyboard to conform to that language.

Change the Default Region

1. Click the Start button, type **region** in the Search box of the Start menu, and click Regional And Language Options to display the Regional And Language Options dialog box.

2. On the Formats tab, select the regional language you want to use.

3. Inspect the sample formats to make sure they're displayed as you want.

4. If you want to change any of the formats, click Customize This Format, make your changes on the Numbers, Currency, Time, or Date tabs of the Customize Regional Options dialog box, and click OK.

5. On the Location tab, select the country or region in which you'll actually be doing your work.

6. Click Apply.

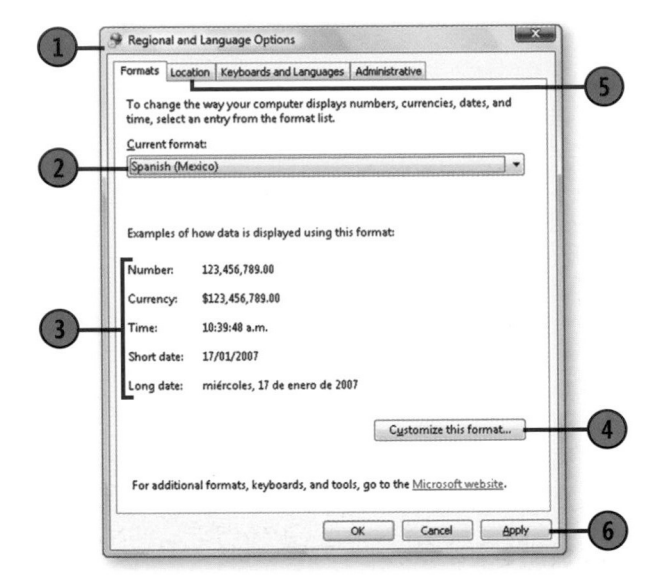

See Also

"Add Keyboard and Language Support" on the the facing page for information about adding languages.

Tip

If you want to use more than one regional setting on your computer, you can add additional languages. When you switch the input language using the Language bar or a keyboard shortcut, the regional settings also change.

Add Keyboard and Language Support

1 On the Keyboards And Languages tab of the Regional And Language Options dialog box, click the Change Keyboards button to display the Text Services And Input Languages dialog box.

2 Select the language you want as the default input language.

3 Click the Add button to display the Add Input Language dialog box.

4 Click the plus sign next to the language you want, and then click the plus sign next to Keyboard to see a list of keyboards.

5 Select the keyboard layout you want. Select Show More if you want to display a list of all the available keyboard layouts.

6 Click OK.

7 On the Language Bar tab, specify the way you want the Language bar to be displayed.

8 On the Advanced Key Settings tab, configure keyboard shortcuts that you can use to switch between languages.

9 Click OK, and then click OK again in the Regional And Language Options dialog box.

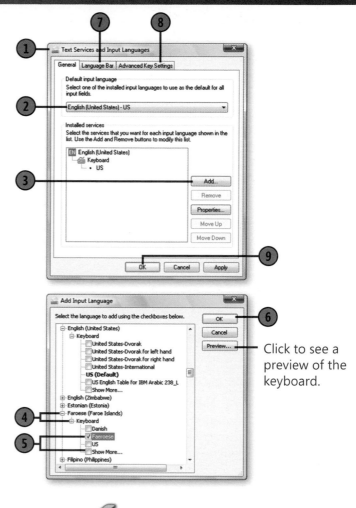

Click to see a preview of the keyboard.

 Tip

To quickly switch between languages, click the language icon on the Language bar, and choose the language you want from the drop-down list; or use the keyboard shortcut you set on the Advanced Key Settings tab.

Tip

To add special keyboards, such as a left- or right-handed Dvorak keyboard, select the language you're using, expand the list of keyboards, and select the keyboard you want to use.

Adding Time Zone Clocks

If you want to keep track of what time it is in a different city or country, you can add a clock set to that particular time zone to the clock that's already on the taskbar. You can add up to two clocks for different time zones. However, note that the clocks, like the calendar, are there solely for your information and can't be used to change the time or the time zone.

Create the Clocks

1 Click the Start button, type **time** in the Search box, and click Date And Time to display the Date And Time dialog box.

2 On the Additional Clocks tab, select this check box to show an additional clock.

3 Select the time zone you want.

4 Enter a short, descriptive name for the new clock.

5 Select this check box, and repeat steps 2 through 4 if you want to add another clock.

6 Click OK.

7 To see the clocks, click the clock on the taskbar.

8 Click anywhere outside the window to close it.

Tip ✓

To quickly see the clock times, point to the clock on the taskbar to show a small window with the time in digital format for each clock.

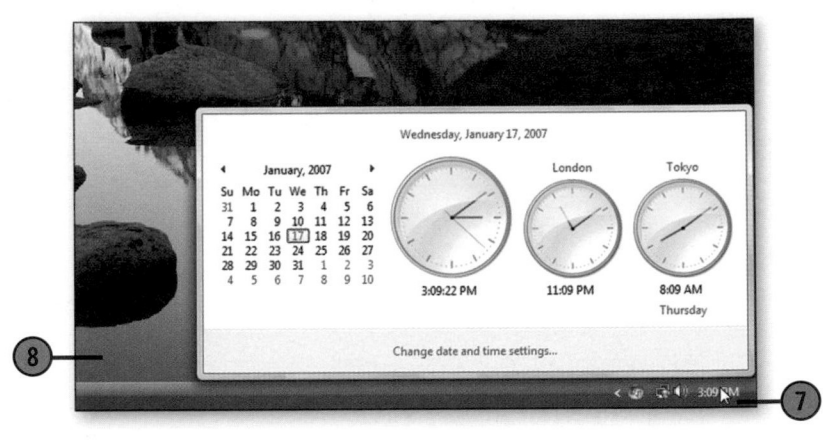

15 Maintaining Security

In days of old, only the administrators of large corporate networks dealt with computer security. These days, with the proliferation of computer viruses, constant connections to the Internet, home networks, and sophisticated hacking techniques used by an ever-growing cadre of snoops and pranksters, everyone should be vigilant. In this section you'll find valuable information about the ways you can protect your files, your privacy on the Internet, and so on. If other people use your computer, you can protect your files from prying eyes by restricting *user rights,* by creating a password that protects the computer from unauthorized access, or by locking your computer.

Windows Vista provides many powerful built-in security features, but you have to do your part too, so in this section you'll find a useful list of things you can do to improve your own security, including checking in periodically with the Windows Security Center to verify that your firewall, virus protection, and software updates are working hard to protect your computer. If several people use your computer (especially if any are children), you can use parental controls to restrict access to games, TV, movies, and Internet sites that contain material you consider inappropriate, and you can apply similar restrictions to movies and DVDs in Windows Media Center.

Know Your Rights

Windows Vista provides several tools to help you effectively maintain security on your computer system. One of the principal ways to maintain security is to assign specific rights to each user of the computer. Those rights can range from simply being allowed to use the computer all the way up to having permission to make changes to the entire system. You specify user rights by assigning individual users to an appropriate group.

User Groups

What you're allowed to do on your computer depends on the user group—Administrator, Standard, or Guest—of which you're a member. You can see which group you've been assigned to by choosing Control Panel from the Start menu and clicking the User Accounts category.

Administrator Group: Users have full control of the computer and can make any changes to the system, including adding or removing software, changing user accounts, and even modifying the Windows Vista configuration. You should log on as an Administrator only when you're certain you know what you're doing, only when you're making extensive changes to your computer, or when you're using certain administrative tools that will run only when you're logged on as an Administrator. As an Administrator, when you choose a command that does something Windows Vista considers a security-sensitive action, you'll be asked to confirm that you want to continue with that action. This confirmation prevents viruses, hackers, and other malicious entities from doing something bad to your computer. The confirmation process, called the User Account Control (UAC), occurs only when the UAC is enabled. Although it's enabled by default, it is possible to turn it off, which is *not* a good idea! For information about the UAC, see "Authorizing Administrative Actions" on page 287.

Standard Group: Users can do most things that don't affect the overall setup of the computer, including running programs, using and creating files, and installing some programs. When a security-related task needs to be executed and the User Account Control is enabled, Windows Vista asks the user to confirm administrative approval by providing the password for an Administrator account; or, if a program won't run unless the user is logged on as an Administrator, the Standard user can often choose to run the program as an Administrator by providing an Administrator's user name and password. Of course, in the latter case, if you haven't been given the password for an administrative account, you won't be able to execute any of those tasks. If the User Account Control has been disabled—which, as we said previously, is a bad idea—a Standard user won't be able to do anything that requires Administrative approval and will need to switch users and log on as an Administrator. Therefore, with the User Account Control enabled, there's no reason for anyone to always be logged on as an Administrator, which makes the computer vulnerable to malicious or accidental actions that can disrupt or even disable all or part of the computer's functioning.

Guest Group: Users are people who don't have user accounts on the computer. By logging on as a member of the Guest group, a user can work on the computer without being able to modify the computer or any files. If you're a Guest user, you're limited in what you can do. You can run existing programs but can't install new programs or make changes to Windows Vista. You can open files that are shared on the computer and possibly shared over the network, depending on the sharing settings, but you can't save changes to those files. You can save or delete only the files you've created yourself. By default, the Guest account is inactive and must be activated before it can be used. There's only one Guest account on the computer, and there's no password for this account.

Setting Your Password

Unless you create a password that allows you to gain entry to your user account, anyone can log on to your computer and access your files. If you want to protect the computer from unauthorized access, create a password that's easy for you to remember and difficult for others to guess.

Create a Password

① Click the Start button, and click your account picture to display the User Accounts window for your account.

② In the User Accounts window, click Create A Password For Your Account to display the Create Your Password window.

③ Type your password, and then type it again to confirm that you didn't make a typing error.

④ Type a hint that will remind you, but no one else, of your password.

⑤ Click Create Password.

Caution

Passwords are *case-sensitive*—that is, *MyPASSWORD* and *mypassword* are two different passwords.

See Also

"Changing Your Password" on page 280 and "Resetting Your Password" on page 281 for information about changing your password.

"Adding or Deleting User Accounts" on pages 302–303 for information about creating a new user account.

Changing Your Password

One of the best ways to prevent others from using your account is to change your password occasionally—especially if you've given it to someone or you suspect that someone might have guessed it or watched you type it. When you change your password, create one that can't be easily guessed (don't use "password" or your well-known nickname, for example), and try to incorporate both uppercase and lowercase letters as well as one or two numbers. Of course, don't make the password so complicated that you can't remember it!

Change Your Password

1. Click the Start button, and click your account picture to display the User Accounts window for your account.

2. Click Change Your Password to display the Change Your Password window.

3. Type your current password.

4. Type your new password.

5. Type the new password again to confirm that you didn't make a typing error.

6. Type a hint that will remind you, but no one else, of this password.

7. Click Change Password.

> **Tip**
>
> For maximum security, use a password that's at least eight characters long and contains upper- and lowercase letters, with at least one number and one symbol, and no real words. This is known as a strong password.

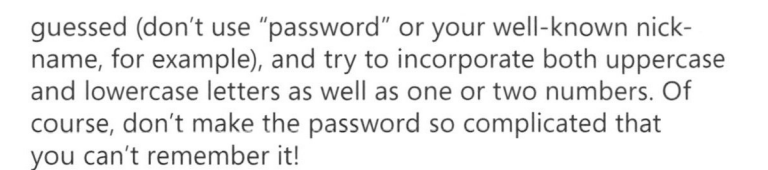

Resetting Your Password

Few things are more maddening than trying repeatedly to log on, only to realize that you've forgotten your password! If this happens, you have two choices: You can reset the password (or, if you're a member of the Standard group, you can ask an Administrator to reset it for you), which means that you'll lose all your settings and any security credentials and

certificates; or you can use your Password Reset disk or USB storage device to log on and reset your password *and* save all your settings and credentials. The latter is obviously the better choice, so you should create a Password Reset disk while you still remember your password.

Create and Use a Password Reset Disk

1. Insert a disk or USB storage device into your computer, click the Start button, and then click your account picture to display the User Accounts window for your account. Click Create A Password Reset Disk in the Tasks list to start the Forgotten Password Wizard.

2. Go through the first two steps of the wizard, and then enter your current password when prompted. Click Next.

3. Wait for the necessary information to be copied to your disk or storage device, and then complete the wizard. Remove the disk or storage device, label it as your Password Reset disk, and place it in a secure location.

4. If you ever forget your password, insert the disk or storage device, and click Reset Password to start the Reset Password Wizard. Step through the wizard, typing a new password and a new (and better!) password hint. After you've completed the wizard, type your new password, and press Enter to log on with your new password.

Tip

To create a Password Reset disk, you can use only a floppy disk (provided your computer has a drive for it) or a USB memory device. You can't use a CD, a DVD, or a removable hard drive.

Caution

Anyone who can access your Password Reset disk (or the storage device that contains your password) can change your password and log on using your account, so be sure to keep the disk or the storage device secure.

Restricting User Rights

One of the surest ways to protect your computer from either malicious or accidental damage is to assign everyone who uses the computer to the Standard group, and allow only one Administrator account for use in executing system changes. Often, however, several people are assigned administrative accounts. You can easily switch those administrative accounts to the Standard group. If you want to further restrict access to specific people, don't assign them user accounts at all; instead, ask them to sign in to the Guest account. Of course, you'll need to activate the Guest account before anyone can use it.

Change the Type of Access

1. Click the Start button, and click your account picture to display the User Accounts window for your account. Click Manage Another Account to display the Manage Accounts window.

2. Click the account you want to manage.

3. In the Change An Account window, click Change The Account Type.

4. Select the Standard User option if it isn't already selected.

5. Click the Change Account Type button.

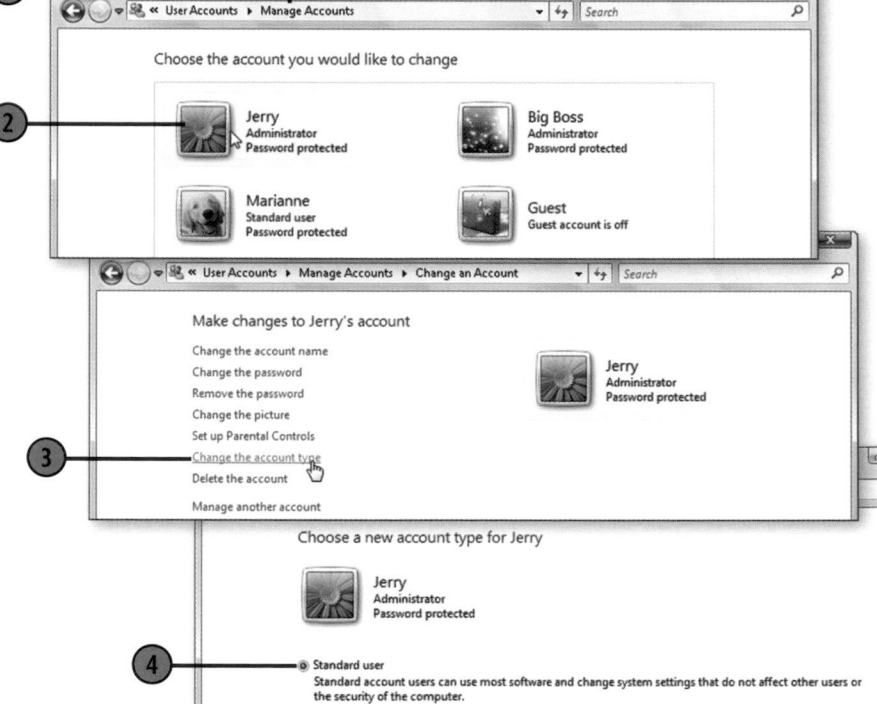
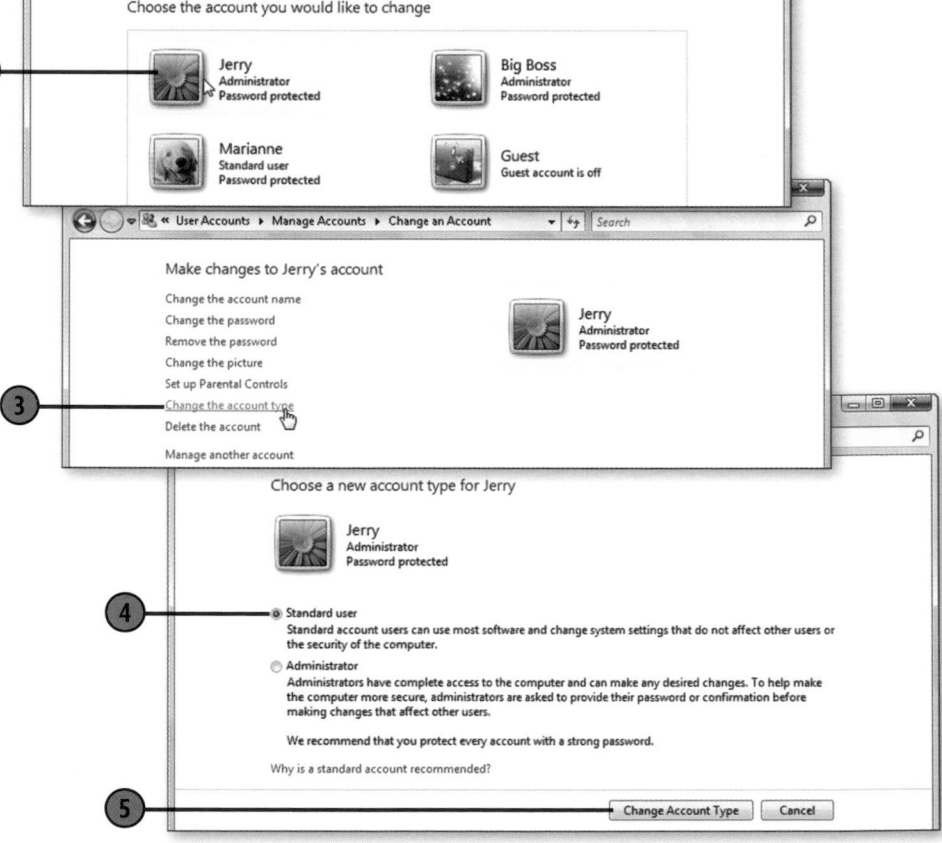

> **See Also**
>
> "Adding or Deleting User Accounts" on pages 302–303 for information about creating or deleting user accounts.

Use the Guest Account

1. In the Change An Account window, click Manage Another Account to display the Manage Accounts window.

2. Click the Guest account.

3. In the Turn On Guest Account window, click the Turn On button.

4. Close the Manage Accounts window when you've finished.

5. If necessary, inform those who want to use the computer that they don't have Standard access, and advise them to log on using the Guest account.

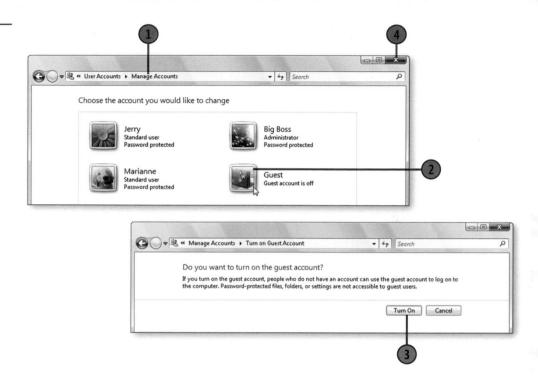

See Also

"Know Your Rights" on page 278 for information about the different types of user accounts.

Tip

If you'd prefer someone who has an account on the computer to log on as a Guest, you can easily delete his or her account. To do so, click the account in the Manage Accounts window, and click Delete The Account. Windows Vista will give you the options of saving any of this user's files (but not their e-mails) to a folder on the Desktop that's accessible only by the person who deleted the account, or of deleting the files.

Protecting Your Account

One of the easiest ways for someone to access your private files is waiting until you leave your computer unattended for a while and then jumping onto the computer using your already logged-on account. To prevent this, you can lock out any access to the computer by other people via your account.

However, you can allow other people to log on using their own accounts and to have network access to the computer. When you lock the computer, all your programs and open files remain running but unavailable until you enter your password.

Lock the Computer

1. Make sure that you have a password assigned to your account.

2. Click the Start button, and then click the Lock This Computer button. The logon screen appears.

3. When you want to resume your work on the computer, type your password, and press Enter. If someone else logged on using his or her account, and your user account isn't already displayed, click your user name, and then enter your password to unlock your user account on the computer.

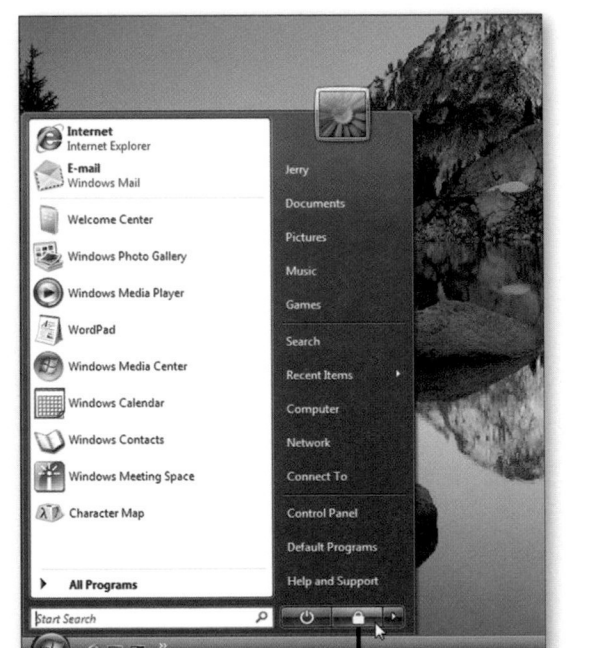

Tip

You can also quickly lock the computer by pressing the Windows key+L.

See Also

"Using a Screen Saver" on pages 258–259 for information about configuring a screen saver to require a password.

See Also

"Starting Up" on page 10 for information about requiring a password when the computer resumes from sleep.

Monitoring Your Security Settings

Although there are many different high-security settings in Windows Vista, there are six big ones: Windows Firewall, Automatic Updating, Virus Protection, Spyware And Other Malware Protection, Internet Security Settings, and User Account Control. In the Windows Security Center, you can easily monitor your settings and can adjust them as needed. All the items shown in the Windows Security Center are part of Windows Vista except for Virus Protection, which you have to obtain separately.

Check Your Settings

① Click the Start button, choose Control Panel from the Start menu, and, in the Security section, click Check This Computer's Security Status to display the Windows Security Center window.

② Check the status of the security features and settings.

③ Click the down arrow next to an active feature to see detailed information about the feature.

④ If you don't have a virus-protection program, click the Find A Program button to go to a Microsoft Web site that features information and links to virus-protection software providers.

⑤ If any other item shown in the Windows Security Center is turned off or is not configured, click the appropriate link, and follow any instructions.

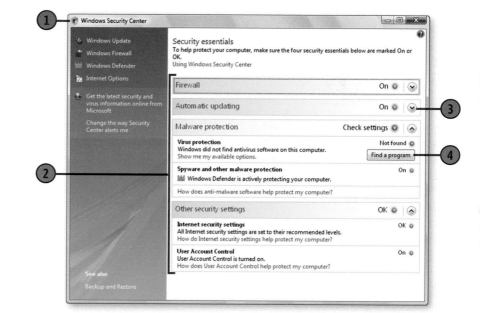

Tip

Windows Defender is a built-in spyware- and malware-protection program. It doesn't, however, protect your computer from viruses.

Configuring the Windows Firewall

A *firewall* is a program that's designed not only to prevent unauthorized and malicious access to your computer over the Internet, but also to prevent unauthorized communications from your computer to the Internet—for example, those that can be made by a spyware program. In other words, a firewall is your defense against hackers, viruses, Trojan horses, worms, and all the other horrors out there in cyberspace. Unfortunately, a firewall can also block legitimate traffic, so you might need to tweak your settings a bit.

Configure the Firewall

1 Click the Start button, choose Control Panel from the Start menu, click Security, and, under Windows Firewall, click Turn Windows Firewall On Or Off to display the Windows Firewall Settings dialog box.

2 On the General tab, verify that the Firewall option is set to On (Recommended). If you're using a public network, select the Block All Incoming Connections check box to increase your security.

3 On the Exceptions tab, select those programs to which you want to grant full access to your network and/or the Internet through the firewall, and clear the check boxes for any programs whose access you want to prevent through the firewall.

4 If the check box for displaying a notice when a program is blocked isn't selected, select it.

5 Click OK.

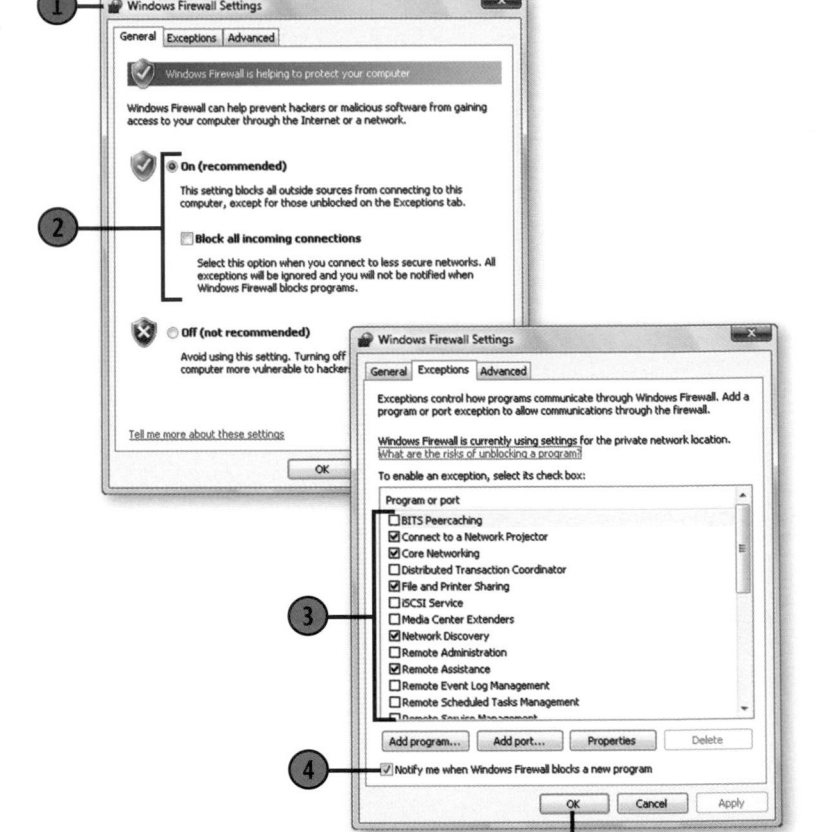

> **Tip**
>
> The first time a program is blocked, a notification appears. You can select the option to allow the program, to always block the program, or to block it this time but to ask you the next time the program is blocked.

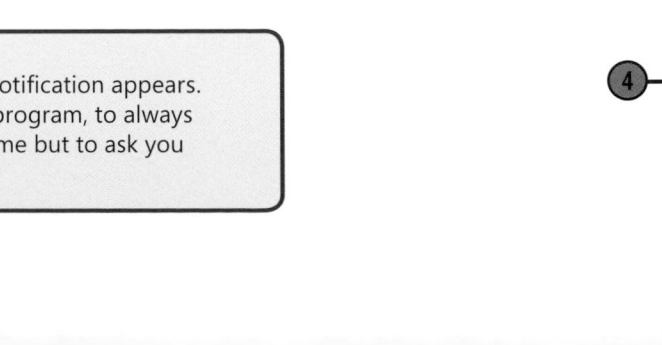

Authorizing Administrative Actions

The User Account Control is a very important part of Windows security and is responsible for all those times a dialog box pops up asking you to verify an action. Although the User Account Control is turned on by default, people sometimes find it so annoying that they turn it off. This action reduces your security and makes it much more difficult to execute actions while you're logged on as a Standard user.

Turn On the User Account Control

① Log on to Windows as an Administrator.

② Click the Start button, choose Control Panel from the Start menu, and, in the Security section, click Check This Computer's Security Status to display the Windows Security Center window.

③ If the User Account Control is shown as Off in the Other Security Settings section, click the Turn On Now button.

④ Click the Restart Now button to restart the computer.

⑤ Log on as a Standard user. When Windows requests your permission to take an action, in the User Account Control dialog box, click an Administrator account, enter the password for that account, and click OK.

Tip ✓

There are four types of situations that require authorization: Windows settings that affect the computer system; running a program that's recognized (digitally signed) but that requires permission to affect the system; running a program that isn't recognized; and trying to run a program that has been blocked from running by parental controls.

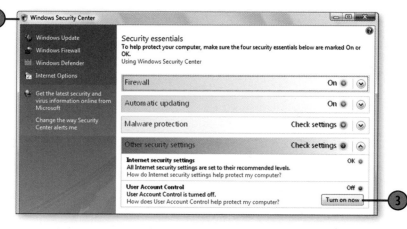

Restricting Access to Web Content

If you're a parent, grandparent, guardian, or concerned relative or friend, a child's access to a computer is a huge source of worry. Fortunately, you can restrict the type of content the child can access, and, if several children have access to your computer, you can make custom settings that are age-appropriate for each child's account.

Set Up Parental Controls

① If any of the individuals whose Web content you want to restrict are logged on, ask them to log off, or log them off yourself.

② Click the Start button, choose Control Panel from the Start menu, and, in the User Accounts And Family Safety section, click Set Up Parental Controls For Any User. In the Parental Controls window that appears, click the account to which you want to apply the controls. If the individual doesn't have an account, click Create A New User Account, create a Standard account for that person, and click Create Account.

③ In the User Controls window, select the On, Enforce Current Settings option to turn on the parental controls if they aren't already turned on.

④ Specify whether you want Windows Vista to keep a record of Web sites visited, games played, programs run, and so on.

⑤ Click Windows Vista Web Filter to display the Web Restrictions window.

Click to view the reports of activities if Activity Reporting is turned on.

Caution

Make sure that all Administrator accounts have passwords and that the person whose access is being restricted doesn't know or have access to a password for any Administrator accounts. With Administrator permissions to change settings, anyone can change or disable the parental controls.

Control the Content

1 In the Web Restrictions window, select this option to enable specifying what content should be blocked.

2 If there are specific Web sites that you want to allow when they're normally blocked, or that you want to block when they're normally allowed, click this option, and add the relevant Web addresses to the Allowed Websites or Blocked Websites list in the Allow Blocked Webpages window. Click OK when you've finished.

3 Select a level of restrictions.

4 If you clicked the Custom option, select the check boxes for the type of content you want to block.

5 Select this check box if you don't want to allow files to be downloaded from the Web.

6 Click OK, and then click OK in the User Controls window.

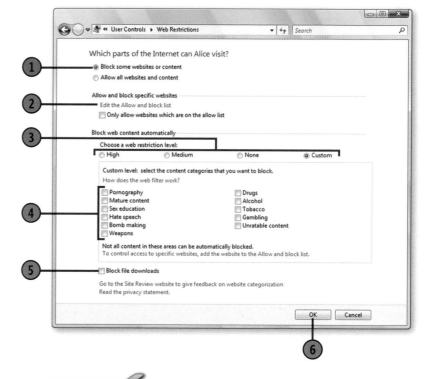

See Also

"Restricting Access on the Computer" on pages 290–291 for information about setting the other parental controls.

Tip ✓

You can create a custom list of allowed and blocked Web sites and then use the list to set the controls for each individual on any computer that's running Windows Vista. To do so, in the Allow Blocked Webpages window where you created your list, click Export, and save the file. When you're setting up any additional parental controls, click Import in the Allow Blocked Webpages window, and import the custom-list file you previously saved.

Restricting Access on the Computer

Not all games are child's play any more, not all programs can be safely used by children, and unlimited access to the computer isn't necessarily the best policy. If you want to restrict the types of games children are allowed to play, the programs they're allowed to run, and the amount of time during which they can access the computer, just ignore the whining and use the parental controls to establish appropriate boundaries.

Restrict the Games

1. Click the Start button, choose Control Panel from the Start menu, and, in the User Accounts And Family Safety section, click Set Up Parental Controls For Any User. Then, in the Parental Controls window that appears, click the account to which you want to apply the controls.

2. In the User Controls window, with the Parental Controls option turned on, click Games to display the Game Controls window.

3. Specify whether this person is allowed to play games.

4. If games are allowed, click Set Game Ratings, specify the rating level allowed, and block or allow any specific descriptors of the game content. Click OK when you've finished.

5. Click here to block or allow specific installed games. Select the games that you want to block or allow, and then click OK.

6. Click OK.

Control which types of games Jerry can play

Can Jerry play games?
- ⊙ Yes
- ○ No

Block (or allow) games by rating and content types

Set game ratings
Maximum allowed rating: ADULTS ONLY, including unrated games
Game descriptors blocked: None

Block (or allow) any game on your computer by name

Block or Allow specific games

Always blocked: None
Always allowed: None

See Also

"Restricting Access to Web Content" on pages 288–289 for information about turning on the parental controls and controlling the content that's accessible from the Internet.

Restrict Access Times

 In the User Controls window, click the Time Limits option to display the Time Restrictions window.

2 Use the mouse to drag out time blocks during which access is permitted. To remove a time block, drag over it again. To change an individual square, click it.

3 Click OK when you've finished.

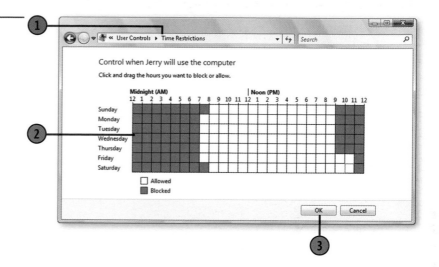

Block Programs

1 In the User Controls window, click the Allow And Block Specific Programs option to display the Application Restrictions window.

2 Specify whether the person can run all the programs or only those that are specified.

 If the option to restrict games is selected, select the check boxes for the programs you want to allow and clear the check boxes for the programs you want to block.

4 To add a program that isn't on the list, click Browse, locate the program, and click Open. Select or clear the check box for the program to allow or block it.

5 Click OK.

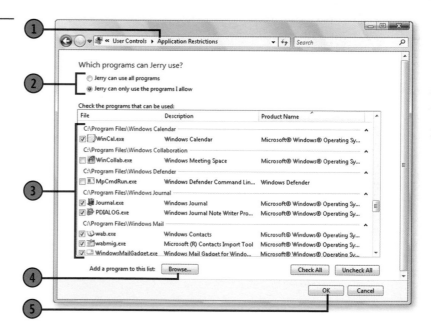

Maintaining High Security

Microsoft Windows Vista itself provides your computer with many built-in security features. However, as powerful as they are, by themselves these security features can't protect you from every type of mischief that can occur. You need to be active in protecting your computer, your data, and your personal information.

Doing Your Part

Here are some things you can do to improve your security:

- Log on using a Standard account instead of an Administrator account, and use the User Account Control to run individual items as an Administrator when required.

- Make sure you have a good, up-to-date anti-virus program installed. This will add protection against viruses and worms that have figured out ways around some of the security features.

- In Windows Mail (or the mail program you're using), read your e-mail in plain Text format instead of using the HTML format. This will prevent any malicious code that's hidden in the HTML code from being executed when you open the message.

- In Windows Mail (or the mail program you're using), don't download pictures and other external HTML content contained on a server unless you trust the source. Doing so verifies your e-mail address to potential authors of spam and can introduce malicious code.

- Make sure that your Web content zones in Internet Explorer are properly set and that you're not using custom settings that provide less protection than the recommended default levels.

- In Internet Explorer, make sure you have the pop-up blocker turned on to prevent code from being loaded, to prevent a hacker from stealing information by making the pop-up look like a dialog box or other content that asks for information, and to keep those annoying pop-up ads from appearing.

- In Internet Explorer, make sure you have the phishing filter turned on to identify illicit Web sites that look legitimate but are designed to steal your information.

- In Internet Explorer, work in Protected mode so that Internet Explorer activities and downloads are isolated from the rest of your computer.

- Keep Windows up to date with automatic updates. Each critical update is an urgent fix to outmaneuver a newly detected software vulnerability.

- Use the Windows Security Center to verify that your basic security settings are properly configured and up to date.

- Stop and think before you do something you might regret: open an attachment, download a file, install a program, or even answer an e-mail message.

- Keep all your important data backed up so that if something nasty sneaks past all your security, you can recover all the data.

Complicated? Absolutely! But don't be intimidated: Windows Vista is designed to be as secure as possible and will take care of most security issues. It also adjusts many of your default settings to maintain the optimum balance between security and functionality. And it monitors your security status and alerts you when there's a problem.

Setting Internet Explorer Security

Although most Web sites pose little security threat to your computer, some sites are designed with malicious intentions. In Internet Explorer, to protect your computer from these sites—and to allow access to additional features for sites you know won't cause any harm—you can set and customize your own security levels and can add sites to your list of trusted or restricted Web sites.

Set Your Security

1. In Internet Explorer, click Tools, choose Internet Options from the drop-down menu, and click the Security tab of the Internet Options dialog box.

2. Click the Trusted Sites zone, click the Sites button, and type or paste an address for a Web site you trust and to which you want full access.

3. Click the Restricted Sites zone, click the Sites button, and type or paste an address for a Web site you believe might be dangerous and from which you want maximum protection.

4. Click in a zone, and do either of the following:

   - Use the slider to adjust the level of security. If the slider isn't visible, click the Default Level button, and then use the slider.

   - Click Custom Level, and select the options you want in the Security Settings dialog box. Click OK.

5. Select this check box, if it isn't already selected, to use Protected mode.

6. Repeat steps 4 and 5 for each of the zones, and click Apply.

7. On the Privacy tab, set the privacy level you want to control the types of cookies that are stored and that contain and/or collect information about you.

8. Click OK.

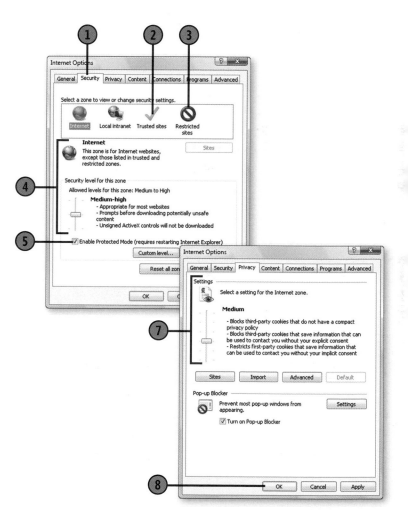

Restricting DVD Movies in Windows Media Player

If there are DVDs that, because of their specific ratings, you don't want to be played on your computer using Windows Media Player, you can block them from being played based on their rating. Note, however, that the blocking can be overridden by providing Administrative permission from the User Account Control.

Specify the Allowable DVD Rating

① With Parental Controls set up and turned on, start Windows Media Player from the Start menu if it isn't already running.

② Click the Now Playing down arrow, and choose More Options to display the Options dialog box.

③ On the DVD tab, click the Change button.

④ In the Change Rating Restriction dialog box, specify the maximum rating you'll allow.

⑤ Click OK.

⑥ Click OK.

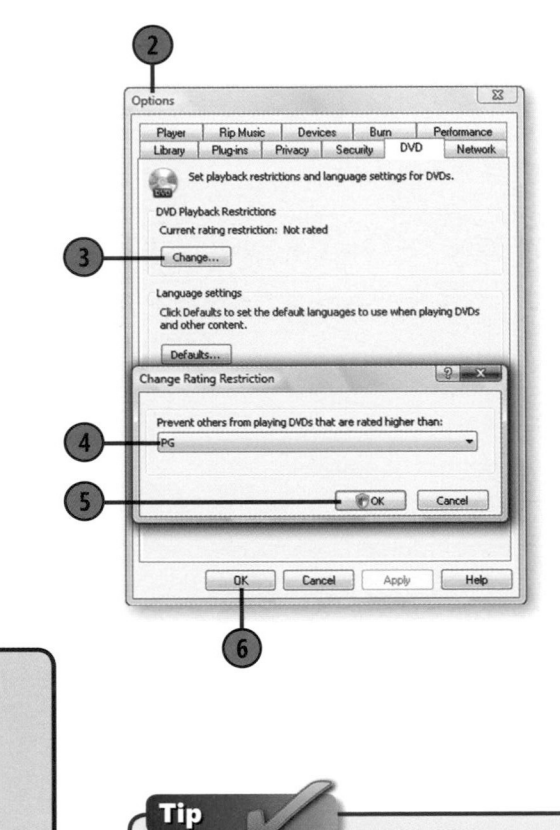

See Also

"Authorizing Administrative Actions" on page 287 for information about using and enabling the User Account Control if it isn't enabled.

"Restricting Access to Web Content" on pages 288–289 for information about setting up and enabling parental controls.

"Restricting Content in Windows Media Center" on pages 296–297 for information about setting access restrictions on playing DVDs and other movies in Media Center.

Tip

To prevent access to inappropriate material, make sure that you set rating restrictions for all the programs on your computer that play DVDs.

Preventing Access While Using Windows Media Player

Although Windows Media Player is great for listening to music or watching videos, you can't do either without being logged on to your computer. Meanwhile, other people can change the music you're listening to or the video that's playing, or—much worse—even take the opportunity to access your files. To prevent this, you can lock out easy access to your computer.

Lock Media Player

1. With Windows Media Player running and playing the playlist you want, switch to Full Screen mode.

2. Click Lock Full Screen Mode. If the controls aren't visible, move the mouse until you can see them.

3. Create and enter a unique four-digit *pin code* to control access, and click the green check mark.

4. Use the controls as you normally would.

5. When you want to access your computer, click the Unlock Full Screen Mode button, type the pin code, and click the check mark.

Tip

If you forget your pin code, press Alt+Ctrl+Delete, and choose to log off. When you log on again, Windows Media Player will no longer be running.

Caution

Locking the full-screen display of Media Player provides minimal protection and is designed mostly to prevent accidental changes to the display and the media being played. To play music while denying access to your computer, start your music, and then choose Lock This Computer from the Start menu.

Restricting Content in Windows Media Center

Windows Media Center has its own tools to control the type of content that can be viewed. Unlike most of the Windows Vista controls, access to the settings is controlled by the use of a pin code rather than reliance on Administrator access. These settings affect all users of the computer.

Set the Movie and DVD Control

1. With Media Center running and the main menu displayed, choose Tasks, and then choose Settings. In the Settings window, select General, and, in the General window that appears, select Parental Controls. Create and enter a unique four-digit pin code to control access.

2. In the Parental Controls window, click Movie/DVD Ratings to display the Movie/DVD Ratings window.

3. Select this check box to turn on blocking.

4. Select this check box to block any movie that doesn't have a rating.

5. Specify the maximum rating you'll allow.

6. Click Save.

Set the TV Control

① In the Parental Controls window, select TV Ratings to display the TV Ratings window.

② Select this check box to turn on TV blocking.

③ Select this check box to block any TV program that doesn't have a rating.

④ Specify the maximum rating you'll allow.

⑤ If you want to specify certain types of content, click Advanced, select your settings, and click Save.

⑥ Click Save, and click the Windows Media Center button to return to the main menu.

Tip ✓

When a movie or a TV program is blocked, you can override the setting by entering your pin code. Therefore, you must make sure that the pin code isn't known by or available to those whose access you're trying to limit.

Creating Trusted Contacts

A *trusted contact* is someone whose online identity you can verify. You do this by receiving contact information from the person that contains a security certificate, which you can then match to the person's online identity. Trusted contacts are especially useful when you're using People Near Me and Windows Meeting Space.

Exchange Contacts

① Click the Start button, type **contact** in the Search box, and click Windows Contacts. Open your own Contacts file, and verify that it contains all the information you want to share, including your e-mail address. Click OK to close the file.

② Right-click the Contacts file, point to Send To on the shortcut menu, and do either of the following:

- Choose Mail Recipient, and send the message that appears to the person whom you want to list you as a trusted contact.

- Choose to copy the file to a removable storage device.

③ When the other person receives the message or the removable storage device, have him or her open the file and choose Add To My Contacts. After your Contacts file has been added, your name appears in the recipient's Trusted Contacts list.

④ Now have the other person send you his or her Contacts file so that you can add it to your Trusted Contacts list.

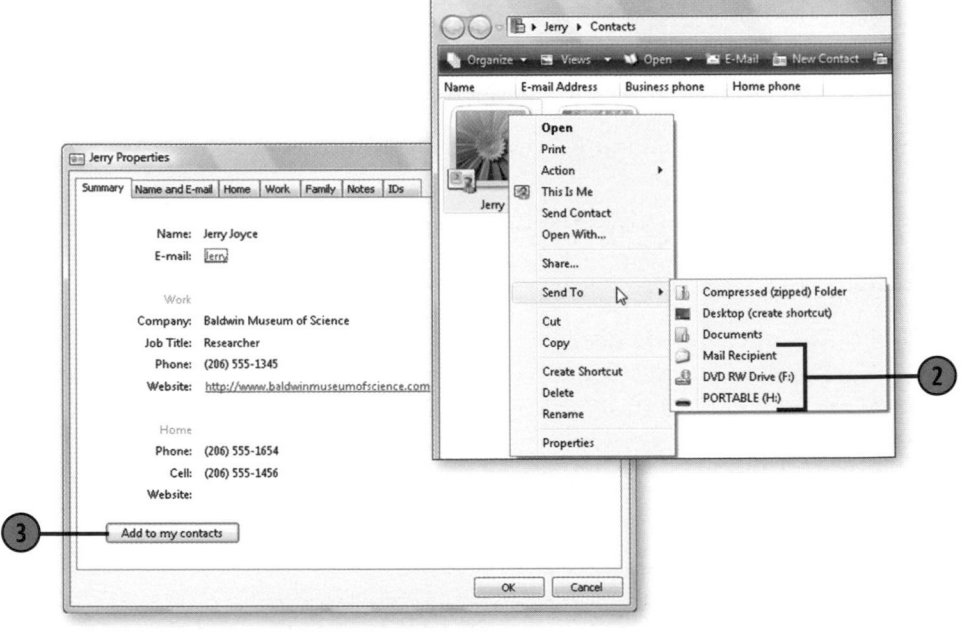

Tip

Contact information is usually sent in one of two ways—as a *Vcard* (a virtual business card) that has the .vcf file extension, or as a Contacts file that has the .contact file extension. Only a file with the .contact file extension contains the security certificate that you need to create a trusted contact, so make sure when you send or receive information that it's contained in a Contacts file.

Foiling E-Mail Viruses

E-mail is your computer's gateway to the rest of the world, and this gateway is what makes your e-mail one of the prime vectors for the distribution of computer viruses and other evils. Fortunately, Windows Mail provides options that can help you detect and prevent the introduction of viruses onto your computer.

Protect Yourself and Others

① In Windows Mail, choose Options from the Tools menu, and click the Security tab of the Options dialog box.

② Select the Restricted Sites Zone (More Secure) option if it isn't already selected.

③ Select this check box, if it isn't already selected, for protection from programs already on your computer that might use your e-mail to infect other computers.

④ Select this check box, if it isn't already selected, to enable inspection of the file type of an attachment and to block any attachment that could contain a virus.

⑤ Select this check box, if it isn't already selected, to stop your message from requesting additional material from an external server.

⑥ On the Read tab, select this check box if you want to prevent any hidden code in HTML-formatted messages from gaining access to your computer, provided you don't mind losing the formatting of HTML messages. Click OK.

Tip

To create even more secure e-mail, you can digitally sign and encrypt your messages, and provide that digital ID to those who'll be receiving your secure mail. To obtain a digital ID, click the Get Digital ID button on the Security tab of the Options dialog box.

See Also

"Creating Trusted Contacts" on the facing page for information about exchanging contact details that can include your digital ID.

Installing Critical Fixes

Microsoft continues to issue updates to Windows, fixing problems and vulnerabilities as they're discovered. To keep your computer running smoothly and to avoid new types of attacks, it's important that you install any critical updates that Microsoft issues as soon as they're available. Fortunately, the Windows Update feature does most of the work for you.

Configure Your Downloading

(1) Click the Start button, choose Control Panel from the Start menu, click Check For Updates in the Security section to display the Windows Update window, and review the status of your updates. If you're not signed up to receive updates for all the Microsoft products installed on your computer, click the Get Updates For More Products button, and sign up.

(2) If the computer hasn't checked for updates recently and isn't set for automatic updating, click Change Settings.

(3) Specify the way you want to receive updates, if at all.

(4) Select these check boxes if you want to include recommended updates as well as critical fixes in the downloads, and if you want to receive updates for other Microsoft products.

(5) Click OK when you've finished.

(6) If you chose to be notified when updates have been downloaded or are available for download, click the message or the download icon in the notification area of the taskbar to install your updates.

16

Managing Windows Vista

Windows Vista provides the flexibility you need to make changes, fix problems, and make your computer work better. With an administrative account, you can create or delete user accounts. If you want to squeeze more items onto your Desktop, you can increase its "virtual" size by changing the screen resolution.

Windows Vista helps you to control the power options on your portable computer, and it provides tools to help you run presentations without embarrassing snafus. Windows also provides disk-maintenance tools to help your computer run at its best. You can schedule these tools to run periodically—they'll find and re-order bits of files that have become scattered or lost, delete unused files, and so on. We'll show you how to get free software and how to remove software you don't want. If Windows won't start properly, you'll find solutions in this section that will either get your computer started or help you diagnose what's wrong. If you want to reverse changes you've made to your system, the System Restore tool will restore your previous settings. We'll also talk about recognizing and removing spyware, and show you how to upgrade to a different version of Windows Vista if the one you have doesn't meet your needs.

Adding or Deleting User Accounts

If you are a member of the Administrator group or can authorize administrative permission, you can grant other people access to the computer by creating new user accounts and specifying what type of access the new users will be allowed. To keep things tidy, you can also delete user accounts that are no longer being used.

Add a Standard Account

(1) Click the Start button, choose Control Panel from the Start menu, and, in the User Accounts And Family Safety section, click Add Or Remove User Accounts. In the Manage Accounts window that appears, click Create A New Account to display the Create New Account window.

(2) Type a name for the account.

(3) With the Standard User option selected, click Create Account.

(4) In the Manage Accounts window that appears, click the new account and, in the Change An Account window, change the picture, add a password, or set up parental controls for the account.

(5) Close the Change An Account window when you've finished.

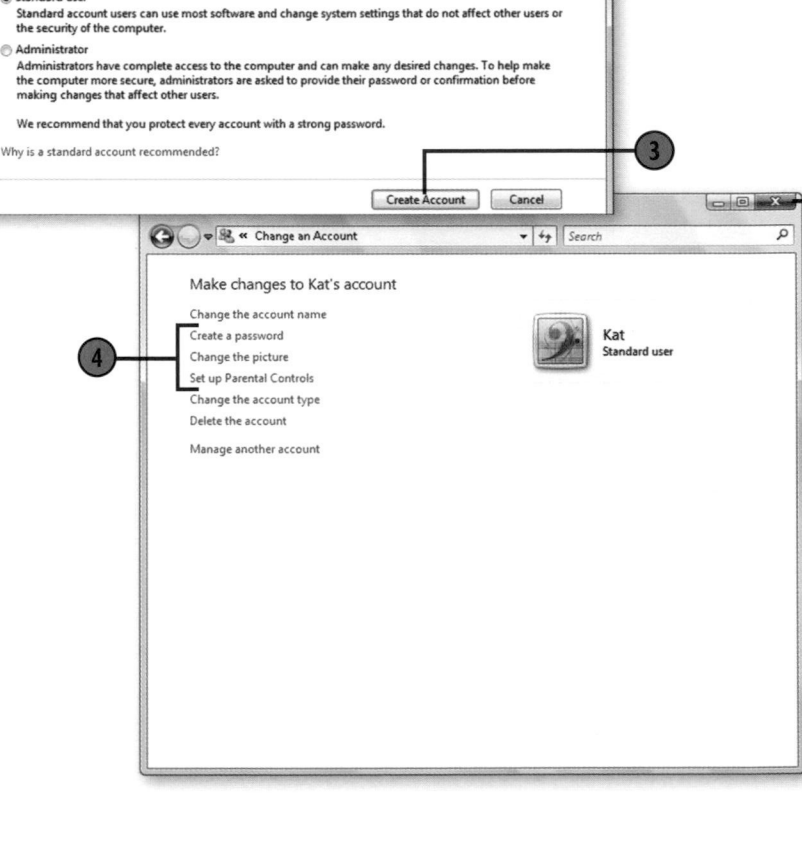

Delete an Account

 Click the Start button, choose Control Panel from the Start menu, and, in the User Accounts And Family Safety section, click Add Or Remove User Accounts. In the Change An Account window that appears, click the account you want to delete.

2️⃣ Click Delete The Account.

3️⃣ In the Delete Account window that appears, click Keep Files if you want all the files in that account's folders saved to a Desktop folder, or click Delete Files to delete all the files.

4️⃣ Click Delete Account to permanently delete the account.

Tip

When files are saved for an account that's being deleted, the files are saved to the Desktop of the person who's deleting the account and are accessible only when that person is logged on.

"Know Your Rights" on page 278 and "Restricting User Rights" on pages 282–283 for information about the reasons you should create only Standard user accounts.

Changing the Date and Time

Windows Vista and your computer keep track of the date and time, using commonly accepted formats to display them. In most cases, your computer routinely checks the date and time over the Internet. However, if the date or time on your computer is inaccurate, or if you travel with your computer into different time zones, you can quickly adjust the settings.

Change the Time Zone, Date, or Time

1. Click the Start button, type **date** in the Search box, and click Date And Time to display the Date And Time dialog box

2. If the date or time is incorrect, click the Change Date And Time button.

3. In the Date And Time Settings dialog box, use the left or right arrow at the top of the calendar to scroll to the current month, and then click today's date.

4. To correct the time, click the hour, the minute, or the second that needs correcting, and then either type a new value or use the scroll arrows to set the value.

5. Click OK.

6. In the Date And Time dialog box that appears, click Change Time Zone if you want to change the time zone. In the Time Zone Settings dialog box, select the new time zone, specify whether you want the time to be adjusted for Daylight Saving Time, and click OK.

7. Click OK.

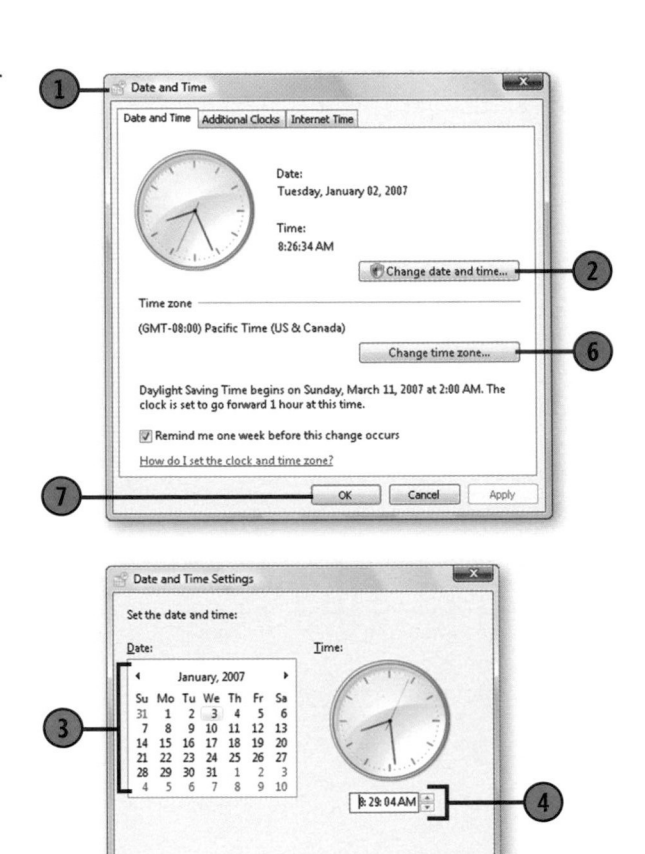

See Also

"Adding Time Zone Clocks" on page 276 for information about displaying additional clocks for different time zones.

Changing the Display

If you want to squeeze more items onto your Desktop, you can change its size...sort of. This is one of those "virtual" realities. You "enlarge" the available space by changing the screen resolution, and thereby the *scaling*, which lets you fit more items onto the Desktop even though its area on your screen doesn't get any larger. Your gain in virtual area comes at a cost, though—everything will be smaller and harder to read. Also, changes to the screen resolution and the color quality change the system demands on the *video memory* (the memory on your computer that's dedicated to producing the video image on your monitor). Therefore, you might need to adjust both the screen resolution and the color quality until you're happy with the result.

Increase the Computer's Screen Area

(1) Click the Start button, choose Control Panel from the Start menu, and, in the Appearance And Personalization section, click Adjust Screen Resolution to display the Display Settings dialog box.

(2) Drag the slider to specify the screen-area size in pixels (the degree of screen resolution).

(3) Specify the color quality you want to use.

(4) Click OK.

(5) If the Display Settings dialog box appears after you've changed the Desktop's screen resolution, click Yes to accept the new settings or No to revert to the original settings. If you don't click Yes or No within 15 seconds, Windows Vista will restore the original settings.

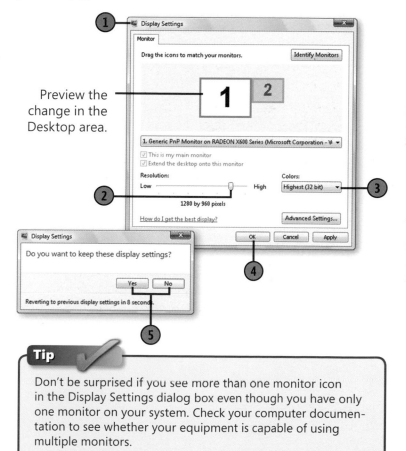

Preview the change in the Desktop area.

Tip ✓

If the screen text is too large or too small after you've adjusted the screen area, right-click the Desktop, and choose Personalize from the shortcut menu. Click Adjust Font Size (DPI) in the Tasks section of the Personalize window, and, in the DPI Scaling dialog box, specify the font size you want; click OK.

Tip ✓

Don't be surprised if you see more than one monitor icon in the Display Settings dialog box even though you have only one monitor on your system. Check your computer documentation to see whether your equipment is capable of using multiple monitors.

Checking the Status of Windows

Windows Vista is available in a wide variety of editions, and it's an operating system that demands a lot from your computer. If you're unable to locate a program or use a feature that you're pretty sure is part of Windows Vista, or if your computer just isn't performing the way you want it to, you should check to see which version of Windows Vista you're running, and find out how well your computer works with it.

Check the Status

① Click the Start button, choose Control Panel from the Start menu, click System And Maintenance, and then click System to display the System window.

② Note which version of Windows Vista you're running.

③ Note the score of your system. You need a score of at least 3 to obtain full functioning of the Aero glass effect, and you need a score of at least 4 to support all the Windows Vista features and programs that demand high graphics performance.

④ Click Windows Experience Index to see how individual items contribute to your score, to view and print details of the score, and to have Windows examine the system again and create a new score.

⑤ In the System window, make sure your computer has been activated.

⑥ Close the windows when you've finished.

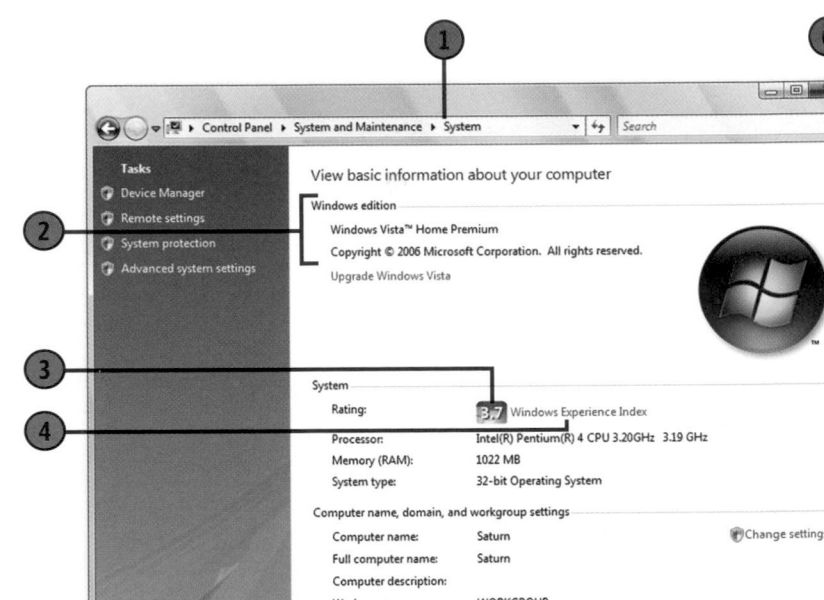

So Many Tools and Settings

Windows Vista is loaded with tools and performance settings, some of which you can use productively and others that require major translation from tech-speak into plain English. In most cases, the settings have already been optimized to achieve the correct balance between power and performance, but they might need some changes based on your computer equipment and your needs.

Although the tools are accessible in several locations, you'll find that you can access many of them in a single location by choosing System And Maintenance from the Control Panel, choosing Performance Information And Tools, and then clicking Advanced Tools in the Tasks list. You can also start many of the tools by typing each one's name in the Search box of the Start menu. We'll discuss some of these tools below, but you might want to spend a little time exploring all of them. Note that in many cases you'll need to be signed in as an Administrator in order to use the tools.

System Information: Provides full details of all the hardware and software on your computer. It's a really good idea to use this tool to print or export to a file all the information about your system, and to save this information for future reference and repair.

Reliability And Performance Monitor: Shows the status of the system and its performance. To run a 60-second test and create an extensive report, choose Generate A System Health Report in the Advanced Tools window. You can save, print, or e-mail the report to diagnose any problems.

Task Manager: A venerable tool over many generations of Windows, Task Manager shows the status of the computer, including running programs, computer processes, Windows services, CPU and Memory usage, network traffic, and logged-on users. Previously, Task Manager was used extensively to terminate misbehaving programs and processes, but Windows Vista has taken over most of those tasks.

Performance Options: Adjusts settings for the best visual effects, the best performance, or a combination of settings. This tool also adjusts the system to get the best performance for running programs or background services and for using virtual memory. It also sets whether Data Execution Prevention is used for essential Windows Vista programs and services or is used for all programs and services except the ones you exclude.

Indexing Options: Identifies and modifies the locations that are indexed. The advanced options can be used to specify whether to index encrypted files, how words with diacritical marks are indexed, the location of the index, and the types of files indexed.

Memory Diagnostic Tool: Examines the physical memory of your computer for problems. It runs after the computer has been restarted, and it generates a report. You can also run this tool from the Windows Error Recovery Startup Options screen if you have difficulty starting up Windows.

Windows Firewall And Advanced Security: Shows the firewall settings and allows creating, editing, disabling, or deleting of rules that govern the way the firewall works with inbound, outbound, and connection rules.

System Configuration: Modifies the way Windows starts up, which services are enabled, and which system programs start at startup. It also provides tools to modify the system, including an editor to change the system Registry.

ReadyBoost: A set of settings to speed up Windows by using virtual memory on a fast USB device. You can configure the ReadyBoost settings in the Properties dialog box for the device, and you can initiate the ReadyBoost feature when you plug in the device using the AutoPlay options.

Controlling the Power Options

Different computers have different power-management requirements and abilities. You might want the monitor on your main desktop computer to shut down after a few minutes of idleness, but you might also want the computer itself to "stay awake" constantly. With a portable computer, you might want everything to go to sleep after a few minutes of idleness.

You can adjust a power plan so that the computer does these things automatically, or you can make the adjustments manually by specifying what you want to happen when you press a power button or close the lid of a portable computer. For protection, you can also require that only you can unlock your account when the computer wakes up from Sleep mode.

Use a Power Plan

1 Click the Start button, type **power** in the Search box of the Start menu, and click Power Options to display the Power Options window.

2 Select a power scheme in the list.

3 Click Change Plan Settings for the plan you want to use.

4 In the Edit Plan Settings window that appears, examine the settings. If you want to modify a setting, specify a new value.

5 If you want to make more detailed changes— for example, to specify when the hard disk is to be turned off—click Change Advanced Power Settings. In the Power Options dialog box that appears, make the changes you want, and click OK.

6 In the Edit Plan Settings dialog box, click Save Changes.

Set the Power Buttons and the Password Requirement

① In the Power Options window, click Choose What The Power Buttons Do (or click Choose What The Power Button Does, if you're using a desktop computer) to display the System Settings window.

② Specify what you want to happen to the items available on your computer when you press a button or close the computer's lid.

③ Click an option to specify whether you want to require a password when the computer wakes up from Sleep mode.

④ Click Save Changes.

⑤ Close the Power Options window.

> **Tip** ✓
> You can quickly switch power plans or access the Power Options window by clicking the Power icon, if it's displayed, on the taskbar.

> **Tip** ✓
> If you want to create a custom power plan from scratch, click Create A Power Plan in the Power Options window.

Define power buttons and turn on password protection

Choose the power settings that you want for your computer. The changes you make to the settings on this page apply to all of your power plans.

Change settings that are currently unavailable

Power and sleep buttons and lid settings

		On battery	Plugged in
When I press the power button:		Hibernate	Sleep
When I press the sleep button:		Sleep	Sleep
When I close the lid:		Sleep	Sleep

Password protection on wakeup

Require a password (recommended)
When your computer wakes from sleep, no one can access your data without entering the correct password to unlock the computer. Create or change your user account password

Don't require a password
When your computer wakes from sleep, anyone can access your data because the computer isn't locked.

Save changes   Cancel

> **Tip** ✓
> If you require a password when the computer wakes up, you'll see the standard logon screen, from which you can log on to your currently locked account.

Managing Settings for a Presentation

Have you ever squirmed uncomfortably as you watched someone struggling to make a presentation from his or her computer, and absolutely everything went wrong? First, the presenter couldn't get the secondary display to work, and then, in the middle of the presentation, the screen saver appeared, or the computer went to sleep. It was a disaster! Don't let it happen to you. With Windows Vista and a portable computer, you can avoid these types of embarrassment by using the Windows Mobility Center to create your presentation settings and external monitor connections.

Prepare for the Presentation

1. Click the Start button, type **mob** in the Search box of the Start menu, and click Windows Mobility Center to display the Windows Mobility Center window.

2. Click the Presentation Settings button to display the Presentation Settings dialog box.

3. Clear this check box if it's selected.

4. Select this check box to make sure the screen saver doesn't appear during your presentation.

5. Select this check box, and use the slider if you want to specify a preset volume level.

6. Select this check box, and click an image if you want a special Desktop background during the presentation. If none of the listed images is what you want, click Browse, locate the picture file you want to use, and click Open.

7. Specify the way you want the image to fit on the screen.

8. Click OK.

9. When you're ready to give your presentation, click Turn On in the Windows Mobility Center window.

Use an External Display

(1) Connect the external monitor. If it isn't immediately detected, and if the New Display Detected window doesn't appear, click Connect Display in the Windows Mobility Center to display the window.

(2) In the New Display Detected window, specify how you want both monitors to work together.

(3) Click OK.

(4) Make any other changes in the Mobility Center as necessary, close it, and then give your presentation.

See Also

"Using a Network Projector" on page 236 for information about using a network projector for your presentation.

Tip

After you've made your changes to the presentation settings, Windows Vista will remember those settings, so you'll just need to click the Turn On button to start using the settings.

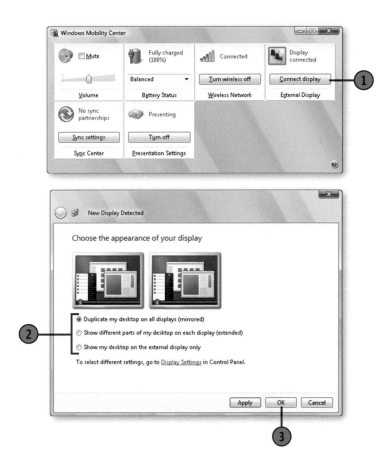

Tip

The items shown in the Windows Mobility Center will vary depending on the computer you use. The items shown here, however, should be available for most computers.

Controlling Your Startup Programs

Sometimes, after you've installed a program, you'll find that it starts whenever Windows Vista starts. That's okay if it's what you want, but if you'd rather have the program start only when you want it to, you can remove it from the list of programs that start automatically when Windows starts. Some of these programs might be in the Startup folder of the Start menu, where you can easily remove them; others are instructed to start from the Windows Registry, an area you probably don't want to venture into. Fortunately, Windows Defender makes it easy for you to access and modify these program settings.

Control the Programs

1. Click the Start button, type **defend** in the Search box of the Start menu, and click Windows Defender. In the Windows Defender window that appears, click Tools to display the Tools And Settings window, and click Software Explorer to display the Software Explorer.

2. Click Startup Programs.

3. Examine the programs. Select a program that you don't want to start when Windows starts, and click Disable.

4. Restart the computer, do some work to verify that the computer runs as you want it to without the program, and then repeat step 1 to open the Software Explorer. Select the program you disabled, and do either of the following:

   - If your computer ran properly without the program, click Remove to remove the program from the Startup list.

   - If the computer didn't run well without the program, click Enable to have the program start when Windows starts.

5. Close the Software Explorer when you've finished.

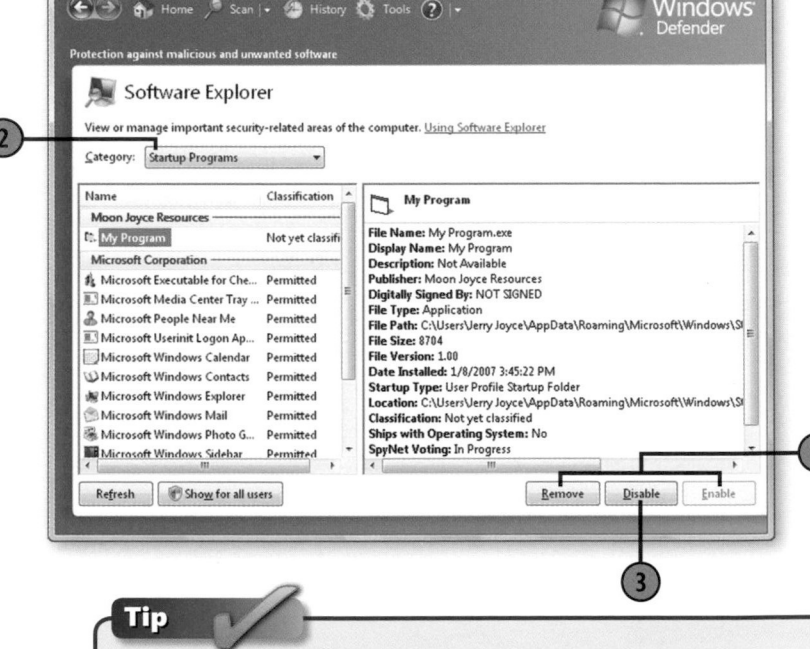

> **Tip**
>
> You can use the Software Explorer to view all the programs running on your computer. Although you can use this tool to help diagnose problems associated with badly behaving programs, the process of correcting such problems can be complex, so you'll probably need some help from an expert.

Maintaining Your Hard Disk

With time and use, your computer's contents can become a bit disorganized. As the information stored in the computer gets used, moved, copied, added to, or deleted, the computer's hard disk, or drive, can become cluttered with useless or inefficiently organized files. Windows Vista provides a group of maintenance tools whose occasional use can make your computer run more smoothly, more efficiently, and (usually) faster. The table below describes what each of these tools does.

Maintain a Drive

① Click the Start button, choose Computer from the Start menu, click the drive that needs attention, and click Properties on the toolbar to display the drive's Properties dialog box.

② Click the appropriate button to use the tool you need, and follow the instructions provided by the program:

- On the General tab, click Disk Cleanup.

- On the Tools tab, under Error-Checking, click Check Now.

- On the Tools tab, under Defragmentation, click Defragment Now.

Tip
By default, the Defragmentation program is set to run automatically every week. If it doesn't run, or if you want to change the schedule, click Modify Schedule in the Disk Defragmenter dialog box.

Disk-Maintenance Tool

Tool	What it does
Disk Cleanup	Checks the disk for unused files that can be deleted.
Error-Checking	Scans the disk to see whether there are disk errors in any files or folders. Optionally, fixes file-system errors and attempts to recover bad sectors on the hard disk. If the disk is in use, error-checking will be scheduled for the next time you log on.
Defragmentation	Analyzes the disk to see whether defragmentation is necessary. Re-orders the items on your disk so that files aren't separated into several noncontiguous parts. Can take a long time to run but speeds up disk performance.

Downloading Free Software

Microsoft and its partners are continually developing tools, utilities, and other items that make it possible for your computer to work better, run more effectively, and just do more things. Many such items are available as free downloads from the Microsoft Web site. True, you'll need to wade through listings of many technical downloads, but it's worth it—your search can yield some pretty interesting items related to just about any Microsoft product, including trial versions of many of Microsoft's games.

Download the Software

① Use your Web browser to go the main Microsoft Web page *(microsoft.com)*, and, in the Resources section, click Downloads to display the Microsoft Download Center Web page.

② Click a download or a category, and then click a download in the Web page that appears.

③ Review the information about the download and the instructions for downloading and installing the item.

④ If you receive a warning in the Information bar, click the bar, and select the action you want to take. In most cases at these Microsoft sites, the warning asks you to install the ActiveX control required for the download.

⑤ Click Download, and follow the directions on the screen.

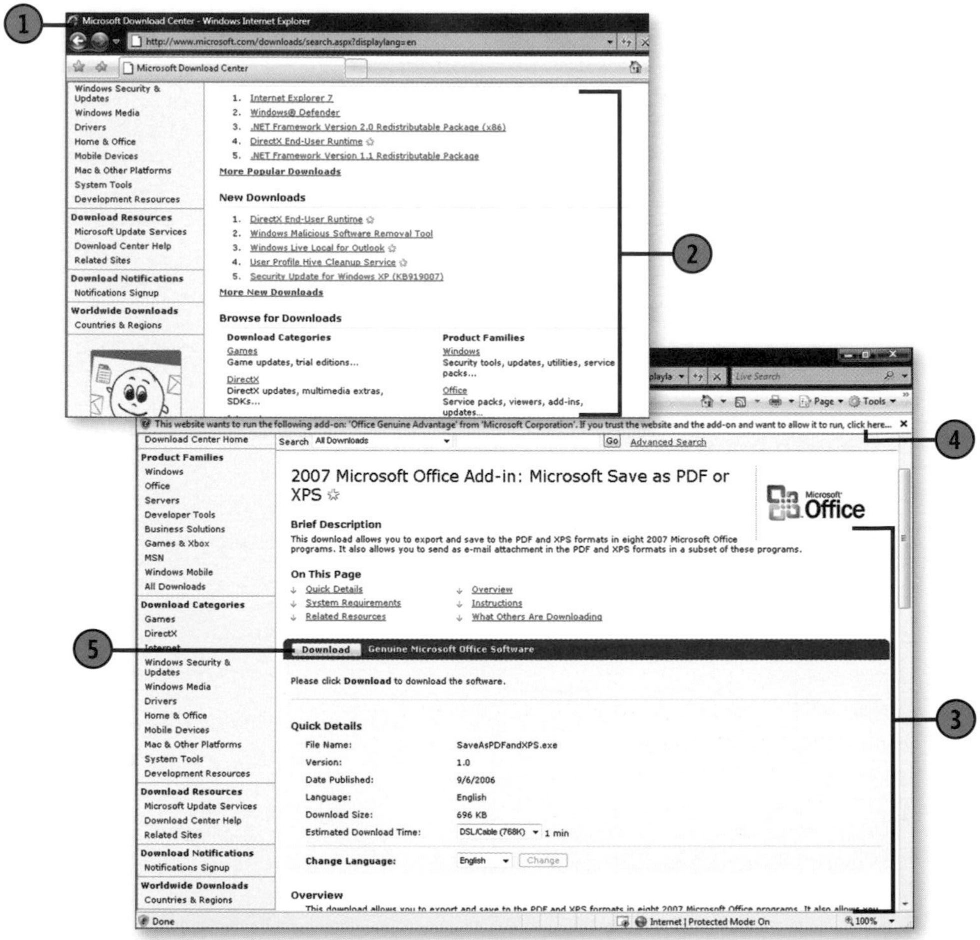

Removing a Software Program

Most programs are *registered* with Windows Vista when you install them. You can—and should—use Windows tools when you want to remove a program. If you simply delete the files, you might leave accessory files you don't need, or delete files you need for other programs. When you uninstall a program using Windows tools, Windows Vista keeps track of the files, and only when a file is no longer needed by any of your programs does Windows Vista delete the file.

Uninstall a Program

 Close all your running programs, and make sure that no one else is logged on to the computer. Click the Start button, choose Control Panel from the Start menu, and, in the Programs section, click Uninstall A Program to display the Programs And Features window.

 Select the program you want to uninstall.

3 Click the appropriate button:

- Uninstall to remove the program

- Change (if available) to modify the installed components of the program or to repair the current installation

- Repair (if available) to reinstall all or part of the program or to correct errors in the current copy of the program

4 If you're asked, confirm the action you took. If another program starts and offers you a choice of actions, use this program to remove the selected program, to change the installed components, or to repair the program.

5 Wait for the program to be removed or modified, and then close the Programs And Features window when you've finished.

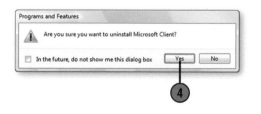

Tip

Various programs provide different ways to remove or modify an installed program. Some programs display only the Uninstall button; others include the Change button, the Repair button, and even an Uninstall/Change button.

Starting Up When There's a Problem

If you have any problems starting up Windows Vista correctly, you can use one of several startup procedures, either to determine what's wrong or to start Windows with minimal features so that you can adjust or restore settings. Then, after you've been able to start Windows, you can use a variety of techniques to fix whatever's wrong with the system.

Control the Startup

 Restart your computer. When the Windows Error Recovery screen appears, press Enter to start up in Normal mode. If the computer doesn't start correctly, shut it down, and wait for the Windows Error Recovery screen to appear again.

2 Use the Up arrow key to select Safe Mode, press Enter, and make changes to correct the problem.

3 Restart your computer, and see whether it starts correctly now.

4 If it doesn't, restart it, and, after the system loads and as Windows starts, hold down the F8 key. The Windows Advanced Options menu appears. Experiment with different settings until you get the system working.

5 If you can't load Windows at all, place the Windows disc in your computer, restart the computer, and, as it starts, press the key for the boot menu (often the F12 key), and choose to boot from the disc. Follow the directions to fix the system.

Windows Error Recovery Startup Options

Option	What it does
Safe Mode	Starts with no network connections and without most of its drivers.
Safe Mode With Networking	Starts with network connections but without most of its drivers.
Safe Mode With Command Prompt	Starts without network connections, without most of its drivers, and with the command prompt only.
Start Windows Normally	Starts Windows as if you hadn't pressed the F8 key.

Additional Options Using Windows Advanced Options Menu

Option	What it does
Enable Boot Logging	Starts normally; records startup information to the *ntbtlog.txt* file (in the Windows folder).
Enable Low-Resolution Video Mode	Starts normally; uses only the basic VGA video driver.
Last Known Good Configuration	Starts normally, using the settings stored in the Registry when the computer was last shut down properly.
Debugging Mode	Starts normally but sends the debugging information to another computer over a serial cable.
Disable Automatic Restart On System Failure	Prevents the computer from restarting repeatedly if a system failure occurs each time the computer restarts.
Disable Driver Signature Enforcement	Allows all drivers to be loaded even if they don't have the proper driver signatures.

Fixing System Problems

An invaluable feature of Windows Vista is the System Restore tool, which makes it possible for you to undo whatever changes you or various programs have made to your computer system. Periodically, and also whenever you make changes to the system, Windows Vista records all the system information. If you've made changes to the system but the effect isn't what you wanted, you can tell Windows to revert to the previous settings.

Restore the System

1. Close all your running programs, and make sure that no one else is logged on to the computer.

2. Click the Start button, type **restore** in the Search box of the Start menu, and click System Restore to start the System Restore Wizard.

3. Specify how you want to restore the settings:

   • Recommended Restore to undo only the last change

   • Choose A Different Restore Point to select a previous Restore point

4. Click Next. If you chose Recommended Restore, click Finish.

5. If you chose a different Restore point, select it, click Next, and then click Finish.

Tip

A Restore point contains a record of the system settings when the Restore point was created, and you can use the Restore point to restore the system settings to the way they were then. Most Restore points are created automatically, but you can create your own Restore points and can modify which hard disks use the System Restore tool. To do so, open the Control Panel, and, in the System And Maintenance section, click System, and then click System Protection in the Tasks list.

Managing Everything

Windows Vista provides a powerful administrative tool called the Computer Management Console, which gives you access to almost everything on your computer system. You can use this tool to explore your computer and learn about the various adjustments you can make, and—armed with a little knowledge—you can then use the tool to maintain and improve your system.

Use the Console

1. Log on as an Administrator, click the Start button, type **man** in the Search box, and click Computer Management to display the Computer Management Console.

2. Click an item to see a subtopic or category, and then click an item to see the details.

3. Use the items in the main pane to gather information or adjust settings. Close the console when you've finished.

Computer Management Console Items

Item	What it does
Task Scheduler	Manages computer tasks that are run automatically.
Event Viewer	Displays system log and other event logs.
Shared Folders	Monitors which items are shared on the network and by whom.
Reliability And Performance	Provides technical data about the running of the computer.
Device Manager	Provides access to manage all hardware devices on the system.
Storage	Provides information and management of all storage devices.
Services And Applications	Provides management of all services available on your computer.

Tip

To access many of these tools without using the Computer Management Console, and to access some additional tools, click the Start button, type **admin** in the Search box, and click the Administrative Tools folder.

Removing Spyware

Spyware and other intrusive programs can gain access to your computer, gather information about you, and bombard you with pop-up ads. Windows Defender is designed to find and remove these types of programs by periodically scanning your files. You can specify when you want this scanning to occur or, if you detect suspicious activity, you can run a scan immediately. However, some spyware programs aren't easily identifiable. If you suspect that there's unidentified spyware on your computer, use another commercially available spyware program to run a second scan of the computer.

Change Defender Settings

① Click the Start button, type **defend** in the Search box of the Start menu, and click Windows Defender. In the Windows Defender window that appears, click Tools, and then click Options to display the Options window of Windows Defender.

② To use Windows Defender, select this check box.

③ Make any adjustments you want to the schedule.

④ Select these check boxes if they aren't selected.

⑤ Look through all the other options, adjusting them so that you get the best possible protection.

⑥ Click Save.

⑦ Click the down arrow next to the Scan button, and select the type of scan you want to run now.

⑧ Close Windows Defender when you've finished.

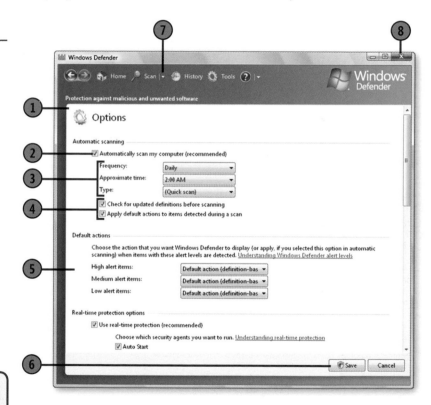

> **Tip** ✓
>
> Defender uses information files, called *definitions*, to identify spyware. To identify the most recent spyware programs that might be on your computer, you need updated definitions. Make sure your computer is set to automatically download updated definitions.

Helping Each Other

How many times have you screamed "Help!" (or worse) when your computer was being an uncooperative brat, only to be met by silence? Now your pleas for help won't disappear into the void. Using the Remote Assistance feature, you can contact someone on your network or over the Internet for help. Your friend or coworker can view your computer Desktop, review your system information, and even chat with you to help you figure out what's wrong. Likewise, if a friend or colleague has a problem that you know how to solve, you can be the expert who provides the oh-so-welcome assistance.

Ask for Help

(1) Click the Start button, type **remote** in the Search box of the Start menu, and click Windows Remote Assistance to display the Windows Remote Assistance window. Click Invite Someone You Trust To Help You. Create an invitation as a file or as an e-mail attachment, create a password for the invitation, and either send the e-mail or provide your potential helper with the invitation file. Wait for him or her to open the invitation file or attachment and enter the password. When you're prompted to allow your helper to connect to your computer, click Yes.

(2) When you're connected, click Chat.

(3) Type a message to explain your problem, and click Send.

(4) If the person asks to take control of your computer, click Yes to allow him or her full access to the computer and permission to make changes to the system. Click No if you want to retain control and make changes yourself. If you've allowed the other person to take control of the computer, click Stop Sharing or press the Esc key when you want to terminate that control.

(5) To send a file, click Send File, locate the file, and send it.

(6) When you've finished (and solved the problem, we hope!), click Disconnect to end the remote assistance.

Tip

To ask for help from someone who isn't in your Contacts list, click the Other tab in the Ask For Remote Assistance dialog box, and type the person's full e-mail address.

Give Help

1 With Remote Desktop Assistance running and connected to the person who needs help, review that person's Desktop. All the actions he or she takes will be displayed, including using programs or changing settings.

2 If you want to take control of the other person's computer, click Request Control. Wait for him or her to confirm that you can take control. Click OK to confirm that you have control, and use your mouse to explore the other computer, to open menus and programs, and to do whatever troubleshooting and problem-solving is necessary.

3 When you no longer need control, click the Stop Sharing button (the Request Control button changes to the Stop Sharing button after it's clicked), and click Disconnect when the session has been completed.

The log of events and messages

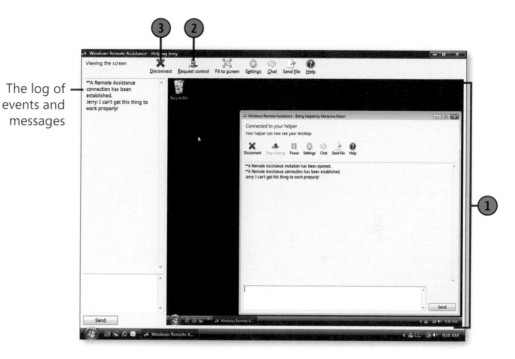

Tip

Your system must have Remote Assistance enabled to establish a connection. If Remote Assistance isn't already enabled, click the Start button, type **system** in the Search box, and click System on the Start menu. In the System window, click Advanced System Settings, and, on the Remote tab of the System Properties dialog box that appears, select the check box for allowing Remote Assistance connections. Click OK.

Tip

Windows Vista also provides the Remote Desktop Connection tool that makes it possible for someone to control your computer from another computer. However, a computer running Windows Vista Home Premium can allow only an incoming Remote Desktop Connection and is unable take control of another computer.

Backing Up Your Files

With all the security features built into Windows, you wouldn't think that you'd need to do anything more. Wrong! What if you have a severe hardware failure—your hard disk just stops, for example, or someone accidentally erases all your files?

What if your computer gets hit by lightning? All your work will be gone forever if you haven't backed up your important files. And, with all the right tools readily available, there really is no excuse for not backing up those files periodically.

Back Up Your Files

① Log on as an Administrator.

② Click the Start button, choose Control Panel from the Start menu, and, in the System And Maintenance section, click Back Up Your Computer. Click Back Up Files to start the Back Up Files Wizard.

③ Specify where you want to save your backed-up files, and click Next.

④ Select the check boxes for the types of files you want to back up, and click Next.

⑤ Specify the schedule you want for automatic backups.

⑥ Click Save Settings And Start Backup. The first time you run a backup, Windows creates a complete backup—called a *shadow copy*. Subsequent automatic backups are *incremental backups*, in which the only files backed up are those that have been changed since the last backup.

⑦ When the backup is complete, log off as an Administrator.

Restoring Backed-Up Files

Have you deleted or otherwise lost files that you now need? If those files were routinely backed up from your computer, you can restore them from the backup onto your computer.

Restore the Files

① Click the Start button, choose Control Panel from the Start menu, and, in the System And Maintenance section, click Back Up Your Computer. Click Restore Files to start the Restore Files Wizard.

② Specify whether you want to restore files from your last backup or files from a previous backup, and click Next.

③ Specify whether you want to add files or folders, locate and select the files or folders you want to restore, and click Add.

④ Continue adding files or folders to the list until all the items you want to restore are selected. Click Next.

⑤ Specify whether you want to place the restored files in their original location or in a different location. If you chose a new location, specify whether or not you want the files to be placed in their original subfolders.

⑥ Click Start Restore. After the files have been restored, click Finish, and then close the Backup And Restore Center window.

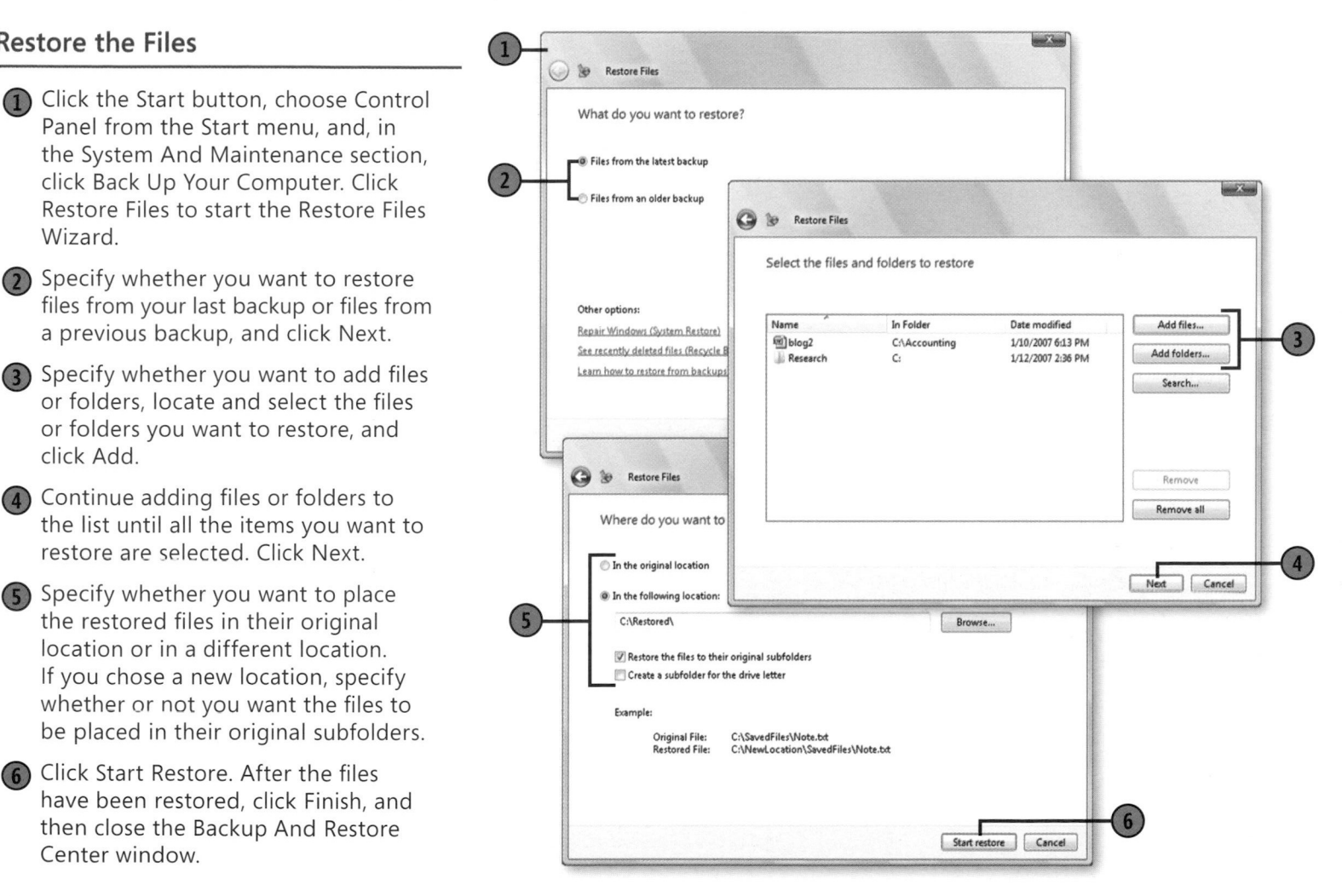

Upgrading Windows Vista

If your edition of Windows Vista doesn't have all the features you want, you can easily (for a price) upgrade to a more comprehensive version. When you upgrade, all your files and programs will remain untouched, and you'll find that you can do a lot more things on your computer.

Upgrade

① Back up all your personal files and settings before you start the upgrade. Then click the Start button, type **upgrade** in the Search box, and click Windows Anytime Upgrade to open the Windows Anytime Upgrade window.

② Click this option to determine which features you'll gain by upgrading.

③ Use the Upgrade Comparison Chart to compare features.

④ If you decide to upgrade, click the Choose button to choose the version of Windows Vista that you want, and, in the Upgrade window that appears, click Begin Upgrade Process. (To upgrade, you must already have a version of Windows Vista installed, and the computer must be capable of running the version you're upgrading to. If you have any doubts, download the Windows Vista Upgrade Advisor, available at *microsoft.com*.)

⑤ Follow the instructions on the Web page to purchase the upgrade, and then download and run the installation software. When prompted, insert your Windows Anytime Upgrade disc. If you don't have a disc, use the instructions on the Web page to obtain one.

Index

W

waking up computers, 10, 308–9
wallpaper, 124, 257
warnings. *See* alerts; cautions
.wav format, 179
Web Archive files, 43, 89
Web browsers, 240. *See also* Internet
  Explorer
Web Filter feature, 288
Web pages
  copying portions of, 96
  graphics on, 89
  opening multiple, 82, 83
  printing, 189
  saving to computers, 89
  sending Journal notes as, 43
  tables in, 96
Web Quick Keys pad, 37
Web sites
  calendars on, 75
  changes in, 87
  clearing history of viewed sites, 84
  controlling children's access to, 288–89
  cookies, 293
  copying portions of pages, 96
  dial-up access and, 244–45
  exporting list of blocked and allowed
    pages, 289
  finding in Internet Explorer, 81
  finding information on, 88
  graphics on pages, 89
  home pages, 81, 83, 87
  illicit, 292
  keeping records of visits to, 288
  Microsoft Download Center Web
    page, 314

newsgroups on, 76
opening multiple pages, 82, 83
phishing, 292
pop-up windows, 90–91
printing pages, 189
privacy settings, 293
returning to, 84–85
RSS feeds, 92–93
saving pages to computers, 89
secure-zone settings, 292
security settings, 293
storing files on, 222
trusted, 293
typing in addresses, 86
Web-based mail, 247
Webpage Complete format, 89
Welcome Center, 4
wheels on pointing devices, 261
WIAs (Windows Acquisition drivers),
  191, 192
windows
  3-D, 18
  arranging, 20
  changing appearance of, 255
  displaying thumbnail images of, 262
  dragging effects, 256
  folders in, 268
  fonts used in, 256
  illustrated, 8
  opening, 18
  pop-up, 90–91, 319
  resizing, 8, 18, 20–21, 145, 198
  sorting files in, 197
  switching to, 18
  toolbars, 214
  transparency of, 255
  view settings for, 194–96
Windows 2000, 238

Windows Acquisition drivers (WIAs),
  191, 192
Windows Aero color and glass
  appearance, 5, 8, 24, 255, 256
Windows Anytime Upgrade disc, 324
Windows Briefcase, 61
Windows Calendar
  comparing calendars, 72–73
  functions, 12
  multiple calendars, 72–73
  publishing calendars, 74
  scheduling meetings, 71
  setting appointments, 69
  subscribing to calendars, 75
  tracking tasks, 70
Windows Clipboard, 26, 30
Windows Contact format, 62
Windows Contacts, 58. *See also* contacts
Windows Defender, 5, 285, 312, 319
Windows DVD Maker, 120, 128–29,
  130, 131
Windows Easy Transfer, 238–39
Windows Easy Transfer Companion, 238
Windows Easy Transfer Wizard, 238, 239
Windows Error Recovery screen, 316
Windows events
  logs, 318
  sounds for, 180–81
  visual cues for, 182
Windows Experience Index, 306
Windows File Associations Web page, 243
Windows Firewall, 5, 108, 285, 286, 307
Windows Import Video Wizard, 130, 132,
  133, 134, 135
Windows Journal, 40–43
Windows key, 4, 19
Windows Live Mail, 247
Windows Live Mail Desktop, 247
Windows Live Messenger, 61

About the Authors

Jerry Joyce is a marine biologist who has conducted research from the Arctic to the Antarctic and has published extensively on marine-mammal and fisheries issues. He developed computer programs in association with these studies to simplify real-time data entry, validation, and analysis that substantially enhanced the quality of the research. He has also had a long-standing relationship with Microsoft: Prior to co-authoring twelve books about Microsoft Windows, Word, and Office, he was the technical editor for numerous books published by Microsoft Press, and he wrote manuals, help files, and specifications for various Microsoft products. Jerry is a Seattle Audubon volunteer and an environmental-representative member of the Washington State Oil Spill Advisory Council and the Washington State Ballast Water Working Group.

Marianne Moon has worked in the publishing world for many years as proofreader, editor, and writer—sometimes all three simultaneously. She has been proofreading and editing Microsoft Press books since 1984 and has written and edited documentation for Microsoft products such as Microsoft Works, Flight Simulator, Space Simulator, Golf, Publisher, the Microsoft Mouse, and Greetings Workshop. In another life, she was chief cook and bottlewasher for her own catering service and wrote weekly food and cooking articles for several newspapers. When she's not chained to her computer, she likes gardening, cooking, traveling, writing, and knitting sweaters for tiny dogs. She volunteers for Seattle Audubon's History Committee, and there's a children's book in her head that she hopes will find its way out one of these days.

Marianne and **Jerry** own and operate **Moon Joyce Resources,** a small consulting company. They've been friends for 25 years, have worked together for 21 years, and have been married for 15 years. They are co-authors of the following books:

Microsoft Word 97 At a Glance

Microsoft Windows 95 At a Glance

Microsoft Windows NT Workstation 4.0 At a Glance

Microsoft Windows 98 At a Glance

Microsoft Word 2000 At a Glance

Microsoft Windows 2000 Professional At a Glance

Microsoft Windows Millennium Edition At a Glance

Troubleshooting Microsoft Windows 2000 Professional

Microsoft Word Version 2002 Plain & Simple

Microsoft Office System Plain & Simple— 2003 Edition

Microsoft Windows XP Plain & Simple

Microsoft Windows XP Plain & Simple—2nd Edition

Microsoft Office Word 2007 Plain & Simple

The 2007 Microsoft Office System Plain & Simple

If you have questions or comments about any of their books, please visit *www.moonjoyce.com*.

What do you think of this book?

We want to hear from you!

Do you have a few minutes to participate in a brief online survey?

Microsoft is interested in hearing your feedback so we can continually improve our books and learning resources for you.

To participate in our survey, please visit:

www.microsoft.com/learning/booksurvey/

...and enter this book's ISBN-10 number (appears above barcode on back cover*). As a thank-you to survey participants in the United States and Canada, each month we'll randomly select five respondents to win one of five $100 gift certificates from a leading online merchant. At the conclusion of the survey, you can enter the drawing by providing your e-mail address, which will be used for prize notification only.

Thanks in advance for your input. Your opinion counts!

*Where to find the ISBN-10 on back cover

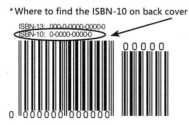

Example only. Each book has unique ISBN.